GREETINGS FROM
SWEETAIRE FARM

A Lifetime of Stories

SECOND EDITION

ARTHUR T. JOHNSON

Copyright © 2025 Arthur T. Johnson.

All rights reserved. No part of this book may be reproduced, stored, or transmitted by any means—whether auditory, graphic, mechanical, or electronic—without written permission of both publisher and author, except in the case of brief excerpts used in critical articles and reviews. Unauthorized reproduction of any part of this work is illegal and is punishable by law.

ISBN: 979-8-89419-683-1 (sc)
ISBN: 979-8-89419-684-8 (hc)
ISBN: 979-8-89419-685-5 (e)

Because of the dynamic nature of the Internet, any web addresses or links contained in this book may have changed since publication and may no longer be valid. The views expressed in this work are solely those of the author and do not necessarily reflect the views of the publisher, and the publisher hereby disclaims any responsibility for them.

One Galleria Blvd., Suite 1900, Metairie, LA 70001
(504) 702-6708

ACKNOWLEDGEMENTS

For years, many of the stories appearing in this book have been part of weekly email messages that we send to our Farmers' Market customers, friends, and family members. These communications continue to be popular among the recipients, and we are often told how much they like our weekly newsletters. And, for years, many of the email recipients have suggested that a compilation of these stories be made into a book. The positive comments that these people gave to us provided much of the motivation for the making of this book. The author is indebted to these people for their support and encouragement.

Many thanks are due to Steve O'Brien and Bernie Mullin for their help and support at the weekly Farmers' Market in Bel Air, MD. When our children were young, they helped Art at the market. After our children were no longer available, first Bernie stepped in to help and then, years later, Steve volunteered. Both were at one time weekly customers, but soon became indispensible helpers nearly every Saturday morning during the growing season.

The author wishes to express thanks to Bernie and Cindi Mullin for their help and suggestions for writing and compiling the first edition of this book. The author is also indebted to his wife, Cathy, and the rest of his family for their experiences that formed the basis for many of the stories that appear inside. Last, the author thanks friend and Farmers' Market customer Ira Silberberg for the beautiful photograph gracing the cover of first edition of this book.

TABLE OF CONTENTS

Welcome to SweetAire Farm xiii

Prologue: Before SweetAire Farm 1
Introduction 2
Charlie, The Belligerent Duck 2
A Name for a Car Mascot 4
Naughty Geese in the Backyard 5
Outhouses and Bathrooms 7
Cranberry Wine 10
Carboy Cowboy 12
Sticky Floor 14
Wine Tasting 15
Finding Four-Leaf Clovers 17
Lo, How A Rose E'er Blooming 17

The Early Years 21
Introduction 22
Ours by a Whisker 22
Farming 24
Hyacinths for Our Souls 25
View from Above 26
A Close Encounter with Dobermans 27
Playing in the Puddle 28
Tootsie Roll Junior 30
Timin I: Woodchuck Hunter 31
Timin II: Falling for a Cat 32
Timin III: Trapped 33
A Reliable Water Supply 34
Amos Stolzfus's Loader 35
Art's Christmas Morning Tradition 36
At the Livestock Auction 36
Our Lawn 38
Silage from Grass Clippings 40

Beautiful Pictures in Catalogs	42
Christmas Eve Tradition	43
Dandelion Stories	44
Turkeys	45
Joy's Song	46
Holiday Surprise	47
Dirt City	48
Meat Comes from Animals, Really!	49
Recipe: Impossible Pie	50
Genealogy of Our Rhubarb	50
George	51
Fence Posts for Castleton	53
Jodi's Pigs	55
Joy and Her Animals	57
Beware of the Ram I	59
Thrown Into the Mud	59
Joy's Sleeping Tree	60
Loud Mockingbird in a Holly Tree	60
Our Live Christmas Tree	62
Holiday Travels to Remember	65
Recipe: Cranberry Relish	68
Our Two Haying Sayings	69
The Parade	69
Barley	71
The Rooster Who Ruled the Roost	72
Failure to Secure Load	74
The Old John Deere Model A Tractor	75
Too Much Help	78
Horseradish for Fun and Profit?	80
Beware of the Ram II	83
Too Much Lime	84
When We Baled Hay	85
Attempt at a Good Deed	86
Being Rich	87
Drinking from My Saucer	88
Out in the Cold	89

Truck Runaway Ramps in the Mountains 90
Listening for Lambs 90
A Ram Called Stolzfus 92
Joe 92
The Trouble Is That They Have To Be Loaded After They Grow Big .. 95
As Good As Gold 100
How We Taught Our Girls to Read 102
Our Old Kitchen Table 103
Back Rubs 105
Dungarees 107
Stuck Without Funds 109
Photos from the early years 112

The Middle Years 121
Introduction 122
A Good Mom 122
Cathy Gets Her Gator 123
Aftermath of a Storm 124
Aircraft Sightings 125
Fence Posts for Castleton 126
Cricket Wars I 128
Recipe: Cathy's Best Ever Chili 132
Animals Love to Eat Apple Prunings 132
Apple Pie Mix 133
Almost a Wether 133
Art's New Gator 134
Lamb in Trouble 135
Bees in the Air 136
Cider-Making and Apple Pomace 140
Cricket Wars II 142
Recipe: Renee's Rhubarb Cake 142
Don't Try This Yourself 143
Farmers' Markets 144
A Year (Almost) Without Peaches 146
When Sheep Got Loose 148
Farmer's Share 150
Cricket Wars III 150

Favorite Apple Choices	151
Feeding a Lamb with a Pail	151
Fox Against Goose	153
It Must Have Been Good for Him	153
Lambs at Play	155
Thorns	156
Lambs Doing Well	157
Mowing with Swallows	158
Feed Bags	158
Lambs Don't Recognize Sheared Moms	161
Musings from the Hayfield	162
The Ram's New Trick	165
Naming Fig Trees After Those Who Gave Them to Us	165
Papers Used for Mulch	166
Paul and Eric Come from Korea	167
Paul's and Eric's First Day	169
Paul and Eric: The Early Years	170
Sheep Are Social Animals	171
Sheep Names	173
Paul and Eric Team Up	174
Stanley the Young Sheep	174
Suspicious Balloon	176
The Parable of the Lost Contact Lens	176
The 23rd Psalm	177
The Road Angel	178
The Twelve Days of Christmas, Revisited	181
Recipe: Linzertorte	182
Use for Wool	184
Deer Ever So Close	185
European Fruit Hornets	186
Did It Taste As Good As Stew?	186
The Miracle Ear Van	188
Checkmate, Or Last Man Standing?	188
Leftovers? There Aren't Any	192
Philosophies from the Field	193
Something to Remember Us By	194

When We Raised Our Own Turkeys 195
Hail, Boys, Hail 198
Paul and Eric Tease the Ram 199
Sooty Blotch on Apples 200
Gregory Becomes Virgil 202
Gregory Learns His Lesson 203
Cathy's Refuge 203
Gotta Keep Movin' 204
Complaining Farmers 205
Gregory's Closest Friends 208
Muscovy Duck Tales 209
Morning Glories, Like Diamonds, Are Forever 213
A Shearing to Remember 214
Running Down the Aisle 215
Put Up Another Building 216
Shadow 219
Buzzing Bumblebees 224
Child Labor on the Farm 226
It Can Be Dark In There 228
Gregory Lies with the Lambs 229
What We Can Learn From Sheep 230
Being Self-Sufficient 234
Photos from the middle years 237

The Later Years 245
Introduction 246
Thunderstorms: Some Like Them, Some Don't 246
Horse Comes to Visit 246
Cathy Has a Bad Fall 248
Mother and Lamb Rodeo 253
Weeding Strawberries 255
Small Houses 256
Where Have All the Wild Animals Gone? 257
Beware of Flying Objects 258
A Dog Incident with the Sheep 259
Almost into the Hornets' Nest 259
A New Lamb for Christmas 260

Recipe: Banana Nut Bread 261
Cricket Wars IV 262
Muddy Feet 264
Gregory Rides a Sheep Into the Fence 264
It Was the Best of Times; It Was the Worst of Times 267
An Arthur Johnson Instead of an Arnold Palmer 267
A Week's Worth of Sheep Tales 268
Art and the Ram 1 271
Art Falls in the Mud, Again 272
Recipe: Blender Oatmeal Pancakes 273
Birds in Our Fruit 274
Caroling with Patients 275
Cathy's Lamb Euphoria 276
Unscheduled Delivery 277
Recipe: Craisins Oatmeal Chocolate Chunk Cookies 278
Cathy's Shuddering Adventure 278
Confused Conversation at the Apple Festival 280
Cricket Wars V 280
Conversation with a Park Attendant 282
Cricket Wars VI 282
Dark Acres 283
Deaf Chef 284
Food Rules 285
Recipe: Morning Glory Muffins 286
Good People are Everywhere 287
Groundhogs Go for a Ride 288
Independence Day Tradition 288
Insect Mating Disruption 289
Cricket Wars VII 289
Introducing Unfamiliar Fruits 290
Recipe: Persimmon Pie 291
Just Us 291
Watch Out, Little Lambs 291
Lost in Thought While Pruning 292
Maneuvers for Feeding the Sheep Their Morning Grain 294
Math in the Berry Patch 294

Mayhaw Magic 295
Mockingbird Nest in the Raspberries... 295
Muddy 2018.. 296
Raccoon Wars I 297
Naming of Our Buildings... 298
Our Maryland State Fair Show Ram.. 299
Recipe: Macaroni and Cheese 301
Papayas for the Sheep 302
Pesticide-Free Fruit... 303
Police Blotter 303
Sheep Out Again... 303
Prices of Our Fruits.. 305
Raccoon Wars II 306
Real Apples.. 308
Return of the Fireflies 308
Reverence for SweetAire Farm 309
Sheep Visit Neighbor's Yard and Are Repelled.............................310
Sheepful Reminiscences 311
Shoveling Snow... 314
Small Berries... 314
Spider Web Season 315
SweetAire Farm Sounds 315
The Most Beautiful Time of the Year.. 318
Raccoon Wars III.. 319
The Sleepy Possum... 320
The Threat of Hay 321
The Trapped Owl 322
Art's First Rule.. 322
Thieving Squirrel.. 324
We Prefer Yellow Sweet Corn.. 324
We Sell Taste, Not Looks... 325
What Global Warming Means to Us 326
When the Big Maple Toppled Over 327
Wild Animals and What to Do About Them 329
Art Is Pinned by a Branch 332
SweetAire Farm Olympics 333

Peppi's Meats	334
SweetAire Farm During the Novel Conrona Virus Pandemic	335
Van No Go	336
Farm Pay	338
Our Old Kitchen Table	338
Father's Day: A Letter to Everyone Close	340
Berry Picker's Lament	341
Our Truck	342
Sunrise	343
The Vultures Will Get You	345
COVID for Christmas	347
New Beginnings	348
Photos from the later years	351
Epilogue	359

WELCOME TO SWEETAIRE FARM

Let me introduce who we are. We were, until retirement from other jobs, part-time farmers. That means we had two full-time jobs, the farm being one of them. Our farm is called SweetAire Farm and is located just outside the little town of Darlington on the edge of the rural-suburban interface in Maryland. That means that where the farm is located is rural right now, but there are signs that urban encroachment could come from two directions: from Baltimore to the south and from Philadelphia/Wilmington on the northeast. In the distant future there may be farms scattered among suburban developments as there are in many locations on the east coast.

This patchwork pattern isn't all bad. The proximity of the population provides a ready market for direct marketing of farm produce, and that's good. Close neighbors don't always understand or tolerate farming operations, and that's bad. But, eventual or not, the encroachment of housing developments hasn't happened yet.

Our family starts with Art and Cathy, and four children: Joy, Jodi, Paul, and Eric, in that order. The children came in two bunches of two each. Joy and Jodi were both born near Ithaca, New York before we moved to Maryland, when Art began active duty in the U.S. Army in 1969. They were in their late teens when we adopted Paul and Eric as youngsters in 1984. We also had our grandson, Greg, live with us for his first six years. This means that the flavor of SweetAire Farm has changed over the years as children with different interests combined with the enlargement of our property holdings and learning from our foibles over the years. These will be made clearer in the pages ahead.

Outside employment is important for most family farms, and it was for ours, as well. Art worked for the government until 1975, when he went into education; Cathy was a stay-at-home mother, occasionally substitute teaching until 1981, when she became the head librarian in Darlington. Art retired from his non-farm job in 2009; Cathy retired in 2010.

SweetAire Farm is a general family farm of 49 rolling acres. That's not really big for the area, but it's a lot larger than many others. On this farm, we have raised some cows (about 10), sheep (10-20 at a time), hay, and many types of fruit. We have since given up the other projects in favor of the fruits that we grow and sell. The animals were fun, but a lot more work at times when we needed to spend our time with the fruits that provide us with most of our opportunities for income.

We have the traditional tree fruits found in the other orchards in the area, such as apples, peaches, pears, and cherries, and other tree fruits not usually grown around here, such as persimmons, paw-paws, and che fruits. In addition, we have a wide range of berries that we produce and sell, such as blackberries, blueberries, currants, elderberries, gooseberries, mulberries and raspberries. Some of the more unusual berries that we grow are Aronia berries, jostaberries, loganberries, and shisandra berries. We have grown grapes, kiwis, and citrus fruits of many kinds. If the pictures of fruits look good in the catalogs mailed to us, and they appeal to Art, then he usually orders some to give them a try and see if they will fit into our scheme of providing a wide range of unusual fruits for our farmers' market customers.

SweetAire Farm started out as a 5-acre piece of property with a house, one small barn, some sheds, and space overgrown with briars and small trees. We cleared the brush and trees by hand, built some fences, and made some pastures. Then we began to plant fruit trees, grapevines, and other fruiting plants until we were tucking something into every available space. We were bursting out of our seams.

By this time, we also had sheep and cows with no place to grow hay and with inadequate pasture. In 1979 we bought 15 acres of land a half a mile down the road from our house. That property had been used to grow corn years before, and the ground was still bumpy where the furrows had been plowed but not quite smoothed. When we bought the ground, however, it had been neglected for several years and was even more overgrown than was our original piece of property.

We had big plans for that 15 acres: we could use some for pasture, some for hay, and we even had visions of pick-your-own strawberries. But first, the trees and brush had to be cleared.

We had very little in the way of machinery at that time, so it was cleared by hand. The small trees were either clipped with shears or cut with a hand saw. The brush was also clipped to the ground. All of this brush had to be moved by hand to the hedgerows. The girls helped a lot with that chore.

One of the best ways to keep the trees and brush from regrowing was to cut the cleared land for hay. We did this with an old John Deere "A" tractor and a sickle-bar mower bought very cheaply from a farm used-machinery dealer. Raking was done by hand and the loose hay was pitchforked onto the back of our Ford F100 pick-up truck. Later, it was loaded onto a trailer, also by hand. We all helped to do this together.

As time went on, we made progress. Things we had done by hand were now done by machines. Things that were done by simple machines were accomplished later by better, more sophisticated, and more expensive machinery. Once cleared, the brush did not grow back; once built, the fences remained. This was bootstrap farming at its purest.

We bought what we could afford, and only when we needed it. Except for a few occasions when we needed large tractors, we did not borrow money to finance our purchases. We didn't know if there would ever be a financial return on our investments, but that was the eventual goal. At the time, we did it because we liked farm life and wanted our children to have farm experiences while they grew up.

We were feeling our way. What methods would work best for us? What things could we do that would be successful? What could we sell that other people might want to buy? What could be possible with the limited amount of time and money that we had to work with? How could we realize some return?

We had many choices. Farms in the Maryland countryside are lush and green. The soil is fertile and rain is usually plentiful. Maryland winters can be cold, but not too cold. Maryland summers are hot and humid, but oppressive temperatures are usually confined to parts of

July, August, and, sometimes, June and September. Springtimes and autumns are several months long and could be perfect except for the excessive pollen that sometimes fills the air and overwhelms the sinuses. Rain is usually well distributed throughout the year, but short periods of dryness have been known to occur. The sun shines a lot. At that time, Maryland could be said to be on the southern edge of the growth zones for northern trees and crops, and on the northern edge of the southern zone. With rising temperatures, northern varieties do not do as well here as they used to. However, the range of choices for what to grow was very wide.

We tried raising cows, sheep, pigs, chickens, ducks, and geese for sale, and had some success. We had regular customers and a stable market, but the financial returns were modest at best, and the amount of work required was huge. So, we tried other things; we even considered selling hay, but soon learned that hay was not for us.

We discovered fruit as a crop almost by accident. We had grown strawberries for ourselves for several years and had some extras that we found could sell quite easily. Other fruits, such as peaches, also seemed to have a ready demand. And, there was something rewarding about growing good, healthy fruit to sell. So, that was the direction we began to see as the right one for us.

We started going to the Bel Air Farmers' Market in 1982, ten years after we moved to our original 5-acre farmstead. At the time, we could only bring excess fruit from the few trees, vines, and plants that we had growing at the time. But, we soon found that to supply a steady availability of fruit to attract regular customers, we needed to plant many more varieties with different ripening times than we had already established. We needed a larger orchard and more plantings.

We did not think we could grow fruit on our property down the road, because neighborhood security for ripening fruit could be a problem. We might have more unauthorized help picking the fruit than we wanted. And, that help would be there when we weren't.

That's when we had the opportunity in 1987 to buy 29 acres adjoining our original 5 acres. It, too, had grown up in trees and brush, but, by this time, I had a chain saw, better tractors, and a Bush Hog rotary mower to attach to the back of the tractor. Clearing of the land took time, but not nearly as long as had our previous two property purchases. We expanded our pastures and our tree plantings. And this area continues to be the main part of our fruit production to this day.

You might wonder about the name of our farm. We needed to identify ourselves somehow, but didn't have a good name. Many of the farms in our area have historical names passed down from generations gone by, but our farm was our creation, and it didn't come with a name already attached.

We talked about this in our family, but really didn't have any good ideas. We considered using "Waggin'-Tail Farm" for a while, based on the many animals that we had, but with our new emphasis on fruit, that wasn't particularly appropriate. The name "SweetAire Farm" was inspired partly by a location in Maryland called Sweetair, which Cathy always liked, partly by the sweet aromas of blossoms in the spring, and also partly by the music that our children played on their instruments they learned to play as they grew up.

There is an old story that goes like this: "How can a farmer become worth a million dollars?" the answer is that "He starts out being worth two million dollars." The point is well made in this riddle that farming is often a losing proposition. It is long, hard work that may not pay off monetarily. But farming is more than just money, and a farmer may be better off than others making ten times as much money.

In this book is a collection of stories drawn from experiences on and around SweetAire Farm and the Darlington, Maryland community. Some stories are funny, some sad, some informative, some unbelievable, and some just plain philosophical, but together they form a picture of our million-dollar life on SweetAire Farm.

So, welcome to SweetAire Farm, and we hope your visit will be enjoyable.

PROLOGUE

Before SweetAire Farm

INTRODUCTION

Art and Cathy both grew up in rural areas in upstate New York: she lived in a house in Windsor, near Binghamton, and he lived on a small family farm in Newfield, near Ithaca. She was the second child in her family and Art was the first of six in his. Both grew up with modest means, and Art's family could have qualified as poor.

They met in 1961 as students of Cornell University; he was in his third year of a five-year program in Agricultural Engineering when she was a freshman Home Economics major. They met as members of the campus Methodist student organization, began dating, and were married while she still had another year of schooling before graduation. In order to allow her to complete her studies after he had graduated with his bachelor's degree, he enrolled as a graduate student in Agricultural Engineering. He earned his Master of Science and doctoral degrees. Cathy helped to support him during his graduate years.

As soon as he graduated, he had incurred an obligation through the Cornell Reserve Officers Training Corps (ROTC) to serve two years as a Lieutenant in the U.S. Army. This is how they came to Maryland. His first duty station was the officers' training course at Aberdeen Proving Ground. He was then assigned to Edgewood Arsenal, nearby.

Whereas there are many stories that we can tell related to the time when we were growing up, and before moving to our little farm in Darlington, Maryland, we have included here only a very few that stand out in our memories.

CHARLIE, THE BELLIGERENT DUCK

When Art was still a graduate student at Cornell University, there was, in the same department, an employee who lived in downtown Ithaca, NY and, for some reason, had a pet duck that he had been keeping at home. And, also for some reason, he wanted to give that duck away to a good home with a family that would not consider the duck to be a candidate for dinner fare.

So, Art, whose parents had a farm in nearby Newfield NY, volunteered to take the duck out of Ithaca and to a new home in

Newfield. When he went to get the duck, he learned that it had a name: Charlie…

Charlie was a Pekin duck, the kind with all-white feathers and a docile personality; Pekin ducks are usually very easy to get along with. They are also the models for Disney's Donald and Daisy Duck.

Charlie was brought to Newfield and released. He had been caged at his old home in Ithaca, so being newly free was, literally, a liberating experience for him. He enjoyed the free run of the farm, and explored all the new places that he could go without restriction.

We soon learned, however, that Charlie had a problem: he hated women, and that also became our problem. It was not known what kind of traumatic experience would have caused such a condition, but Charlie definitely hated all women. He did not bother men, but, whenever he spotted a female human, he would spread his wings as a gesture of aggression, and run or fly as fast as he could in the direction of his prey. Once close, he attacked her ankles with his bill, and did his best to frighten her; and, he relentlessly persisted with the attack until the woman escaped somehow to a place of asylum out of reach or out of sight for Charlie.

On one visit by Cathy and Art to see his parents at home, Cathy and Art had become separated, Cathy stayed outside and Art visited with his parents inside their house. Charlie had not been at the farm for long, and his belligerent reputation was not well known at that point.

So, as Cathy wandered by herself outside, she was spotted by Charlie, who recognized her as a woman; he attacked. Taken by surprise, she ran to the steps to the upper part of the barn, and climbed as high as she could. She stayed marooned there, safe for a while because Charlie could not climb the steps. Charlie continued pacing at the foot of the steps and tried to figure out a way to get closer to harass Cathy.

After a while, Art did notice that Cathy was not around, so he went to see what was keeping her. There he saw her, a hostage atop the steps, and Cathy not knowing how to get out of there without being attacked by Charlie.

Art hurried over and chased Charlie away; Charlie did not go willingly; he knew that he had a conquest and wanted to assert complete dominance. He had evil in his eyes at that point.

Art's rescue of Cathy that day earned him the status of hero, at least for a short while, and Cathy learned not to go wandering outside without first carefully checking around for any sign of Charlie. Even if he was nowhere to be seen, extra caution had to be exercised, lest Charlie sneak up from behind.

We never really knew what eventually became of Charlie. One day, he came up missing, to everyone's relief, actually. A telltale small scattering of white duck feathers indicated that Charlie may have met his match in the form of a bigger and hungrier fox. Charlie couldn't deal with that situation, no matter how belligerent and aggressive he was.

A NAME FOR A CAR MASCOT

When Art was a young man, just graduated from high school and prior to his freshman year at college, he needed to find transportation to his summer job working for a landscaping business in Ithaca, N.Y. He was fortunate to be able to purchase a used 1949 Chevrolet two-door coupe from a graduating university student for the price of $50. Without extra funds to his name, this was a price that he could afford.

Although drivable, his "new" car needed some work. There was bodywork that needed to be done to repair the damage that had been caused by Ithaca winters with lots of snow and salted roads. There was also some engine work needed to correct its tendency to burn oil. Over time, Art learned by experience about body repair and about replacing piston rings in an engine.

He had a small plastic figure of a caveman that he glued to a magnet and placed it on the dashboard of his car as a kind of mascot. That figurine went everywhere that Art went. But that little creature needed a name.

One day, Art was in the car with his younger sister, Lynda, driving for some purpose when the issue of a name for the mascot came up as a topic of conversation. Lynda had some suggestions, but none suited Art's fancy. He told Lynda that he had been considering the name "Urgle" as appropriate for the name of a caveman. She agreed that Urgle could be a good name.

"Then Urgle it'll be", said Art. And that was the name assigned from then on for that mascot, "Urgle-itel-bee".

NAUGHTY GEESE IN THE BACKYARD

Back in the olden days, when Art was growing up on a farm in Newfield NY, there were many animals to care for. There were chickens, cows, sheep, and Guinea fowl. And then there were geese.

The number of geese in the flock varied, depending on the number of young that hatched that year, or on the number taken by the local wild predators. There were at least four geese in the flock, and as many as six or eight.

The geese roamed all over the area near the house. All day long they could be either seen walking around with their heads held high, here and there reaching down to sample an attractive morsel of vegetation, or they could be heard honking just to make themselves known to anybody who didn't know that they were present. They acted like stately kings and queens of the property. They were in charge, and nothing happened without their approval.

As they wandered around, they, of course, left behind their manure droppings, plenty of them. They were well fed, and they left plentiful evidence to prove it.

One of the hazards when a family member or friend walked around outside in the summer was that goose manure could not easily be avoided. Its color was the same shade of green as the vegetation, so, unless one walked around with one's eye constantly on the ground, it was easy to miss –that's easy to miss seeing, not easy to miss on one's shoes, or, Heaven forbid, one's bare feet. Stepping in goose manure was so common, that Art's mother required everyone to wipe his or her feet each time they entered the house after walking outside.

Art's father used to cut the grass around the house with a string trimmer. He apparently preferred this method over trying to keep a lawn mower in operation throughout the season.

However, using a string trimmer on grass and weeds with occasional piles of goose manure can have consequences. One feature of using a string trimmer is that small pieces of vegetation can fly anywhere.

Hitting goose manure with a string trimmer sometimes results in goose manure flying high. Art's dad was quoted as saying, "Goose [manure] doesn't taste so good!" The word in brackets was actually uttered with more colorful language.

There were only two places around the house from which the geese were excluded. The first was our vegetable garden, and the second was the yard behind the house. Wire fences surrounded each of these areas. If the geese ever got into the vegetable garden, then they could eat all of our good food before we had a chance at it, and we needed that food to preserve for the winter.

The second place, the back yard, was the domain of Art's mother. It was there that she hung the laundry to dry and it was there that she cleaned household objects and did many other chores that had to be done outside. It was also in the back yard that she felt safe from walking in goose manure and tracking it into the house.

There were two gates in the fence that surrounded the back yard. One on the upper side and the other on the lower side. The lower gate was hardly ever used, but the upper gate was used often to bring things into the yard or into the back of the house. Art's mom often reminded, in no uncertain terms, anyone using the gate to be sure it was closed after using it. She was very protective of her back yard, and, she did not want geese in there to spoil it.

But, occasionally, the gate was inadvertently left open by someone, and that was bound to bring down her wrath. The reason for such sensitivity is that, as they wandered around the yard, the geese could tell when the gate was opened. And, they could see on the other side of the fence all that fresh, tasty new grass and weeds that had not been selectively grazed. There were juicy morsels to taste and enjoy. So, it didn't take very long for the geese to find the open gate and rush in. As they did so, they would honk loudly as if celebrating at a party.

Mom would either hear the noisy geese, or, a few minutes later, peer out the window and see them in her sacred back yard. Out the back door she would fly, shouting loudly, "Shoo ... Shoo ... Shoo!", and flailing her arms wildly as she ran. Those words, said loudly and forcibly, could not be ignored by the feasting geese, and they flew out the same way they got in. They knew that they did not belong there, and they also knew not to stand and challenge this determined wild woman chasing after them.

Once the geese were gone, and the gate reclosed, tranquility returned to the back yard.

All was again peaceful in this small area of sanctuary. And, the geese resumed their rounds outside of the back yard, watching for the perfect blade of grass that had yet to be plucked.

OUTHOUSES AND BATHROOMS

When Art and his family moved to upstate New York in 1955, our new home had no bathroom. There was an outhouse in back, near the barn and somewhat in front of the chicken house. It wasn't too big, being a two-seater, and constructed of gray and worn wooden planks. We all had to use it whenever nature called, and we would hope that nobody else was in there if there was an emergency.

I don't remember how much time it was that we tolerated that condition. It was probably at least a year, because I do remember how we used to bathe in the meantime. There was no bathtub or shower for us, so we bathed in the kitchen in a galvanized metal tub that was meant to be used to water livestock. It had been purchased at the local feed store in Ithaca. The tub was probably about 4 feet long, two feet wide, and 2 feet deep. The tub came out (from wherever it was stored) every Saturday evening for our weekly baths. Water for the bath was heated on our wood and coal stove in the kitchen. There were four children in the family at that time; and three of us who were given baths. We took turns in that tub. My sister Linda, being the youngest at 9 or 10 years old, was first in line. My mother made my brother and I stay in the living room while she was in the tub and until she was dressed afterward. After she was clean and dressed, my brother Don, the next youngest, had his turn. Mom poured heated water into the tub to add to the water that Linda had bathed in. After Don, then it was my turn for a bath. Again, more heated water was poured into the tub, and I was able to bathe in water that had already been used by Linda and Don. That was our weekly ritual for at least the first year in that house.

Tolerance for that situation wasn't easy for my mother, in particular. Mom and Dad decided that a bathroom had to be constructed for the house. There was no obvious place in the house to repurpose as a bathroom, so they decided to add a new room on the back of the house.

Constructing the new bathroom was a big project. Dad and we kids were not enough to complete the job in a short enough time, and money for materials and labor was in short supply, so my grandfather and uncle came to lend a hand. I don't remember all the details of the construction, but a foundation of concrete blocks and mortar had to come first. Then the room was framed, sided, and roofed. Inside, a toilet, sink, and bathtub had to be installed once the floor was finished. A door was cut through from the interior of the house to the new bathroom.

My Uncle Don had worked as a plumber at some time, so he knew how to install the fixtures and the drain to carry wastes away. He had a gas-fired pot to melt lead that he used to connect and seal the ceramic drain pipes together. A ditch was dig from the new bathroom to drain the wastes away.

With a new bathroom finished, and water supply hooked up, we were able to take our weekly baths in private, and to eliminate our bodily wastes without having to go outside first. Such luxury! The only worry now was the reliability of our water supplied from a spring up the hill from the house. Soon, after some dry summers, we had a new well drilled to eliminate that worry.

And, before we leave the outhouse entirely behind us, there is another story that comes to mind. Next to the outhouse was a hill slope. At the time, we had a vehicle that we called a "Doodlebug" that we used for various chores around our farm. The Doodlebug was an old 1937 Chevy automobile with the body largely cut off using a metal chisel; on the back of the Doodlebug was a flat platform constructed of bolted planks. We would sometimes carry things on the back of the Doodlebug; at other times, we just used the Doodlebug for transportation around our 60-acre farm.

One problem with the Doodlebug was that the electric starter did not work. There was no money to fix it, so, when we were done using the Doodlebug, we parked it at the top of the hill that ran next to the outhouse. We could start the engine of the Doodlebug by forcing it into gear as it rolled down the hill (it had a manual transmission that was standard at the time). The Doodlebug almost always started that way.

There was one other big problem with the Doodlebug: the clutch would not release. That means that, in order to shove it into gear, the driver would have to take it out of gear before the engine was running, release the parking brake (which did work!), and start the Doodlebug rolling down the hill (sometimes needing an extra shove, which required getting out of the driver's seat, pushing the vehicle at little bit, and quickly jumping back into the driver's seat before putting it into gear). Because the clutch did not work, the gearshift lever, located on the floor, had to be pulled with a good deal of force after the Doodlebug was rolling downhill fast enough, but before it was rolling too fast to pop it into gear. Most of the time, the required force was so much that two hands and arms were needed to pull the gearshift out of the neutral position and into a gear. A lot of grinding of the transmission happened during this maneuver.

Once the vehicle was in gear, and still rolling, the engine was connected directly to the wheels, and the engine would turn over and start.

So, picture this: the vehicle was rolling downhill by its own accord, the driver had two hands on the gearshift lever, trying to get the vehicle into gear as quickly as possible, and certainly before the vehicle reached the bottom of the hill and stopped. If the vehicle stopped rolling, there was no way to start it or get it back up the hill except by pushing it uphill by hand. There were a few times when we boys had to push it back up the hill.

With all this going on, there were no hands available to steer the Doodlebug. The driver could only hope that he could correct any inadvertent misdirection quickly enough once the engine started. One day, it didn't happen.

My brother Don hopped on the Doodlebug, and tried to start it. With both hands occupied with the gearshift lever, no hands on the steering wheel, and pulling with all his might to get the vehicle in gear, the Doodlebug ran into the far corner of the outhouse, breaking some boards off.

All of a sudden, Grandpop came out of the outhouse, scared and convinced that something bad had happened. He had been inside using it, and it took just a few (not many!) seconds to get his pants back up before he could pop out the door.

A little later in the day, after the Doodlebug had been started and parked back at the top of the hill, and the damage to the outhouse repaired, the same thing happened once more. But, this time, no one was inside to imagine that the world was coming to an end. The new damage to the outhouse was repaired, and potential users from then on always checked to be sure that no one had plans to start the Doodlebug while the outhouse was in use.

CRANBERRY WINE

A long time ago, when Art was still single and free to do such things, he experimented with wine-making. He made wine from almost anything that could be fermented. Inspired by wine recipes in books that he borrowed from the library, he even made wine from potatoes and beets. About the only fruit that he did not ferment were grapes.

In those years, cranberry sales were very seasonal. Cranberries were sold during the Thanksgiving and Christmas seasons, but were not usually available in grocery stores at other times of the year. Any unsold bags of cranberries were placed on sale immediately following New Year's Day. Bags full of cranberries were labeled "Reduced for Quick Sale", and placed on tables near the produce department.

This was an invitation for immediate action. Art did not have a lot of discretionary money in those days, so the cheap prices of the berries beckoned him to purchase them and turn them into wine.

Wine made from cranberries had a good flavor, and was one of Art's favorites. He did not make much cranberry wine, and did not consume a lot of it, but what he had he remembers fondly.

To make wine from cranberries, he first went through the berries in the bags to remove those that were spoiled, moldy, or unsound. If he had not been quick enough to visit the grocery store when the cranberries were first put up for sale, then there might be a large number of bad berries that had to be removed. Too many bad berries, and it was not smart to buy them in the first place.

The berries were ground into little pieces, and sugar, water, and yeast were added; the mix was placed into a container to ferment, a gallon at a time. The container was then placed high on a shelf in the kitchen of the apartment that he shared at the time with two other male college students. That way, the fermenting mixture was out of everyone's way, and was close enough to the ceiling that the temperature was a little warmer and the fermentation could proceed unabated at a fast rate.

The gallon container was topped with a rubber stopper with hole for a glass tube. Attached to the glass tube was a short rubber tube ending in a small jar of water. This arrangement formed an air-lock that allowed carbon dioxide gas produced during the fermentation to escape, while blocking unwanted air from leaking back into the fermentation vessel. It was fun to watch the bubbles in the glass jar while the juice was being transformed into wine. The bubbles came especially fast at the beginning of the fermentation process, when the available sugar was most abundant and alcohol was at a minimum.

While all this was going on, Art still had college classes to attend, and it was during one of these classes that it happened. To explain, we start with the fact that Art's wine-making was not sophisticated enough to use special wine yeast in the fermentation. Instead, he used regular bread yeast, which was easily and cheaply available. One difference between yeasts used for making bread or wine was that bread yeast is supposed to produce more carbon dioxide gas, to make bread rise, than wine yeast makes.

The fermentation in one container was so vigorous, producing so much gas, that it made a froth of the cranberry pieces in the mixture and forced them into the glass tube at the top of the stopper, blocking further gas escape into the jar of water. All the while, however, fermentation was proceeding at a furious pace and producing more gas. Pressure in the vessel built up so much that it burst the small glass tube.

Art returned from class to find a mess. Small pieces of bright red cranberries were everywhere. The ceiling looked like it had a bad case of measles. There were bits of cranberries on everything in the kitchen – on the shelves, on the cabinets, on the clean dishes in the rack, on the floor, on the walls, on the stove, on the refrigerator, and on the table and chairs.

The mess had to be cleaned up fast before his apartment-mates came home from their classes. He did not want to anger them by letting them see what a mess he had made. He even had to wash the dishes again and scrub all surfaces.

It never happened again, although Art continued to make cranberry wine whenever he could. But, he was more careful after that about filling the gallon containers quite as full. And, he still enjoyed every sip of that wine.

CARBOY COWBOY

When Art was in his college days, and had nothing better to do than to study engineering, he dabbled in making wine. His winemaking was fairly successful for certain types of wine, although he never was able to make wine from traditional grapes. Some wine he made a gallon at a time, but some kinds of wine he made in three- and five-gallon batches. Finding fermentation containers of the right size and of proper materials was not always easy. Glass containers were perfect: they were able to be cleaned between uses, did not add extra flavors to the fermenting wine, and the wine inside them was able to be watched closely during the fermentation to make sure that everything was progressing according to plan. Art was able to purchase a three-gallon glass jug from a science supply catalog, but anything larger was too expensive for him to afford with his limited discretionary budget. He needed to find an affordable source for additional glass jugs that he could use to make his wine.

And, that's when serendipity came into play. Art was one day walking past the nuclear reactor on the campus of Cornell University when he noticed in the refuse a five-gallon glass container. They were throwing away exactly what he needed! So, the first chance that he had, he grabbed that container, called a carboy, and brought it back to his apartment.

The carboy needed cleaning, so he used a lot of water with ammonia liquid, bleach, and detergent, all used separately, of course, to thoroughly clean his new-found potential fermentation vessel. The wash water was dumped into the toilet and flushed down the drain. Once cleaned in that fashion, he was able ferment his wine substrate into tolerable wine five gallons at a time. The cost of the cleaning materials was a lot less than would have been the cost of a comparable carboy.

He continued to keep his eyes on the trash behind the nuclear reactor, and was able to retrieve several more carboys. In each case, he brought them home and cleaned them up. He was then able to make wine ten, fifteen, or twenty gallons at a time. This was big-time winemaking.

It may have been the last carboy that he brought home, and maybe not, but at least one of the last carboys that he retrieved was a little different. Before that carboy, Art had not seriously questioned what they had contained, how they were used, or why they were being discarded by personnel at the nuclear reactor. Answers to both of these questions became perfectly clear once he attempted to clean this carboy of whatever had been inside it.

He went through his cleaning ritual, dumped the dregs into the toilet, and flushed. It was then that he noticed that some of what he had dumped into the toilet was not removed with the rush of water. In the depression at the bottom of the toilet, a metallic substance remained. He flushed again. And again. Nothing changed. The metallic stuff was still there.

He had seen this stuff before – it was mercury, and it was heavy and not wetted by water. And, because this mercury had come from a carboy that was thrown out by people at the campus nuclear reactor, he assumed that it was radioactive mercury. It had to be removed somehow.

He tried everything he knew to remove that pool of mercury from the bottom of the toilet. He first tried Saniflush, then Drano, but nothing worked. He knelt next the toilet and tried to spoon the mercury out, but the mercury would not stay on the spoon. It was determined to stay there. Exasperated and without any more ideas about how to remove the hazard, he resigned himself to acceptance of its presence for an indefinite duration.

What else could he do? There was one thing, and he did it. He found a sticker on the outside of the carboy with a radioactive symbol imprinted on it. He removed the sticker from the carboy, and posted it on the bathroom door. We had the only radioactive bathroom east of the Mississippi!

The story doesn't completely end there. Over time, the mercury eventually disappeared. Another result is that mercury reacts with iron to form a soft metallic amalgam, and some time after, a few of the pipes underneath the bathroom began to develop some leaks. The last additional outcome is that all of these carboys, which are of heavy glass, have remained with us through every relocation move we made thereafter; Art was, for valid reasons, not present for most of these moves, so Cathy had to handle all of these heavy carboys by herself. They remain stored in one of our sheds on SweetAire Farm.

STICKY FLOOR

In his college days, Art experimented with wine making. He was inspired by several library books on the subject of wine-making that included recipes for making wine from exotic sources, such as potatoes and beets, among others.

His very favorite homemade wines were fermented from elderberries or wild black cherries, both of which grew wild near his home in upstate New York at the time. He would wait until these fruits were fully ripened, pick them, and bring them to his apartment where he lived while taking college classes. The wine was made, usually many gallons at time, in glass containers big and small.

Once the wine had finished fermenting, it had to be transferred from some of these vessels into others, and then into bottles and sealed with corks. Empty champagne bottles had been found freely available in the garbage cans of fraternities on the Monday following Spring Weekend parties at the university. They were good, sturdy bottles that would take a lot of abuse if it came to that.

With all this pouring and decanting of the wine, it was inevitable that spills would occur, especially when pouring from large, 5-gallon carboys into other vessels and then into bottles. Champagne bottles were of dark green glass and it was hard to see when the wine level in the bottle neared the top. So, there were spills.

Most of these spills were sopped up relatively quickly, but there were times when the bottling operation demanded undivided attention. At those times, the liquid was allowed to stay on the floor for a short time until it could be attended to.

There was tile on the floor in the apartment kitchen, which was held in place with tile cement, probably water-based. What happens to water-based cement when wine seeps under the tile? The cement weakens and releases its hold on the tile. What happens when wine is allowed to stay on top of the tile for a short time before it is cleaned up? The tile becomes sticky. This combination led to tile that was loose from the underlying flooring, but would stick to the bottom of shoes when someone walked on it.

The hazard this created was that, when one walked through the kitchen and came out of the kitchen, a square of tile would be stuck underneath each foot, making for very difficult walking. It was just like walking wearing snowshoes.

WINE TASTING

In the old days, when Art considered himself to be a master wine maker, he had many adventures worthy of recounting. This one led to some confusing results.

He never had the opportunity or inclination to make wine from grapes; about anything else that could be fermented was attempted as a source of wine. All that had to be included in the mixture (called the "must", according to the books that he read on the subject) was some base fruit or vegetable, sugar, and yeast. Then stand back and watch the must turn into wine, either good, or terrible, as the case might be.

Two of his favorite kinds of wine were elderberry and wild black cherry. Copious quantities of both of these fruits were readily available growing wild on the family farm. Elderberries grew as umbrel-like clusters on tall bushes, while wild black cherries grew as grape-shaped bunches on trees. Both of these ripened toward the end of summer, just in time to be brought to his apartment that he shared with two other guys while attending college classes.

Wine made with either of these fruits was delicious. They were similar in many respects, taste, deep red color, and alcohol content. When they had finished fermenting, and were subsequently bottled in the dark green colored champagne bottles that he had obtained from dumpster-diving and garbage-picking the many fraternities on campus, both wines were so similar that one could not tell them apart from looking at them through the bottles. It was important to label the bottles as soon as they were filled in order to identify positively the kind of wine that was contained inside. Unfortunately, there was an instance when labeling was not done at the right time.

It must have been a time when Art was busy with other things, after all, he had classes to attend, that the labeling was postponed for later. Normally, that would not have been a problem, because two kinds of wine would not be ready to bottle at the same time, or, if there were several kinds of wine to attend to, they could be separated until there was time to label them. In this case, however, the elderberry wine and the cherry wine bottles were intermingled somehow.

The only way to separate them was to uncork each bottle, pour a very small amount into a cup, taste the wine, and decide which type of wine that it was. When a decision had been made, the bottle was recorked and labeled on the outside with the type of wine written on a paper sticker.

So, Art and Cathy took on this tedious chore.

At the beginning, it was easy to classify each bottle of wine. This one was cherry, that one was elderberry, and so on. But, as the number of samples increased, so did the amount of alcohol ingested. And, there were still a lot of bottles to classify. It soon became harder to discriminate between the elderberry wine and the cherry wine. Very quickly, they began to taste the same. Was that one elderberry, or cherry? Who knows? Who cares?

Art and Cathy had a great time trying to discern the two kinds of wine. It became fun, and neither of them cared whether the wine bottle was labeled correctly or not. Toward the end of this tasting and labeling session, both were in really good moods.

Tasting party, anyone?

FINDING FOUR-LEAF CLOVERS

Whatever it was, young Cathy had the knack. She could spot four-leaf clovers almost automatically. Although it is said that only one out of 10,000 clover leaves has four lobes, the way Cathy could locate them made them seem so commonplace.

When they were younger, and had the time to do such things, Cathy and Art would stroll across fields and over lawns populated with clover plants of many varieties. Once he found out about her talent, Art invariably challenged Cathy to find him a four-leaf clover. Usually without hesitation, she would bend down and pick something up from the ground. In her hand would be a four-leaf clover.

This frustrated Art somewhat, because he could stare at the ground forever, and not spot a clover leaf with four lobes. And, when he was ready to abandon the search, Cathy would just bend down and come up with a four-leaf clover to show him how easily it is to find one.

This didn't just happen once or twice, but many, many times. Cathy could just find four-leaf clovers as easy as that. It was one of her gifts.

Art figured that anyone who had such a gift was someone to keep around, so he married her. Even after that, she still found four-leaf clovers with abandon.

Almost always after finding her special clover leaf, she would hand it to Art, perhaps to show off, or perhaps just to share her luck with him. And what did he do with each and every four-leaf clover that she handed to him? He ate them, every one.

LO, HOW A ROSE E'ER BLOOMING

It was going to be a lonely Christmas for Art in 1970 in Cam Rahn Bay, Vietnam. There was a war going on, including sporadic rocket attacks launched from the other side of the bay. Not aimed at any particular place, most of them caused only property damage, but there were casualties. One Sergeant was killed by shrapnel while sitting behind a desk in a Quonset hut during a nighttime rocket attack. Art had walked by that exact location just a couple of nights before as he attended to his responsibilities as nighttime Duty Officer. In Vietnam, there were no guarantees of survival, or anything else for that matter. Coming to grips with one's own mortality had to happen, or we all would all go crazy with worry.

Art was 12,000 miles away from home, with a wife and two young daughters back there. Joy, the elder at three years of age was at a cute stage in her childhood. Jodi, his second daughter, was not yet two; she would never remember her dad after an absence of a year. Art missed them both, almost as much as he missed Cathy. Art and Cathy corresponded daily by audio cassette. Cathy would respond to what he had recorded and he to hers. It was nice to hear her voice, even if it was not live.

Although they each sent a cassette to the other on a daily basis, sometimes the mail service would cause a back up, and cassettes accumulated for up to a week. On a day when no message came from Cathy, it was a bad day. When, at last, the cassettes came in a bunch, there followed a blissfully indulgent marathon of listening to her voice for hours at a time.

Christmas would be especially hard. They had never missed celebrating with their families, even when Art was stationed in Maryland and they had to travel back home to upstate New York to be with them. But this year there was to be none of that. Although nobody in Cam Rahn talked about it, most felt the loneliness more acutely at this time of the year than at any other.

Art had occasionally attended Sunday chapel services led by Chaplain Bob Slimp, who thought it would be nice to form a choir to sing at a 2300 hours Christmas Eve service. There wasn't a choir at the Sunday morning service, so the choir was completely ad hoc. Art had sung at his hometown of Newfield, NY, and at their adopted Presbury Methodist Church in Edgewood, Maryland so he volunteered to sing with the Christmas Eve group.

He has no recollection of the identity of the choir director, but the director chose a hymn appropriate for the season: "Lo, How a Rose E'er Blooming". Art had heard the song before, but had never sung it. It was a pretty song, but Art had not paid it as much attention as he had a lot of other Christmas carols and songs.

They practiced several times before the scheduled evening service, and it was consoling to be part of the group. Art particularly liked the syncopation in the bass part and practicing singing with others in this environment was distracting me from his feeling of aloneness. He was sure that the distraction was shared.

Christmas Eve came, and they all worshipped and sang. They sang carols and they sang their anthem. "Lo, How a Rose E'er Blooming". There was never a piece of music any prettier and more meaningful. It was reassuring and consoling at the same time. For just a few minutes, the seasonal loneliness was relieved. Art still missed his family, but he would be with them again next year and the year after, and all the years after that. Everything would be alright.

Whenever he hears that song, the memories of that Christmas Eve return in full. There may have been fighting going on, and there were men and women somewhere not too far away who were being injured and killed, but in that little chapel thousands of miles away from home, on that evening, there was peace.

The Early Years

ARTHUR T. JOHNSON

INTRODUCTION

Art and Cathy moved to Maryland from upstate New York in 1969, when Art went on active duty with the U.S. Army. With them came their two very young daughters, Joy and Jodi. After Art returned from VietNam and they spent a year in a rented apartment, the small family bought their five-acre homestead in Darlington, Maryland. Both Cathy and Art had grown up on farms, so it was natural that they would begin to turn their few acres into a farm to supply the fruits, vegetables, and meats needed by their family. The girls had enough room to run around outside and were given responsibilities to help care for the garden and animals that now lived there also.

Art had an outside job during this period, and Cathy stayed home to care for the family. After a couple of years, Cathy was an occasional substitute teacher at the local elementary school and also worked for a time for a local veterinarian. Toward the end of this period, fifteen acres located a half mile down our road were added to our land holdings. This ground was used for summer pasture, growing hay, and, for a while, growing horseradish roots for a local condiment company. Brush and young trees growing there were cut and removed by hand by Art with help from the girls.

OURS BY A WHISKER

Our house and the surrounding five acres almost belonged to someone else. The fact that it didn't attests to our belief that this place was meant for us and only us. This is the way it happened:

Art, Cathy, and their two young daughters had been living in the area around Edgewood, Maryland since 1969 when Art went on active duty in the Army and was stationed at Edgewood Arsenal. Art returned from his tour in Vietnam, and was discharged from the U.S. Army in 1971. Art began searching for a civilian job once released from the military. The job search net was widely cast, with no place in particular that he would locate. One possible job was as a government employee in the same laboratory at Edgewood Arsenal where he had served during the first year of his military obligation. He had interviews in places far away, but his application at Edgewood Arsenal was the one that resulted in a job offer that he decided to accept. The small family moved to a rented apartment in Joppatown, Maryland.

Although both Art's and Cathy's families remained in upstate New York, the couple had become comfortably accustomed to Maryland, and looked for a house to buy in the area. They had driven through the small town of Darlington, MD, and liked the rural flavor of the vicinity. Both Art and Cathy had grown up in farming country, and wanted, if possible, to purchase a house with enough property around it for them to feel comfortable raising their daughters there. They soon found a place that was on the market that fit their expectations. The house had recently been refurbished and had five acres of mostly unimproved property around it. There was a small barn and a couple of sheds on the property. It was exactly what they were looking for.

So, they inquired about the possibility of purchase. They were told that the place was available, but that a down payment was required. This was a problem. The couple had very few bills and other financial obligations, but had not had time to save enough money for a down payment. They were also naïve potential buyers who were not sure of the entire property-purchase process. They proposed that Art use his eligibility to get a VA mortgage that would not require a down payment, but the seller would not accept that offer. They disappointingly gave up on that house.

Art made up his mind that he was not going to be denied again if another house-buying opportunity presented itself. He arranged for a bank loan that was enough for a reasonable down payment, if needed. There would be no problem paying off the loan, because Art and Cathy had not obligated all their income for other purchases. All this took several months to complete.

With some money in the bank, and with the self-assurance that they would not be blocked by the lack of a down payment, they began looking again for a house, and, perhaps, with some property to go with it. It was then that they found out that the same house that they had looked at previously was still unsold. They were dismayed, but pleased, that such an attractive house was still on the market after all this time. It had been several months, but they had not given up hope to make that house their own. They contacted the realtor, and set up an appointment.

This time, when a down payment was discussed, Art and Cathy were ready. They had the cash. They met one evening in the office of the realtor and signed a contract to purchase the house with its five acres in the Darlington area that they had particularly liked. After all this time and maneuvering, this house would be theirs.

An hour later, someone else in a different real estate office had also signed a contract on the same house. After months of no activity, they had beaten the other potential buyer by one hour.

FARMING

We found a quote by John F. Kennedy that is very appropriate to farming:

"The farmer is the only man in our economy who buys everything at retail, sells everything at wholesale, and pays the freight both ways."

And another from Dwight D. Eisenhower:

"Farming looks mighty easy when your plow is a pencil and you're a thousand miles from the corn field."

We can add that farming looks much easier when looking out our windows than when immersing ourselves in the great outdoors where the work is.

Adding to all this are several excerpts from a Paul Harvey talk, entitled "So God Made a Farmer":

God said, "I need somebody with arms strong enough to rustle a calf and yet gentle enough to deliver his own grandchild. I need somebody willing to sit up all night with a newborn colt. And watch it die. Then dry his eyes and say, 'Maybe next year.' I need somebody who can shape an ax handle from a persimmon sprout, shoe a horse with a hunk of car tire, somebody who can make harness out of haywire, feed sacks and shoe scraps. And who, planting time and harvest season, will finish his forty-hour week by Tuesday noon, then, in pain from 'tractor back,' put in another seventy-two hours." So God made a farmer.

God had to have somebody willing to ride the ruts at double speed to get the hay in ahead of the rain clouds and yet stop in mid-field and race to help when he sees the first smoke from a neighbor's place. So God made a farmer.

God said, "I need somebody strong enough to clear trees and heave bails, yet gentle enough to tame lambs and wean pigs and tend the pink-combed pullets, somebody who will stop his mower for an hour to splint the broken leg of a meadow lark. It had to be somebody who'd plow deep and straight and not cut corners. Somebody to seed, weed, feed, breed and rake and disc and plow and plant and tie the fleece and strain the milk and replenish the self-feeder and finish a hard week's work with a five-mile drive to church.'" So God made a farmer.

Farming is a way of life as well as a means of employment. Farmers are free to make their own decisions, and reap the rewards when they are successful, but also to pay the penalties when things don't turn our just right because of weather conditions or external markets that collapse through no fault of their own. They are good stewards of the land they feel tied to, support local programs, help their neighbors even without being asked, and are good, solid citizens of their communities. They represent the essence of the salt of the Earth. That is why God made a farmer.

HYACINTHS FOR OUR SOULS

*If of mortal goods thou art bereft,
And of thy slender store two loaves alone to thee are left,
Sell one, and with the dole,
Buy hyacinths to feed thy soul.*
 - Omar Khayyam

This poem has been one of our favorites since we learned it many years ago. Since then we have believed that hyacinths were necessary to feed our souls; even during times when money was tight, and there was none to spare, we could always find a little bit to buy hyacinths for our spiritual well-being.

Hyacinths for the soul can take many forms. Years ago for us, it could have been a particular LP record with treasured music. It has also been a special painting or print to hang on the wall, or an outstanding book or short story, or maybe viewing an exciting movie. These indulgences were infrequent when we had little money to spare, but they made life worthwhile. The point is that it is important to care for one's psychological well-being, especially during times of stress or hardship.

Today, our hyacinths often take the form of our flowers growing in beds around the house. Both of us enjoy seeing them when driving in the driveway, or when looking out the window, or when going to retrieve the mail from the mailbox alongside the road. At other times, we walk together out through the orchards for the same purpose, just to enjoy the beauty of our surroundings. So often, especially in the long, hot summer days, the orchards and plantings mean sweaty work for long hours. It is hard to really appreciate the beauty of our farm during those times. But it is good, every now and then, to see things through different eyes. Hyacinths for our souls, indeed.

VIEW FROM ABOVE

Soon after we bought our first five-acre portion of SweetAire Farm, Art thought it would be a great idea to photograph the house, buildings, and property from the air. He had a friend, Ed Meseke, where he worked who had a pilot's license and was an enthusiastic pilot, so Art arranged for his friend to rent a small plane from the local flight club, and take an hour off from work to fly to Darlington with Art on board to photograph our new farm. Ed was only too happy to have a chance to get some flight time in.

So, on the appointed day and at the prearranged time, they both took off in the rented plane.

They were soon over Darlington, and Art discovered that things on the ground look a lot different from the air than they do from his normal perspective. Nevertheless, he spotted our house and property, and requested that Ed fly around in circles above the farm while Art used his camera to shoot photos. Ed dipped one wing of the plane and did wheelies in the air above the farm. Around and around they went, with Art looking through the viewer of the camera to make sure that he got the shots that he wanted.

It must have been the combination of the circling while being tipped on his side, along with the restricted views of his surroundings that soon made Art start to feel uneasy. Unease soon turned to vertigo and worse. If Art had been able to keep sight of the horizon, then maybe he would not have felt so bad, but he couldn't look out the window at the horizon and still shoot the photos he wanted.

Art pleaded with Ed to return to the airport as fast as possible. Art managed to keep the contents of his stomach where they were intended to be, but it was not because they did not have other tendencies in mind. Art had never felt sicker at any time up to that point in his life. The trip back took a lot longer than Art would have liked, but they made it, and landed safely.

Art managed to exit the plane and stumble to his car. He eventually recovered, but the memory lingered. And that was the last time that he even remotely considered photographing the farm from above.

He never again had such an "air-brained" idea.

A CLOSE ENCOUNTER WITH DOBERMANS

Many of our early fences and other buildings were built with used boards that usually went cheaply at local auctions. There was one time, at an auction in nearby Aberdeen, MD, when Art bought a couple of pick-up loads of old boards. He brought one load home, but had to return later that afternoon to the auction site to load the rest. The auction had been held at a farm, and nobody lived there anymore. But, the farm was guarded by a couple of extra big and mean-looking Doberman dogs. When Art returned for his second load, all the people at the auction had gone and left the dogs in charge.

Art had brought our daughter Jodi with him for her company. She was only 4 or 5 years old at the time.

When she discovered that there were wooly-bear caterpillars hiding in the wood pile, she got very excited and wanted to collect all she could find. The only container that we had to put them in was a plastic Tupperware container that had held some cookies that we finished on the way to the farm. So, as Art was loading the boards on the truck, Jodi was collecting caterpillars and putting them in the container. Art kept a wary eye on the dogs, but they had kept their distance. However, there must have been some residual smell of cookies emanating from the container, because, as Jodi looked under another board for caterpillars, one of the dogs was attracted to the container. It came over to investigate the container that, by now, held several wooly-bears. Jodi saw that, and screamed to her Dad that the dog was after her caterpillars.

Responding to her cries, Art turned toward the container and the dog. That was a mistake. The dogs, which until this point had largely put up with us intruding on their territory, now bared their teeth and growled menacingly. When Dobermans bare their teeth, they are very frightening. What could he do? Art did not want to turn around or even back away, because then he would have been mauled mercilessly. And there were no other people around to help (this was also in the days before cell phones, so no calling 911). He told Jodi to get into the truck.

He stood his ground and sternly and repeatedly told the dog to go. For a time that seemed forever, the dog stood there, still baring her teeth and growling. Finally, after several years, or maybe not quite that long, the dog quietly turned and slunk away. And Art retrieved the container for Jodi, who, by now, had been watching from the relative safety of the truck.

Later, when Art asked Jodi what she would have done if the dog had attacked her Dad, she said that she would have climbed into the truck and locked the door!

PLAYING IN THE PUDDLE

For many years, our driveway, as with most farm driveways, consisted of packed dirt with a grass strip running down the center. The driveway was somewhat uneven, with high and low spots that formed over the years with use. At the end of our driveway, where vehicles had to turn to either park in their designated spots or to exit our farm, was a slight depression in the ground. The depression was caused when the dirt there was pushed aside by the right front wheels of the turning vehicles. Despite Art's periodic efforts to fill the depression with new dirt, the depression reformed almost immediately because all vehicles turned in the same place.

Whenever it rained or the snow melted, this particular depression filled with water to form a puddle lined with mud. Whenever a vehicle tire then hit that puddle, it splashed mud out of the depression and made it deeper.

The bottom of this puddle seemed to be impervious to water penetration, and so the only way that the puddle would ever dry was through evaporation. With the amount and frequency of precipitation that we normally had through the year, evaporation was highly unlikely; the puddle persisted.

That small pool of muddy water was a siren song to each of our children to play there. Temptation lay so close to the house that it could not be resisted. So, if any of them was playing outside, chances were that child would end up sitting either next to or in that puddle, slapping, swishing, or splashing the muddy water. And, a good deal of that muddy water would end up on the clothes or skin of the child playing there. Sometimes, enough of the muddy water ended up on the child that it was hard to tell where the puddle began and the child ended.

It was even worse when two children played in the puddle at the same time. Somehow, the splashing became more vigorous under those circumstances, and it was difficult to recognize that there were little humans under the coatings of mud.

Cathy was unhappy to see her children so messy. She sternly required each child to remove their disgusting clothes outside the house, and leave them in piles outside the door. Then, if it was warm outside, she might try to rinse off the rest of the mud from their bare bodies with a hose or pail of water. If it was not so warm that she could justify rinsing off outside, then she escorted the children quickly to the bathtub. It is possible that the temperature threshold for Cathy to rinse them outside may have been lower than comfortable for the children, or that the temperature threshold might have depended on her mood, which did not vary a lot when dealing with muddy kids.

All of our children went through this stage in their life. And that particular play puddle stayed there until 2003, when we finally paved our driveway. Asphalt does not form mud in which to play, which would have made life less fun for any children that we happen to have had around at the time. But, by then, all of our children had grown out of the desire to play in that old mud puddle anyhow.

TOOTSIE ROLL JUNIOR

Cats are very useful around a farm for controlling the spread of mice and rats drawn to stored feed supplies for livestock, and for the abundant places of shelter in which to make themselves comfortable. Of all the cats we have ever had, Tootsie Roll Jr. was the best hunter. She was thin with mottled fur of black, brown, and yellow. Seen from a distance, she looked about the same color and shape as a piece of Tootsie Roll candy. Hence her name, which was bestowed by one of our two girls.

Not only did she catch mice, rats, moles, and birds, but she caught them on schedule. Every morning without fail, the body of her latest victim would be found on our doorstep, and each morning the cadaver was of a different species. Once, when Cathy fell into the habit of leaving her clothes basket under the clothes line that we had at the time just across the driveway from our door, Tootsie Roll Jr. left the carcasses in the clothes basket. We neither encouraged nor discouraged her practice, but she was very punctual in the timing of her deliveries.

We got Tootsie Roll Jr. as a nearly full-grown kitten as a replacement for other cats that we no longer had. Not all cats are good hunters, so it came as a very pleasant surprise when she developed into a super varmint killer.

Sometimes we watched her on the prowl, and she seemed to hunt for the sheer pleasure of hunting. She would catch her prey and play with it for hours before she finally put it out of its misery. When it was dead, she no longer had interest in it, and she would leave it for the other cats to eat.

There was nothing, it seemed, that Tootsie Roll Jr. wouldn't try to catch. Most other cats do not kill moles, possibly because they dislike eating them, but Tootsie Roll Jr. caught moles for days on end. She caught wild rabbits as large as herself, and caught birds unlucky enough to have landed within her field of view. Most of these ended up on our doorstep in the morning.

Once, we trapped a young rat in one of the metal barrels in which we kept our bags of sheep and cattle feed. The feed bag in this barrel had been emptied enough so that the rat could not jump back out of the barrel. We tried putting some of our other cats into the barrel with the rat, but none would have any part of that. They clawed and grabbed and wouldn't even notice the vermin in the bottom of the barrel. Tootsie Roll Jr. had the same reaction at first, but caught the smell of the rat, pounced onto the rat, grabbed it in her mouth, and jumped back out of the barrel with the rat held in her mouth, all in one quick motion. Thereafter, whenever we opened up a barrel to get feed, Tootsie Roll Jr. would jump in to look for more rats.

Despite being a keen hunter, Tootsie Roll Jr. was very affectionate and not as aloof as are many other cats. When we would weed the garden, she often visited us, and rubbed against our legs and hands until we petted her. One of her favorite buddies was our dog at the time, Ollie. When he was left unchained, Ollie would sometimes play roughly with her, and she might scream and claw at him. But, she returned time and again to frolic with him. If Ollie was on a chain at the time, she often came over to rub against his leg and offer sympathy.

We have had many cats on SweetAire Farm, but none any more memorable than Tootsie Roll Jr., hunter extraordinaire.

TIMIN I: WOODCHUCK HUNTER

Every farm ought to have a dog, so, within months of moving to our new farm, we acquired our first dog. Like two of the other three dogs that we have had, we got her as a puppy from the animal shelter. She was named Timin. The origin of the name has been lost to us, but it was suggested by one of our girls. Timin was a small mixed-breed beagle-type black and white dog.

She was Art's buddy. When she grew to be an adult dog, she and Art made a great team chasing and catching woodchucks. There really isn't too much wrong with woodchucks as long as they live on some other farm, but on SweetAire Farm they caused trouble in hayfields by digging holes and mounding dirt at their entrances; hay mower knives dulled when the mower ran into them. In the garden, they ate everything they wanted and left none for us. They tunneled under buildings and our porch, and made a mess of everything. So, woodchucks were not wanted around our farm.

Some people get out the shotgun when stalking woodchucks. Art and Timin used to take a more visceral approach. When it was time to hunt a particular woodchuck which was out in the open, Art would call Timin and she would position herself on one side of the woodchuck and Art would maneuver himself to be on the other side; the woodchuck would be between them. They would try to move themselves to be between the woodchuck and its hole in the ground. When that happened, they had that woodchuck.

Timin once came upon a litter of baby woodchucks that were motherless and hungry. She grabbed them one-by-one in her teeth and shook them so hard that they expired. After that experience, she had the idea that woodchucks were easy prey.

She may have thought otherwise when she once cornered a large woodchuck in our pasture. The woodchuck was as large as was Timin, and Art was not close enough to help. She was a valiant fighter, and really attacked that woodchuck, but it was a match for her. She was bitten badly on the nose, face, and legs. She eventually won, but that woodchuck was no pushover.

TIMIN II: FALLING FOR A CAT

Our dogs and cats had always had an interesting relationship. The dogs, naturally, have liked to chase the cats, but the cats not only tolerated it, but actually seemed to like the excitement of the encounter. When lying around sleeping or lounging as dogs sometimes do, the cats often came over to nuzzle the dogs, rubbing on them until they captured the attention of the dogs. Then the dog would grab the cat in its mouth and shake the cat. Instead of running away, the cat would stay close, and sometimes yell if the dog was too rough. Then, if the cat tried to run away, the dog would grab that cat by the tail and drag it backwards around the yard. There was no use in scolding the dog or separating the cat from the dog, because, as soon as things had quieted down, the cat would again be taunting the dog. This has happened with all of our dogs, and our dog named Timin was the first.

Cats that were not ours ran as fast as they could when they spotted Timin running toward them. That made the chase for Timin more fun. Timin may have had visions of eventually catching one of these foreign felines and chewing on it as she did the cats that belonged around here.

One day, Art was on our deck, about 10 feet off the ground, and Timin was there next to him. They could see far into the sheep pasture from the deck, and, for an animal as low to the ground as Timin normally was, the improvement in perspective was probably much better than it was for Art. Just then, a strange cat started running across the far end of the pasture. Timin spied it, and became immediately alert. She forgot where she was, however, and when she saw that cat, she charged full speed ahead, right off the deck. She landed on the ground more startled than injured, and forgot to resume the chase.

TIMIN III: TRAPPED

When our first dog Timin was old, there came a period of about two weeks in January when she didn't return to our house at the end of the day. We usually let her outside in the morning, and she stayed pretty much stayed around the house. But when she didn't come when she was called in the evening, we thought that something really bad must have happened to her. After a few days when she did not come when called, we thought that she was likely dead.

But, one night after that long absence she showed up \at our door, almost as if nothing had happened. We let her inside and then saw that her hind leg had been injured. It appeared that she had been caught in an animal trap, and the skin and tissue on her leg was missing in a ring entirely around her leg. Bare bone was showing.

There was nothing we could do. The wound was not fresh, so surgery would not have helped. We took her to the vet, and he advised that she would probably lose her leg, but gave her a shot of antibiotics to prevent any further infection.

Timin had spunk, though, so we cared for her as best as we could. This consisted mainly of feeding her huge appetite and letting her rest. One day, the leg beneath the wound fell off, as predicted, and we had a three-legged dog. She wasn't a good hunter after that, but she still made her rounds in the morning to check on events in the neighborhood. She lived for several more years, generally adapting to her handicap and still accepting any and all petting that we gave to her.

A RELIABLE WATER SUPPLY

Through all the hot summer weather, there is one thing that has remained dependable and with which we could not have endured. That thing is water. We don't usually think about our water, but without it, we would have been the opposite of "up the creek without a paddle".

It wasn't always this way. When we first moved to our house, and the small five acre beginnings of SweetAire Farm, the supply of water for our house and farm was a spring located in a small concrete enclosure next to our driveway. The spring supplied our water needs on a tentative basis; there was usually enough water if we were judicious about its use. During rainy periods there was enough water; during dry periods we had to be especially careful. When it rained hard, our water had a murky sediment in it, and sometimes it smelled and tasted like the good Earth from which it sprang. The water must have been very acidic, because there were several occasions during which we had to replace foot valves on the pipeline from the spring to the house because they corroded and wouldn't hold the priming of our pump. We had to be alert that the pump did not burn out before we could shut it off when it ran dry.

There were some dry summers back then, and sometimes the spring went dry, or almost went dry. We could remove the heavy concrete cover over the spring and look down to see how much water was stored inside. If there was little to none, then the word would go out to all members of the family to conserve, conserve, conserve. Showers were limited to five minutes or less, baths to a couple of inches deep. Fortunately, we had a running stream several hundred feet from the house. The stream never ran dry. We would go down to the stream with two pails to fill with water for uses such as flushing our toilet. We posted signs in the bathroom saying "Flush with a friend." We used what water we had from the spring for drinking, washing, and brushing our teeth. It never occurred to us to buy bottled water for some of these purposes; bottled water was not as prominent back then.

We endured this situation for about 20 years. Those were tough times, but we made do.

When we finally could afford to have a well drilled in 1991, we were very excited. It was during a dry period, and our spring water supply was running low. We asked around about well drillers, and settled on the Barber Brothers as the firm to call. The week that it took them to drill the well, install the well casing, dig a trench from the well to the house, install the connecting pipe and the electric wire to power the pump, backfill the trench, and test the water seemed to us to last a very long time. We were so excited with anticipation.

The new well, the one we still use, could supply all the water we could ever want. Right after it was hooked up to our household water system, our daughter Jodi celebrated with a luxurious 20-minute shower. We all thought that we were in heaven. And we were, but we have not taken water for granted ever since.

AMOS STOLZFUS'S LOADER

When we needed rough cut building lumber for fences or buildings, we bought it from an Amish man named Amos Stolzfus, who lived with his sawmill just up the road in Peach Bottom, PA.

Amish people are prohibited by their local bishops from having modern machinery to help them get their work done. Especially not allowed are tractors with rubber tires that could be used as mobile power sources, or, especially, means of transportation. If Amish people have tractors or other equipment with rubber tires, they are supposed to replace them with steel wheels so that the machinery is clearly to be used on the farm and not as a forbidden conveyance on the road.

Amos had a great big front-end loader to help him handle large logs and bundles of sawed lumber around his sawmill. The loader had huge rubber tires on all four wheels. Art did not think that was allowed for an Amish person, so he asked Amos how he could get away with keeping a loader with rubber tires.

"It's okay", replied Amos, "it's for sale".

Several years later, Art returned to the Stolzfus sawmill for more lumber. The same front-end loader was still being used. Again, Art asked the question.

"It's okay", said Amos, "It's still for sale."

ART'S CHRISTMAS MORNING TRADITION

Art carries on a Christmas breakfast tradition handed down in his family through two prior generations and continues somewhat for two subsequent generations, for a total of five: his Christmas breakfast consists of a bowl full of bananas cut into pieces, sprinkled with sugar, and bathed in evaporated milk. It is said that this tradition started with his grandparents during the Great Depression of the 1930's, when they operated a small neighborhood grocery store in Oceanside, N.Y. Bananas and evaporated milk were luxuries at that time, and they could only afford to indulge in them very sparingly. Art was told that his grandparents lost the store because they extended credit too liberally to their customers, many of whom could not pay their bills. So, this tradition also carries with it the remembrance of sacrifice and benevolence.

Our daughters, Joy and Jodi, added their own style to the bananas and evaporated milk Christmas breakfast. Another family tradition had been that a jar of maraschino cherries was always an item found on Christmas morning in each stocking that had been hung the night before. Joy and Jodi added maraschino cherries to their breakfast bowls along with the bananas, evaporated milk, and sugar. And that is the way the tradition continues to this day.

This tradition connects each generation of the family to those that have gone before us, and helps each of us to remember when people didn't have as much as we do now; it helps us to appreciate the bounty in our lives that too often becomes so very familiar that it can easily be overlooked.

AT THE LIVESTOCK AUCTION

We used to raise cattle as well as sheep. In the first few years that we lived on SweetAire Farm, we used to go to the Sechrist Auction on Monday nights in Stewartstown, Pennsylvania, and buy calves to raise for our own consumption. If you have never been to a livestock auction, and most of you have not, there is a pit about eight feet below the bidders' gallery in which each animal is brought in through a gate from one side and exits on the other. The floor of the pit is covered with a layer of sawdust to make it easier to clean after the auction has ended. There are two or three men in the pit with the animals; one keeps the animal moving so that all the bidders can all get a look at it, and the others watch the audience to spot when a bid is being made. When they see someone who attempts to enter the bidding, they shout loudly and point in the direction of the bidder.

The auctioneer is located in a little booth elevated toward the back of the pit and faces the audience where he can see when a bid is made. Behind him is a person, often the only woman working in the auction, who records each transaction on a sheet of paper as it is completed. The animal, a cow, sheep, pig, goat or other, usually spends very little time in the pit because the auctioneer needs to make the sale quickly.

The audience is seated surrounding the pit, with about six or eight regular repeat buyers from large meat-packing companies seated up front. They often have reserved seats, and can easily be spotted with their clipboards or note pads to jot down the animals that they purchase. At least one typically chews on an unlighted stub of a cigar. They know each other very well, usually sitting and joking with the others one or more times each week. If no one else bids on an animal, then these are the representatives who the auction house counts on to buy it.

Behind the steady buyers sit the others in auditorium style, with each semicircular tier of seats higher than the one in front so that everyone can see the animal up for sale and the auctioneer can see the bids when they are made. Some of these people have come to buy, and others have brought animals to sell and are hanging around to see what prices their animals would bring. There are others, including whole families with little children, who have come for a family outing. This is how they entertain themselves on a weekday night after a day working on the farm. They usually sit high in the back, and make good use of the food concessions located off the main level.

Bidding is usually accomplished by some means such as raising one's hand or waving a hat. Once a bidder has the attention of the auctioneer, then a simple nod of the head is all that is necessary to make a new bid. Shaking the head "no" lets the auctioneer know that he or she is no longer interested in bidding on an animal. If the animal has received no bids, or the bids do not meet a minimum amount specified by the seller, then the animal maybe assigned to one of the regular buyers in the front row by prearranged agreement. They hardly ever signal a bid except to face the auctioneer sometimes. Otherwise they may talk among themselves or just look off into the blue. You can tell when an animal has been sold to one of these regular buyers because the winner jots a note down in his note pad. That's the only clue anyone has that one of these regulars bought the animal. Anyone else in the audience who has successfully bought an animal must show a numbered card that has been registered beforehand, or, in some cases, shout out his name to the person recording the transactions.

If we successfully won the bid for a calf, we would load the calf into our pickup truck and bring it the roughly 30 miles home. If the weather had been warm, the calf would be transported in the bed of the truck. If the weather was cold, the calf would be pushed and shoved into the cab, and would usually not take well to riding alongside the stranger who was driving the truck. This led to some awkward moments when the calf would try to scramble on to the seat, then try to escape the uncomfortable situation it had been forced to endure. There were times when the calf interfered with driving, and Art would have to shove the animal aside to maintain his position behind the wheel and keep control of the truck. There were many other times when the calf would erupt with disgusting emissions that would have to be endured until everyone reached home and the mess cleaned up later.

OUR LAWN

> *"So many have a lawn with manicure*
> *That never knows the joy of giving seed.*
> *It's conquered, cut, enslaved for civic pure,*
> *A waste of earth in crew-cut green indeed."*
> *- Laurel Patterson*

We have some lawn area around our house on our farm – but not too much - because a lawn represents ground that could be used to grow other plants, and also because lawn care is not as productive a use for our time as caring for other types of plantings. Our lawn is the natural kind. It has grass, to be sure. But it also has dandelions, clover, ground sorrel, some kinds of creeping plants, and many other species that can establish themselves and remain in harmony with all the others.

Our lawn is interesting. In the spring, it is punctuated with bright yellow dandelion blooms. Art picks one of these every now and again, and eats the petals. He claims it has a slightly sweet and slightly bitter flavor. And, he claims health benefits, too. There are also smallish blue flowers in our lawn, and, in just a little while, purple violets. In the heat of the summer, white blossoms on wild clover make their appearances. Our lawn is a kaleidoscope of different colors and textures that makes for an interesting experience.

Pollinators love our lawn, too. There are things for them to eat all over our lawn. We need to care for these little partners for our farming efforts, and as with the flowers in our flower beds, we try to provide a good selection of delectable fare for their survival at all times through the growing season.

We don't fertilize our lawn, either. There is no need, because the diversity of flora in our lawn is based on mutual support; clover fixes nitrogen that is used by other plants, and other plants provide nutrients for the clover. Too much applied fertilizer only leaches through the ground into the groundwater, which is not just wasteful of fertilizer, but also harmful for the groundwater. We have the suspicion that a lot of the nutrients polluting the Chesapeake Bay attributed to farms comes instead from suburban lawns surrounding agricultural areas. We, at least, will not contribute to that problem.

We sometimes pass by houses with vast expanses of green grass, mowed to certain height specifications, and devoid of diversity. We look at each other and talk briefly about the waste of good land going for no particular good. This is not sustainable. We are not attuned to the reasons why some people would want to spend so much time and effort caring for such expanses.

SILAGE FROM GRASS CLIPPINGS

Keeping cows and sheep fed required a lot of hay in the wintertime, and even in the summer during very dry conditions when pasture grass was in short supply. We were not always as successful with haymaking as needed, so sometimes we had to buy supplemental hay to keep the animals adequately fed in the winter. When that happened, it was sometimes difficult to find someone with enough hay who was willing to sell it. In any case, it was expensive to buy hay, especially in years when there wasn't much local hay to be had. On top of that, many farmers who baled hay now made very large round bales and not the small, square bales that we could easily handle. There had to be a better and less expensive solution to this problem.

Having had to deal with this problem for about 10 years after we moved to our farm, Art hatched what he thought was a brilliant idea. There was, in the summer, an abundance of grass clippings from areas around our house that we mowed on a regular basis. If only this surplus could be preserved until the winter, when the animals really needed it, then we might not have to make or buy as much hay.

He knew that grass silage could be made from chopped grass fermented in the absence of air, and the organic acids and alcohols that resulted could keep the clippings from spoiling and losing nutrient quality. He also knew that grass silage made on a large scale by dairy and livestock farmers usually smelled horrible, but that the animals to which it was fed ate it without hesitation.

With grass silage in mind, he began to plot the details about what would be appropriate for a farm five acres in size at that time. Large-scale farmers used upright or trench silos in which to store their silage. That would not work for our small farm. Instead, a convenient storage container could be had in the form of a 55-gallon barrel. These were readily available and inexpensive; with luck, he could find some available for free.

The top of the barrel had to be covered as hermetically as possible so that the oxygen still entrapped in the grass clippings would be rapidly drawn to zero by initial aerobic processes and then anaerobic processes would form the acids and alcohols that would preserve the grass as silage. Done correctly, the silage could be kept for many months, if not years. A double layer of plastic was chosen as the appropriate cover, and the cover was to be sealed around the barrel by a rubber band cut from an old inner tube.

Newly-mown grass clippings had to be packed tightly in the barrels by stomping them after they were placed in the barrel. This ensured that as much air as possible was expelled from among the blades of grass.

With this system in place, Art proceeded to acquire the necessary equipment and supplies. He found 20-30 barrels to start with, was able to obtain old inner tubes from a local tire store, and made enough rubber bands to fit all the barrels. He would need a mower with a grass catcher to collect the clippings, and, for that, he needed extra funds. He was able to secure support from the United States Department of Agriculture (USDA) small farms grants program for a mower and the help of University of Maryland graduate student Geof Schoming. Each week, Geof came to SweetAire Farm to mow grass, pack it in barrels, and seal them.

The results were as successful as we had hoped. As long as the grass was packed tightly in the barrels and the sealing was adequate, the grass ensiled nicely. On the top of only a couple of barrels, the silage had mold growing in it; this was a sign that the silage was exposed to the oxygen in the air. These layers of moldy silage were easily removed before feeding to the animals. In the vast majority of cases, the silage formed exactly as expected.

When ready to feed to the cows and sheep. The barrels were uncovered and tipped on their sides. The animals could eat their way into each barrel as they satisfied their hunger.

And, the animals loved it; they often fought over who would get first crack at the delicious forage inside the barrels. Instead of dry old grass hay, here was moist grass silage that was preferred over hay or wintertime pasture grass. Sometimes, the ram at the time could push the cows aside and eat his fill; at other times, a dominant cow would prevail. The calves and female sheep usually had to wait their turns. The animals could eat *ad lib* until the barrel was empty, and, when there was no more silage inside, another barrel could be opened for them. The silage went fast, but the dry hay fed at the same time to the animals lasted a long time.

All-in-all, the idea of turning surplus grass clippings into grass silage to be used as animal feed was successful. We kept making grass silage for several more years, but, eventually, we planted orchards where grassy areas had been, and also the work of making enough grass silage became more than we could handle. It was, however, an idea that could be appropriate for a very small livestock farming operation.

BEAUTIFUL PICTURES IN CATALOGS

Each winter is again catalog season. Catalogs come to our farm in bundles at this time of the year, giving the mail lady a reason to have to lift weights the rest of the year. The pictures in all of these marvelous catalogs always look so good: the beautiful cherries, the prized apples, the golden pears, and the perfect peaches. This is how we got started in the fruit business, seduced by beautiful pictures during the time of the year when the trees outside are bare and good fresh fruits are only a memory. Yes, there are fruits available in the supermarkets (how spoiled we have become), but the first bites of those purchased peaches and plums from halfway around the world always disappoint so much. Contrarily, the fruits pictured in the catalogs always look like they taste wonderful!

So, there developed a positive feedback loop: from the enticing pictures come desires, and from the resulting desires come plant orders, and then, at some point, the plants arrive on our porch, brought there by one of several package-delivery trucks. But, our plant purchases reward the nurseries putting out the pretty-picture catalogs, and that begets more catalogs, and the loop repeats. That's how this orchard grew from a couple of trees to hundreds, one or two catalogs at a time.

Prices of fruit trees, vines, and plants pictured in these catalogs, as with most other things used around our farm, have skyrocketed in recent years. Trees that used to be $5 each when we started ordering in 1972 had became $60 each by 2015. There are grape vines available for $100 each! Years ago, Miller's Nursery used to have a motto, "A five-dollar tree deserves a ten-dollar hole." Following that logic, a $100 grape vine would need a hole valued at a small fortune. Compensation for our own labor time has not kept pace, so a $200 dollar hole would take a week or more to dig.

CHRISTMAS EVE TRADITION

Soon after we moved to Maryland from upstate New York, we realized that Christmas Eve was a time of mixed emotions. There was the anticipation of the next day, there was the boredom that comes from waiting when you have done everything you can to get ready and you have nothing left to do, and there was the letdown of being so busy for so many days and then, all of a sudden, all that was left was to wait. Cathy had to prepare a dinner for the family when she was tired from all the Christmas preparations. We needed something different, and decided as a family to go out to dinner on Christmas Eve; this would give us something fun to do before the big day and before the 11 pm Christmas Eve service at our church. In between the dinner and the church service we would drive around neighborhoods to enjoy all the Christmas decorations lit brightly that night.

We have continued this tradition since the early 1970's. In those days, the Colonel's Choice restaurant was operating in Aberdeen, MD, and it was at that restaurant that we enjoyed many Christmas Eve dinners. We have since changed restaurants several times, mostly because they have closed or changed management. None of these were our fault. We don't think so, anyway.

The meals that we had were good, but it was the family celebrations that were more memorable. There was one year, many years ago, when we all came down with the flu. We were sick on Christmas Eve, so staying up until the 11 pm church service was out of the question. But were we to give up on our traditional Christmas Eve dinner? No way. It was a family tradition. So, we all bundled up and went to the restaurant. The problem was that no one in the family was hungry.

There may still be some servers out there who remember the family of six that came to the restaurant and ordered only cups of tea, and ate only a few pieces of bread. That was us, that Christmas Eve many years ago.

DANDELION STORIES

When spring comes in earnest, we have multitudes of dandelions popping up all over the place – in our pastures, in our flower beds (where they will be removed as quickly as possible), and, especially, in our lawn. We know that many people do not like dandelions to sully their immaculate lawns, but we have a lawn that is made of anything that grows there. This means that our lawn features purple ground ivy flowers in the early spring, white clover blooms in the summer, and, especially, cheerfully bright yellow dandelion flowers at this time in the spring. Until they turn into gossamer seed puffs a few days later, and dissipate in the wind to lodge seeds in the most inauspicious locations, they are lovely.

And, they are nutritious. When we used to buy calves at the animal auctions many years ago, we used to pick dandelion blossoms to feed to the calves to ward off the scours that calves usually developed after having been exposed during their brief appearances at the auction houses. Although the calves were young, and fed only milk replacer, we knew that the calves would be fine once they had been administered their prophylactic dosages of dandelion blossoms. If the blossoms did not appear for a week or three after the calves were brought home, we would hope that the calves could hold on long enough until the blossoms were available to cure the calves. Until then, the calves' health could deteriorate very quickly. So, dandelion blossoms are miraculous.

Art still goes outside and samples some of the blossoms himself. He picks the blossoms and nips the yellow portion from out of the green base. The flavor is a little sweet and a little bitter, but a free snack with, at least, significant carotenoids and a taste of early spring.

Even more years ago than we care to admit, when Cathy and Art were both students at Cornell University, they used to spend a sunny early Saturday morning of the Cornell University Spring Weekend clambering around the open athletic fields to gather large feedbags full of dandelion blossoms to be used to make dandelion wine. They were usually the only people around, because the remainder of the students, especially those who were members of fraternities and sororities, were still in their beds nurturing their hangovers from the late-night bacchanals they had attended during the wee hours of the night before.

Once the bags were full, then the pair of pickers took them back to Art's apartment to convert, with the aid of citrus juices and wine yeast, into an alcoholic elixir reminiscent of early spring. Dandelion wine, by the way, is bitter and not worth drinking, but, at the time, it was the activity to engage in on Spring Weekend.

TURKEYS

One advantage (!) to living on a farm is that there is a lot of work to be done, and the work never seems to be finished. When the girls, and, later, our boys, were growing up, their father believed that the children needed to share in this experience. He assigned them jobs to do each day when they were not in school. He believed that it was good for them to learn responsibility and appreciation for the things we had and did. When their jobs were done, they could look back at what they had done that day and appreciate what their efforts could accomplish. It may have taken many years for them to feel this sense of accomplishment, but, at least by the time they grew into adults, they knew how to work.

'Most of the time, each girl was assigned to her own job for that day. In that way, they could work at their own paces, and when they had finished, they were free to do whatever they wished to do. But, one job they had to do together was to move the turkey cages to new grass every day. It took the two of them to move the cages.

We did not learn until much later the stories that came from this task. It seems that there was occasional rivalry between the two girls, and that sometimes led to some friction between them. When they moved the turkey cages in warm weather, which was most of the time, they were often barefooted. They liked to run around outside without shoes if the opportunity presented itself.

When they moved the turkey cages, each girl lifting one side of the cage, they would try to maneuver the cage such that the other girl was pulled into the space from which the cage was just moved. That way, one girl or the other would walk in turkey manure with bare feet, much to the devilish delight of the other sister. That may have helped to grow bigger feet, but it also added to the grudge that one daughter held against the other.

JOY'S SONG

When the girls were just a few years old, we had a ritual when we were traveling in the car for hours at a time. Art would quiz them, as we rode, on the sounds of the letters of the alphabet. He did this so that they would soon be able to sound out written words when they saw them. This worked. Both girls learned early to read. Joy was reading the entire book, *Wizard of Oz*, before she started school, when she was only four years old.

A few years later, a jingle with a very catchy tune was played repeatedly on a local radio station that we listened to, especially when driving in the car or truck, and singing along became a tradition between Joy and her Dad. The song was "Shaddap-a you face" by Italian singer Joe Dolce. The chorus went like this:

> Whats-a matta you, HEY
> Gotta no respect HEY
> Whatta you tink you do HEY
> Why you look-a so sad HEY
> It's-a not so bad, HEY
> It's-a nice-a place
> Ah, shaddap-a you face.

Joy and Art would sing with gusto, in their loudest voices. He usually sang the words written above in small letters, and she would sing the "HEY"s. Sometimes they changed parts, and he sang the "HEY"s. He would sometimes forget all the words, or mix them up, and she would correct him with a laugh. The chorus would be repeated many times, or until the song ended on the radio. Many times the two of them would just break out in song while at home or outside on the farm. This song was especially called for after some complaining about work that had to be done, or how hot it was, or some other grumbling. But, each time when they finished the song, they laughed loudly and vigorously, and went on smiling for quite a while afterward. Joy's song was a powerful mood enhancer. [To appreciate the song better, look it up on YouTube on the internet.]

HOLIDAY SURPRISE

It was a nice Independence Day. Art's brother, his wife, and their three sons had come from their home in Delaware to our place for a mid-day picnic. The weather was beautiful, not too hot, and it was comfortable in the shade. They had brought some food, and Cathy supplied the rest.

We sat down for our meal. Cathy offered a choice of drinks: water, iced tea, or Coke. Some of us like iced tea on a warm summer's day, and that's what we drank. Some of the others, especially the kids, chose Coca Cola, a real treat for them. Cathy and Don's wife, Janet, also drank Coke. There were enough soda drinkers that we quickly went through two bottles.

But, what was that in the bottom of the second bottle? It was a solid mass, and hard to see. Cathy shook the bottle upside down. There it was, the hairless carcass of a mouse. Yuck. Those who had had Coke poured from the second bottle quickly dumped their glasses. They also turned a little green.

Nobody had ever seen anything like it before. A mouse, nonetheless. And, if there ever was any question about what immersion in Coca Cola could do to a mouse, here was the evidence. At the very least, the mouse drowned, and the acid in the Coke ate away all the hair on its body. The mouse probably never knew what hit it after it had crawled inside that cozy bottle for a little snooze.

What should we do now, we all asked. A whole bottle of Coke had been wasted, and the Coke from the other bottle didn't taste as good any more, either. After some discussion, we decided, at the very least, to stick the bottle in our freezer and to inform Coca Cola about what we found.

The next day was a normal business day, and Cathy sent a letter to the Coca Cola company. It didn't take them too long to respond. A Coca Cola representative soon showed up on our doorstep. In return for the bottle with the embalmed mouse still in it, he gave Cathy a voucher for free bottles of Coca Cola and several nice trays with the Coke symbols painted on them. Cathy took them up on their offer, and handed over the bottle with the frozen hairless mouse.

And, that's how we could have become rich, but missed the opportunity when the bottle containing the mouse passed from our hands.

DIRT CITY

Small rural towns are good places to live, and Darlington, Maryland is no exception to this. There are maybe 500 residents of the town, living on either side of Main Street or one of several small side roads. The houses of Darlington are not spectacular in any way, being mostly medium in size and colored in various shades of white. There are a few picket fences and some sidewalks here or there, but the sidewalks don't really go from here to there as much as they are located in random stretches along the road. Some of the older sidewalks are made from slabs of slate.

Darlington has an elementary school, three churches (United Methodist, Episcopalian, and Friends (or Quaker); others are located a bit out of town), a Post Office, a two little antique and craft shops (open for business at times, and not at others), a pharmacy, a firehouse, a small library, two car repair garages, and Scarborough's general food store. In the old days, there was a hardware store, a sub shop, and an orchard outlet. The town would be very quiet except for the state highway traffic that goes through Main Street.

Dirt City is a nickname for Darlington that some residents consider derisive, others consider affectionate, and still others consider amusing. It was popular in the 1970s among teens who lived in town. To them, Darlington was a very unexciting place to spend their time. But, the same small, quiet town environment that was boring to them at times was also what protected them from hazards faced by their peers in larger locales. Everyone in Darlington is a neighbor and everyone knows everyone else. There is nothing that goes on in town that is not known to everyone in town. There is a communal responsibility for children's upbringing. This has truly been the village that it takes to raise a child.

The social structure in town is relatively simple. There are no social strata except for one thing: newcomers are treated somewhat differently from those residents who can trace their lineage back several generations. It's not that newcomers are looked down upon, but they are not consulted in the same ways as are those from established families: families with relatives that have been part of the community fabric forever. It takes living in town at least 15-20 years before newcomers are fully accepted in the same way as the established families. Raising a family here helps to shorten the residence time for full acceptance.

One other thing: as in most small towns, once a person has an identity, it is theirs for a long time, if not forever. So, someone who is known as a generous person will always be known as a generous person; someone who sings well in the church choir will always be expected to sing well; someone who knows how to repair cars will always be expected to know this; someone who has been a leader in the community will always be consulted to be a leader. Once you have a job or position in the community, it is yours for life. Try to get out of that job, and you are out of luck unless you can convince other residents that you don't like them anymore.

So, Dirt City: it has its own identity, and that isn't a bad thing at all.

MEAT COMES FROM ANIMALS, REALLY!

Few children have the opportunity to realize that the food they grow in the garden this summer is the food they will eat next winter. Nor do many children appreciate that steak does not grow with plastic wrap around it, and that pork chops do not originate in a supermarket. The first meat that we ate that our girls realized came from animals that we raised and nurtured was pork from our pigs. At first, the girls didn't know what to think about it, but we explained that all meat comes from animal flesh and that the meat they had eaten before had also come from animals somewhere. They accepted that explanation quite well, and, for a time, we went through a period where they called the hamburger and lamb chops by name, but that was short-lived.

It is healthy for children to know what they are doing when they care for animals and eat them later. That way there are no illusions about nice animals disappearing and delicious meat suddenly appearing. We still appreciate the beauty and cuteness of the animals when they are small, but cute babies soon enough grow into no-so-cute adults: baby pigs are cute, but adult pigs are definitely not; lambs are cute, but adult sheep may butt or threaten you; calves are very cute, but adult cows break through fences; baby geese are cuddly, but adult geese hiss and pinch. By the time the animals have grown the attachment for them has greatly diminished. They can be eaten without regret and maybe with a little relief, even.

IMPOSSIBLE PIE

We made this pie almost every week for many years. We ate it in the evening while entertaining Bob and Laura Lee Knight; we ate it in the field as a meal during haying. The recipe is easy to make and forms its own crust.

Ingredients:

4 eggs
½ cup sugar
½ cup self-rising flour (or ½ cup regular flour plus ½ teaspoon baking powder plus ¼ teaspoon salt)
2 cups milk
1 teaspoon vanilla
½ stick margarine or butter, melted
1 can (7 oz) coconut

Beat the eggs with the sugar. Add the rest of the ingredients and beat until well mixed. Pour into a greased 10-inch pie plate. Bake at 350°F for 30-40 minutes.

GENEALOGY OF OUR RHUBARB

Our rhubarb, as we have told some of you, is descended from plants that his grandfather gave to Art when he was a teenager, many, many, many years ago. The variety name is long forgotten, but our rhubarb has nicely colored red stalks. The plants given to Art had been divided from plants growing in the backyard of Art's grandparents' house on long Island, and were planted in the soil on his family's farm in upstate New York. They remained growing there for many years. When Art, Cathy, and daughters moved to Darlington in 1972, some of the plants were brought to Maryland. Over the years, they have been divided and divided again many times until now we have several long rows of rhubarb plants. Even more divisions are usually made each year. Based upon the demand for our rhubarb, we still don't have enough. We like to be somewhat gentle with the plants, not pulling too many stalks at once, so that we can continue to bring rhubarb until October. The hot, dry summer weather is not the best for rhubarb growing, but the plants will tolerate it as long as they are mulched and have not too many stalks removed from them at a time.

GEORGE

One year we bought a calf with at least half Angus breeding. As it turns out, we found out from this calf why we never again wanted to have anything to do with Angus cattle. We named this male calf George.

Although George was castrated, he was still more than a handful. At that time, we had very poor fences, so we put a collar on him and each day we would move George to a different location in the pasture, tied to a steel stake with a nylon rope attached to his collar. When it was time to move him, Art would pull up the stake, pull George to the new location, and pound the stake in the ground with a 2-pound hammer. For a while this worked well, but soon George figured out that the sharp sound of the hammer hitting the stake meant that he was going to be tethered to a specific place where he was not always pleased to be. He soon began to attempt to run quickly away from the rope while the stake was being pounded into the ground. If you can imagine this scene, then you realize that it takes three hands to accomplish the staking procedure: one to hold the stake with the rope attached, one to hold the hammer, and a third to hold the rope with George pulling on the other end. What Art would do was to release the rope tied to George, hold the stake, and hit the stake as quickly as he could before George started to run away. If all went according to plan, the stake would be deep enough in the ground when George tried to escape that Art could hold his rope in one hand, usually his left, and the hammer in the other hand, usually his right, while he buried the stake deep enough into the ground that George could not pull it up. But George became so very sensitive to the sound of the hammer hitting the stake that he often began to run with the very first hit. If the stake was not sunk deep enough in the ground on that very first hit, then George could, and sometimes did, pull it out of the ground before Art could deliver the second hit. Art had to be deliberate with the hammer and fast when reaching for the rope.

It happened once that Art was going through this well-choreographed movement, hold George's rope-release rope-hold stake-hit stake with rope attached-release stake-grab rope, when the stake must have hit a rock just below the surface and was not able to stand by itself after the first hit. George began to run with the first sound, and Art grabbed his rope with his bare hand. George had a good head start, and the nylon rope was pulled through Art's clenched hand. Nylon rope can do a job on flesh, and Art now had a deep rope burn. But the worst was yet to come. Art either did not want to let George run free or was so concerned with the rope wearing away the skin on the palm of his hand that he forgot to drop the rope. As soon as the stake reached his hand, it pivoted around and the other end gave his elbow a good whack. His elbow suddenly tingled with intense pain. Ow, ow, ow, ow, ow!

Art does not remember how this episode ended. His memory stops with the pain in his elbow, but that memory is seared into his head. Art probably let George go temporarily and called Cathy to help; George was eventually restaked and life went on, but George had more in store for us later.

George grew into a large animal, and the staking was no longer an option, so we built wire fences around the pasture to keep George inside. George, however, did not respect wire fences, and, when the grass looked greener on the other side, he just leaned into the wire, bent it down, and walked through the fence. When we had reached our limit of forbearance, we replaced the wire fence with wooden fences. We made sure to nail the boards on George's side of the fence so that he could not lean against the boards and push the nails out. These fences, at least, looked stronger. And they were. For a while they managed to discourage George from wandering where he was not welcome. However, he eventually found out that if he got a good running start that he could break through the boards. In time, Cathy would be home alone when George needed to be chased back through the fence and the fence repaired.

Cathy has her own style of fence repair. Her style is utilitarian, not artistic. She uses lots of boards and lots of nails. When she is finished, the fence is sturdy, but looks a lot different from what it looked like before the episode.

She managed to chase George back through the hole that he had made, located a hammer, brought a bunch of new boards, and all the nails that she could find, and started to repair the fence. But George knew what was going on and continually put his head in the way so that he interfered with Cathy, and she could not get a good swing on the hammer. She had a very hard time nailing new boards on the fence because George was continually in the way. She eventually managed to fix the fence, but George had done everything he could to interfere.

George caused us a lot of trouble, and convinced us to raise more docile Hereford cattle from then on. We later brought George to the slaughterhouse with no regrets, and with relief even.

He tasted good.

FENCE POSTS FOR CASTLETON

Each of the three parcels of land that we purchased, and were eventually united into what is now SweetAire Farm, were badly in need of improvements. Among those that were needed were good fences to surround pastures and contain the livestock animals that we had at the time. Our original five-acre plot did have a few old and dilapidated barbed-wire fences, but they would have given no challenge for animals determined to break through. So, we began our fence building projects right there, close to home.

When we purchased our second land parcel, a half mile from our house and called by us "Castleton" after the name of the crossroads nearby, there were no fences that had ever been erected on that site. We needed more summer pasture land to for our cows and sheep, so we needed to get busy with fence-building.

Pasture fences require posts at a spacing of eight feet between them, and the fence was to be several hundred feet long, so a lot of posts had to be located. There were mature locust trees on the land, and locust posts last a long time, so that was to be the source of the fence posts.

That would save the money that otherwise would have been needed to purchase that many posts,

Art had asked friend Jim Caldwell to bring his chain saw and help with felling the trees and cutting the posts. Jim agreed without hesitation.

The trees that we chose to cut had to be mature enough to have enough old wood because new locust wood does not last long in the ground. The trees that were cut were at least eight inches in diameter and as large as twelve inches in diameter. They were at least 50 feet tall or taller.

The posts had to be six feet in length. This would allow them to be sunk about two feet into the ground with four feet sticking up above ground for the fence wire to be nailed to. The woven wire stock fence that was to be used was four feet in height.

In order to cut the trees into six-foot lengths, Art used himself as a measure by briefly lying down beside the fallen tree and marking where the top of his head was located. This gave the necessary six foot length. Jim then cut the log at the mark, after Art had moved out of the way, of course.

Once they were cut, the new posts had to be moved to a pile uphill from where they had been cut, and close to where they would be used later to build the fence. Newly cut posts of this size are not even close to being lightweight. It took a good deal of strength and energy to move them from where they were cut to where they had to be piled. Both Jim and Art did the carrying.

The day in which all of this was done was a cold, blustery day with occasional snow squalls all day long. The two of them hardly noticed the temperature, however, because all that heavy work generated lots of extra body heat.

Over the course of the day, the pile of posts grew, but energy levels of both Art and Jim began to flag. Toward the end of the day, they both found it harder and harder to move the new posts. They tired.

It was after dark that they finished their work. By then, the snow squalls had ceased, and the sky had cleared, displaying many stars and a beautifully bright full moon. The two men were too tired to move.

So they remained there until they could muster enough energy to leave and go to their homes to eat supper.

Back home, Cathy began to be concerned about the welfare of the two of them when they did not return at the end of daylight. She had waited supper, but they still did not show up at home. So, worried that something really bad had happened to them, she got into her vehicle and drove to our Castleton land. She got out of her car, and walked the length of two fields to see if she could find them, and to give help if needed. She was apprehensive about what she would find. And there she found them, two exhausted middle-aged men slumped down on the cold, hard ground with no more energy reserves to move even a muscle.

JODI'S PIGS

Our younger daughter Jodi had traditionally taken care of our turkeys and pigs, while number one daughter, Joy, usually cared for baby chicks and rabbits. Baby geese or ducklings were assigned to the one who had the smallest amount of work to do. We frequently found one girl or another in the pen with baby chicks, turkeys, or ducks, playing with them and talking to them, teaching them to perch, or just enjoying their presences. Whereas their enthusiasm for contact with animals diminished as the animals grew and became less cuddly, there developed a visible pride in the animals as they grew and matured. When we dressed the turkeys and they all exceeded 30 pounds, with some over 35 pounds, Jodi was noticeably proud of the job she had done to get them to that point. Joy lost track of the animals in her care a little more easily, but still learned responsibility.

Jodi loved raising pigs. Each spring we would buy feeder pigs from a livestock auction or from a Darlington farmer named John Archer, and grew them in time to show at the 4-H Fair. Jodi was good about feeding them and about cleaning their pen, and she was always interested in their welfare.

Bringing them back from the auction was sometimes interesting. The pigs were often sold in batches of 2 to 8, and were about 15-20 pounds each. If we could get them into the back of the truck and close the gate, then they could be transported back home without a problem – as long as it was warm enough outside that they wouldn't get too cold. We bought them in the springtime, so the temperatures were usually mild enough. On the trip home, the piglets would snuggle together in front of the truck bed near the cab to keep themselves warm and, probably, to provide comfort for each of their siblings in this time of uncertainty for them. On occasion, we may have bought a single pig, in which case it may have ridden in the cab of the truck being held by the lucky person in the passenger seat. The pig may not have liked that arrangement, and would squirm and fuss all the way home. So would the human passenger.

Pigs are interesting animals. They are very intelligent, and look for things to play with to occupy themselves. We sometimes gave them beach balls or other toys to play with. If we didn't, they would inevitably tear something off the wall of their pen or move their large feeder around so that one of us would have to move it back to its proper place before they could be fed again. They would run around the pen, grunting and chasing each other. When they slept, they usually slept together, all lined up next to each other like sausages. How ironic!

They could also be bad little boys and girls. Some pigs would bite the tails off their penmates, and sometimes they could be cruel to one of their number. This didn't happen too often, because they were usually happy and friendly. Different pigs had different personalities.

Jodi had some of these pigs for her 4-H project. She was in charge of feeding, watering, and cleaning them. Cleaning a pig pen is a smelly job, and the odor of pig manure can persist on the skin through several morning showers. But, she was sure that her mother loved her anyway.

Jodi had a very close relationship with her pigs. She named her pigs after her best girl friends, and spent a lot of time with her pigs named Gabrielle and Kirsten.

When it came time for the 4-H Fair, we would load on the truck the pigs that Jodi were to show, and she would take the hose, some soap and a brush, and turn those dirty, stinky animals into pink, sweet-smelling cuties. To watch Jodi clean those pigs was fun. Jodi ended up as wet and clean as the pigs, because the pigs, although confined to the enclosed area on the bed of the truck, were not completely happy about all the attention and were certainly not at all cooperative. They liked the brush on their backs (Ahh!), but the water from the hose got a little cold, so they would run as best as they could in circles around the back of the truck. Sometimes Jodi would be up-ended when they did that, and it wasn't entirely clear who was washing whom.

When they were finally as clean as Ivory soap, they were bedded in clean straw and kept as clean as possible until show time. Immediately before showing, they were given a coat of baby oil and some baby powder to make them appear wholesome and pure. Then, they certainly did not smell like pigs.

In the show ring, it was the responsibility of the youngsters to keep the pigs moving slowly around the ring while the pigs were being judged. There were at least a dozen, and maybe as many as 20, youngsters and their pigs at a time in the confined space of the show ring. The scene was set for confusion and chaos, as neither the youngsters nor their pigs knew exactly what to do in that situation. Quite often, all these strange pigs in the same close confines had to settle their pecking order right then and there. Perhaps some pigs didn't like how other pigs smelled all prissy and genteel. No matter what the cause, there was always at least one and many times more pigs in the ring than youngsters controlling them. Fights broke out and pandemonium would ensue. The young handlers were often unprepared to deal with the chaos.

That's when some of the adults jumped in. They held panels of plywood in their hands, which they tried to insert between disputing pigs to separate them. Once separated, the pigs would quiet down until they again came too close to one another, and the entire scene would begin anew.

In the end, Jodi didn't do badly. Her pigs came in fifth one year and third another. She was able to sell them at the 4-H Fair animal sale, and the money that she received impressed her and motivated her to continue raising pigs for several more years.

JOY AND HER ANIMALS

After seeing our children grow up on our farm, we are convinced that a farm is a very good place to raise children. The animals that they cared for helped to teach responsibility. Some non-farm children are taught responsibility in the family by being assigned to take out the garbage, or to wash dishes, or to do some other chores. Whereas those tasks may teach some responsibility, they don't have the same impact of an animal that is hungry or thirsty because it lacks food or water. Dishes not washed can wait until later, but an animal that doesn't have water can suffer. Garbage not taken out may smell, but a hungry animal invokes a feeling that cannot be elicited from a neglected garbage can.

Joy, in particular, loved small animals, especially baby chicks. Whenever we couldn't find her, we had only to look for the moveable chicken pen; she was always in there, with chicks on her hands and arms, and perched on her knees. She taught them to fly, she claimed, and was very proud of her accomplishment. She must have done well, because, when the chicks had grown large enough to release, they spent their nights high up in a chestnut tree. They had to fly to get up there. Joy really liked those chickens, but we had to get rid of them after they spent their days in the garden eating strawberries.

She took up raising rabbits. We bought some black and white Dutch Blue rabbits from a family in Pennsylvania, built some nice cages and nest boxes, and bought waterers and feed. Joy had chosen this particular type of rabbit because they were small and furry, but she was less enthusiastic when they scratched her as she held them. We kept them for several years, but were never very successful breeding them (did you ever before hear of rabbits that wouldn't multiply?). We finally sold them to some other unsuspecting young 4Her.

Because joy really liked small animals, we tried to interest her in caring for honey bees. Honey bees, after all, are small and fuzzy. Art had wanted for several years to try beekeeping, and thought that this night be one way to finally do it. Joy seemed interested when we ordered our first bees and they came by postal mail. She was initially attracted to them, but they buzzed and acted menacing; she wasn't quite convinced that they were the cute and fuzzy little animals like the other kinds she liked so well. Even wearing her new veil and canvas gloves did not allay her fears. She dutifully watched from a safe distance whenever Art worked with the hives, but she was never convinced that they could be hers; they soon became Art's only.

BEWARE OF THE RAM I

Rams are usually either gentle, or at least pacific, except during breeding season, when they become downright obnoxious, or worse. We had a close friend, Bob Knight, who let us keep some sheep at his place in the middle of Darlington during the summer when the pastures at home were too bare to support the sheep we had at the time. Bob would tend to the animals when they needed feed or water. One day, he was giving some water to the ewes when he made the mistake of turning his back on the ram, also with the sheep. Bob soon found himself looking at the water pail from the bottom side, wondering where the truck came from that had hit him. For a man in his late forties, there aren't usually a whole lot of completely new experiences in his life, but Bob had one that day. After that, he made sure to know where the ram was at all times.

THROWN INTO THE MUD

Cathy was out feeding the sheep one winter's day when the mishap occurred. She had chased the sheep out of the corral area and closed the gates, as usual. The only real difference was that the mud on this morning was sticky and deep rather than mostly frozen. She waited until the anxious sheep running back and forth on the other side of the closed gates had cleared the gate behind which she stood. She figured that if she opened the gates at the right time, the sheep would push open the other gate rather than the one behind which she was standing. Bad figuring! The sheep pushed both gates and she was unprepared for the onslaught. When the sheep pushed her gate, the gate opened into her, and Cathy flipped backward, right into the wet, sloppy, disgusting mud. Plop!

She was able to grab something to help get up (with a big sucking sound). She could have been described as "mad as a wet hen", but that doesn't quite do it. By then, the sheep had already run by her and fought their way into the shed to gobble their grain, so she couldn't even kick a ewe in retribution. She was reminded about all those words her mother had admonished her never to say, but which she had heard anyway when other people had muttered them on special occasions.

She walked stiffly and uncomfortably back to the house, and shed her soaked sartorial accouterments in the back room, where they stayed until she could take them to the Laundromat. There they would have their own washer all to themselves.

JOY'S SLEEPING TREE

There was an old apple tree behind the house with the frame of an old aluminum chair leaning against it. That's the tree that daughters Joy and Jodi liked to climb and play in. The trunk of the tree was about two feet in diameter and the very first branches were about a foot in diameter and located off the main trunk about four feet off the ground. It was easy for them to use the chair to climb onto those limbs and then stay on them because the branches were so big and broad.

Joy, especially, liked to sit in that tree when she was about six or seven years old. She would either read books or play with the cats when up there. She stayed there for hours, and the cats, having nothing better to do than to be petted, would gladly stay with her.

One fine summer day we called Joy for supper, but she did not come. We called some more, but she still didn't come. We began to worry, and started looking all over for her. Had she had an accident? Was she lost? Was she in trouble? We were concerned for her safety.

After a bit of searching, we found her. She had taken her favorite baby blanket, to which she had become attached since babyhood, and laid it neatly and carefully in the crotch of her apple tree, and had fallen asleep on it. There she was, arms and legs dangling over the edges of that limb, sleeping as peacefully as could be.

After that, we first looked for her in that tree, and were hardly ever wrong.

LOUD MOCKINGBIRD IN A HOLLY TREE

When we first moved to our house in 1972 there was a smallish holly tree growing about 12 to 15 feet outside our bedroom window. It was a nice tree of good proportions and it supplied branches and berries during the Christmas season for several years after we moved in. However, there came a time when that holly tree became an *arbor non grata*. This is the story of its fall from grace.

Several years after we moved in, a male mockingbird took up spring and summer residence in that holly tree. He was no ordinary mockingbird; he liked to sing more loudly than his compatriots, and he liked to wake early in the morning. We are talking about 2 to 3 am when we say early in the morning.

We are used to an open window in the bedroom, especially at night in the warm evenings of late spring, summer, and early fall. The nighttime air outside usually cooled enough to provide some respite from the temperatures of the hot summer days.

This worked for a few years until the mockingbird flew in. All of a sudden, in the middle of the night, the mocking bird would begin to emit the loudest song that could be heard, much louder than could be tolerated by the people trying to sleep inside the house. This was especially loud contrasted with the peaceful nighttime silence that usually existed outside our window.

Once the mockingbird started his virtuous performance, there was no sleep possible. He was so loud, and so persistent, that he easily ruined many a good night's sleep.

In response, Art, suddenly awaken, and not in a very good mood, would do all he could to discourage that avian Casanova from continuing his aria of many decibels. At first, Art tried shouting out the window, without effect. Next he tried clapping loudly, also without effect. The bird just would not stop singing. Art would have tried throwing cold water in the direction of the holly tree, but the window screen prevented that. And the window screen was all but impossible to remove, even during the daylight when everything could be seen and understood clearly.

Upon being unceremoniously awakened by the sudden unwelcome musical outburst, Art soon took to going downstairs and out the door, walking around to the back of the house, and attempting to physically discourage that bird from residence at the top of that holly tree. Art soon found out that walking in his bare feet outside next to that holly tree was not such a good idea; old holly leaves are stiff and prickly. So Art usually slipped on a pair of rubber boots before he left the house.

By now the tree had grown to about 15 feet tall, and the bird could not be seen in the darkness. Art first tried the old standby method of clapping, but that had no more effect than it did when he clapped inside the house. Art tried to shake the branches of that tree to scare the bird away, but shaking the bottom branches had absolutely no effect. He couldn't reach the top branches without help. So, he kept a garden hoe propped against the back of the house so that he could locate it in the dark. Holding the hoe end in his hand, and, using the hoe handle and stretching his arm as far as he could, he beat the branches of the tree high enough so that the bird would eventually, and quite reluctantly, fly away into the night. The mockingbird did not like to move, and it took a lot of striking the branches to motivate him to do so.

Finally, after several years of this nonsense, Art finally cut down that tree. He did not want to do that, because the tree itself did nothing wrong. But it had to be done if we were ever going to sleep peaceably through the summer night.

OUR LIVE CHRISTMAS TREE

We now decorate only minimally for Christmas. We hang Christmas ornaments from the hooks on the porch that in the summer are used for hanging baskets of flowers, and we have some colored Christmas lights strung around the edge of the ceiling in the living room. These stay up all year, and can be turned on anytime we need a little cheer in our lives (Art calls it a "Whoopidie Doo-Dah Day"). Cathy hangs all the Christmas cards that we receive at the kitchen portal, and we may have a small Pointsettia somewhere around, but that is about the extent of our Christmas decorations ever since the kids moved out of our house.

It was not always that way. We used to set up a Christmas tree every year, and decorate it with lights, ornaments (some with extra memories attached), and tinsel. It was beautiful.

But this wasn't just any tree. Cut Christmas trees are fine… for someone else. No, we had to have a live tree, one that would live long after Christmas in a spot selected somewhere in our yard just for an evergreen tree. We had planted spruce seedlings on the back of our farm to grow our own Christmas trees, but they were so slow to grow and there were always weeds growing among them and vines growing up them, so that they did not work out as well as could be hoped.

So, one year we rode over to the other side of our town of Darlington to purchase a live tree from the plantings of Bob Hostetter. We picked out a nice tree about 6 feet tall, and dug it up. That wasn't so easy to do. You have to dig around the roots of the tree, and then under the roots by tipping the tree over slightly. Done correctly, most of the dirt around the roots is held in place by the tree roots. A piece of burlap can then be slipped under the root ball, and, with some difficult maneuvering, around the ball. The burlap can then be fastened with nails so that the tree is ready to pull out of the ground.

Dirt is not light weight. It is even heavier when it is wet. Add to that the weight of the tree of considerable size. The secret to digging a live Christmas tree is to make the ball as small as possible. Unfortunately, Art did not figure that out until he had already dug up this tree. It took several of us all we could do to lift the tree out of the ground and on to the truck.

There were some early years when we set the Christmas tree up in our living room on our ground floor. Unfortunately, that was several years before we decided that it was nicer to have the tree upstairs on the second floor in the front room outside of all the bedrooms. That was where the live tree had to go.

Art was much stronger then. He had to be with that tree. Getting it through the front door and into the house was a chore. The tree was wider than the door, and the root ball had to be lifted over the threshold. Needles and dirt were scattered all over the place. But getting the tree upstairs proved even more difficult. Progress proceeded one stair step at a time: lift, rest, lift, rest, lift, rest, lift, …, breathing hard and struggling all the way. Finally, when the tree had cleared the last step, the tree could be dragged across the floor to its final position and decorated. There it would stay from sometime before Christmas until January 6th, when we undecorated the tree and took it back out. Going down the stairs was easier than going up, not only because of the gravity assist, but also because the ball had dried in the time that it was in the house; it weighed much less. Outside, the tree was planted where it could stay and grow for many years.

One year, he had an epiphany. Instead of buying a new tree every year, he would dig up the tree that he had planted the year before, wrap the ball of dirt that came with it in burlap, and bring it inside to use again as our Christmas tree for that year. This worked almost as well as he thought it would. The only problem with that idea was that every year the ball kept getting bigger and bigger. Art doesn't always do things the easy way. It is one thing to carry a tree and ball of dirt that may weigh 60-70 pounds; it is another to lug a tree and ball of dirt that weighs up to 250 pounds. If it had recently rained, the extra moisture in the dirt could make the weight of that tree even heavier.

Art would struggle getting that tree in the house. The first obstacle was to drag it down from the hill where it was planted. Not too bad ... it was all downhill and could slide across the grass. Sometimes he loaded it into a wheelbarrow and wheeled it down, but that was usually unnecessary. The next obstacle was lifting it up the three steps to get it into the house. This happened only slowly, with a huge effort for each step, and time out to recover in between each lift. When the tree was finally at the doorstep, it had to be lifted one more time over the door jam, and into the front room. By this time, the burlap would have split and started leaking dirt all over the place.

Now, there were 12 more steps to climb before the tree could be located upstairs where it was supposed to go. Lift, climb, huff and puff, try to avoid losing any more dirt. Repeat twelve times. It took a Herculean effort and an eternity to get the tree into place where it belonged. By the time he was done, he was really done. It would take some recovery time before he could participate in the decoration of the tree.

So, this was what it was like to have a perpetual live Christmas tree. The only real problem was lugging it up the stairs one step at a time. It never got easy.

The idea of a cut tree had always occurred to Art as he struggled to lift that live tree up each step, one step at a time to the top of the stairs. Finally, there came a year when he was unwilling to repeat the strenuous workout made necessary by always having a live Christmas tree in the house. It took him many years before he came to this revelation. He may be slow, but he does come to his senses ... eventually. Most times.

Our perpetual live tree eventually lived out its life with its roots in the ground where it was supposed to be all the time. The annual dislocation had taken its toll, however, and it died within a few years. Some say it missed the excitement and exhilaration of its annual visit into the house and the adoration of the children at Christmastime. It may have died of loneliness.

HOLIDAY TRAVELS TO REMEMBER

Years ago, when our parents were still alive and living in upstate New York, we used to travel from our farm to Art's parents' house for Thanksgiving on Thursday and then on to Cathy's parents house for another Thanksgiving meal on the Sunday after. This went on for many years.

When we started out on our journeys, the first thing we did was to cross the Conowingo Dam and the Susquehanna River, and then drive along the highway lined on both sides with trees. Of course, at that point, we all had to break out in loud and gusty voices, the song, "Over the river and through the woods, to grandmother's house we go."

We also drove up to see family at Christmas time. With two sets of parents to visit, Christmas morning was usually spent with Art's family near Ithaca, and Christmas afternoon was spent with Cathy's family living near Binghamton. The 75-mile separation between the two locations was driven in an hour and a half. On the way, we listened to traditional Christmas stories and music on a local Ithaca radio station, WHCU-AM.

With the climate moderation we have had recently, the weather across the mountains of Pennsylvania and in upstate New York has become a lot more tame compared to how it was in the past. But during the times when we trekked to New York for the holidays and back home to Maryland, at least one of these trips was occasioned by nasty weather: snow, freezing rain, fog, or ice.

One of the most memorable of these trips occurred in 1971, after Art had just finished serving his tour of duty in the U.S. Army. On the trip up to New York at Christmas time, the forecast for Maryland was for heavy rain; the forecast for central Pennsylvania and upstate New York was for heavy snow. It turns out that the word "heavy" was an understatement.

Undaunted by the threat of snow, Art, Cathy, Joy, and Jodi piled into their car, at that time a Plymouth Valiant bought in 1965. They brought some extra blankets, a small shovel, a few snacks, and some extra water, just in case they became stranded somewhere along the way.

All was going fine until it started to snow above Pine Grove, Pennsylvania. There is a high mountain over which PA Rte. 501 goes. We had always considered that mountain to be the separation between our mild weather down south and the rough weather up north. On the uphill southern side of the mountain, there would be rain; on the downhill portion of the mountain, there was snow. By the time we reached I-81, it was snowing in earnest, and snow plows were nowhere to be seen. The highway was officially closed.

Despite the snow, we were able to keep going. Art was used to driving in the snow, and made good enough time while still being careful. At some point just south of Hazleton, PA, the traffic stopped in front of us. There was a long line of cars ahead, and, at the head of the line, on an uphill grade, was a Cadillac automobile trying to spin its way up the hill. The driver of the car obviously had not had much experience driving on slippery roads in the snow.

We sat there in the car for about a half hour or more. There was no progress being made; the driver of the Cadillac continued to try to spin up the hill without success. The car was blocking the only highway lane that was passable to any degree. Realizing that something had to be done, and there was nobody else doing anything about this situation, Art got out of the car and trudged through the snow toward the Cadillac. When he reached the immobile car, he tried to talk the driver into moving his car out of the way of the rest of the line. It took a bit of persuasion, but the driver finally agreed as long as he could be allowed back into the lane if the cars behind him could get by. On the way back to his own car, Art talked to the driver of a tractor-trailer truck located not too far from the front. Art thought that the large truck might have enough traction and enough under chassis clearance that it could break a trail for the rest of the cars to follow. The truck driver was only too glad to help if he could. With all that arranged, we were all hopeful that we would be moving again. Just at the time when Art returned to our car, a snowplow came along and plowed one lane of the highway. Everybody started up the road.

Our car had been idling to keep Cathy and the girls warm all the while that we had been stopped, so we needed to refill with gasoline. We stopped at a gas station just off I-81 in Hazleton. Getting off the highway was easy; the exit ramp had been plowed. But, I-81 was still officially closed, so the on-ramp had a foot or more of snow covering the roadway. Trying to negotiate the on-ramp would only have been more trouble, and we were already late for our destination, so Art made sure his headlights were turned on, and headed down the exit ramp with the intention that he would make a sharp right turn once he reached the highway. Cars on the highway flashed their lights at him as he came at them from the wrong direction. But, he successfully reached the highway, and continued driving to Cathy's parents' house. The original intention was to drive to Art's family first, but Cathy's parents were closer, so that's where we headed.

We stayed at Cathy's parents' house for four or five days. It kept snowing.

Cathy's father worked for a local highway department, so he was on snowplow duty for the whole time we were there, and we did not see him for the entire time. He came home for a couple of hours rest and food in the middle of the night and left again very early in the morning. Wanting to be of some help, Art shoveled out the driveway so that he would have an easy time coming in at night. He certainly would have been exhausted by the long hours spent plowing snow. The snow at the end of the driveway was packed and heavy, and piled to about three or four feet in depth. There was almost no place for the plows that were clearing the road to deposit the snow, so it naturally filled the opening at the end of the driveway. Cathy's father still couldn't get home easily when he tried. Every time the plow filled the driveway with snow, Art shoveled it out. The piles of snow on either side of the driveway were getting high enough that the shoveled snow had to be carried back from the end of the driveway to be deposited. This cycle repeated for all the days we stayed at their house: shovel snow, plow fills it in, shovel snow, plow fills it in, over and over again. Art was still young at the time, but he was beginning to feel tired. But, he was still sympathetic towards the plight of his father-in-law who had to work many, many hours plowing snow.

Finally, after the persistent snow stopped falling, we left to go to where Art's family lived. It was only 75 miles away, and the main roads had finally all been plowed. All was relatively easy until we reached about a mile away from his parent's house. The roads further on had not yet been plowed. So, we parked the car in the driveway of a neighbor whom we had known for years, and Art walked through the snow to his parents' house. He came back with a galvanized sheet metal tub with rope attached into which the girls and some of our belongings could be slid like a sled to the house, and there we stayed until the roads were plowed the rest of the way.

The trip back was, thankfully, much less eventful.

CRANBERRY RELISH

This has been a Thanksgiving staple in our house since we were first married. The recipe came originally from Cathy's mom, Vera Throop. Art likes this relish so well that he often asks for it at other times of the year besides Thanksgiving and Christmas, and often puts it on his morning cereal with or without other fruit.

Ingredients:

2 (12 ounce) packages of fresh cranberries, frozen
2 oranges, 1 peeled and 1 unpeeled
2 large apples, cored and unpeeled
2 cups sugar

Put all the fruit through a grinder. Add the sugar and mix. Allow to thaw before serving.

OUR TWO HAYING SAYINGS

We used the have two slogans when we did hay: "make hay while the moon shines", and "cured in the bale". There were many times when we needed to get the hay back to the barn before the next day, and the only way to do that was to bale hay and pick it up after dark. So, there were times when the only light we had to do the work was the lights on the tractor and that coming from the moon. It was better if the moon was full rather than in any other stage. One advantage to loading bales at night was that at least the hot sun was not beating down on the workers.

It seemed that many times that we cut hay, no matter what the weather forecast, it would rain. Again, we sometimes did not have a choice about whether to leave the hay in the field to be wetted again or get it up as best as we could. There were those occasions when Art would be soaked as he baled hay during a thunderstorm. The bales, of course, would be at least damp inside.

There are several dangers with putting away wet hay. First, the hay was likely to mold, and would not be nutritious enough for animals to eat. The second danger was more immediate: metabolic reactions in wet hay could heat up enough to flare up into fire. That is the cause for many barns burning to the ground after being filled with wet hay.

When we put wet hay into the barn, Art was careful not to stack the hay bales too close to each other so that there were air channels that could carry excess heat away and cool the hay. Even so, he made several trips to the barn during the night to check on the hay. He would stick his arm into the pile as far as it would go, and gauge the temperature. If too hot, he would move the hay around, and even remove some if warranted. We had many occasions to put in wet (or moist) hay, but were lucky and vigilant enough not to lose a barn.

THE PARADE

If the neighbors only knew the adventures that we have, they would die laughing. Come to think about it, some neighbors have participated. Take the time we were going to bale hay and had to move the baler on the road from the house to the hayfield one-half a mile away. Our road is quite narrow in places, and the baler was not. Neither of our tractors at the time was very speedy, and therefore, Cathy often followed Art with the truck with emergency flasher lights on to warn auto and truck traffic that we were in their way.

We left the driveway without incident, Art on the tractor, followed by the baler, and Cathy and kids in the truck. As we passed the neighbor's house, the temptation to join the parade was too great for the neighbor boy, Kevin. He came out of his driveway, following us on his bike. It was already mentioned that the tractor was not too swift, and it wasn't difficult for him to keep up.

This entourage continued down the road, with Art trying to avoid running into mailboxes with the baler, Cathy trying to go slow enough in the truck to keep from running into Art and the baler, and Kevin showing how fast he could peddle.

There wasn't much traffic at that time, but the day was very hot. Sweat poured down Art's forehead. Cathy and the kids had the truck windows open for ventilation.

All was going fine until we were close to the halfway point. Several days earlier someone had run over a cat in the road, and it had festered over the hot days as it had lain there. As fate would have it, a car came from the other direction just at that time, so there was no maneuvering around the cadaver.

Over the putrid carcass went the tractor tire, leaving a very smelly residue on the tire. Within a flash, the wheel of the baler hit the ugly thing, but, instead of going over it, the baler wheel dragged it along. By now, the car had passed, but Art could not separate the baler from the remains of the cat. Cathy closed the windows on the truck (without air conditioning), and Art was wishing that the tractor could go faster.

The baler was finally able to roll over the thing, but, as it did, it bounced and jarred the baler hay pick-up loose. The pick-up hit the road with a loud crash.

Oh, no! We couldn't continue down the road until the pick-up was re-secured on the baler.

Art stopped, Cathy stopped, and Kevin stopped. Art jumped off the tractor to put things right, Cathy kept the windows closed and sweltered, but poor Kevin, behind it all, couldn't see why everybody was stopped, nor what was causing that awful smell. So, he waited there.

Art never worked so fast in his life, and on a very hot summer's day yet. But, by the time we moved again, Kevin was gone.

BARLEY

Lambs born in the winter usually had an advantage over lambs born later in the season in that the earlier lambs had more time to grow before the hot temperatures of summer drained their appetites and made them listless and passive all day long. Sheep really do not like to eat very much in the summer when they just lie around and suffer. Lambs born in the winter, however, are sometimes chilled by cold wind, especially when born outside the barn. This often happened after we noticed that keeping pregnant ewes inside was not good for their health, nor for their offspring.

Lambs that suckle soon after birth are usually fine. Mothers dry their lambs, and the warm milk in their tummies gives them the strength to survive the trauma of birthing. They need to drink within a half hour of birth in order to have a good chance at survival. Cathy was especially good at helping newborn lambs drink from their mothers.

We found out that newborn female lambs are hardier than newborn male lambs, and females usually drank by themselves, whereas male lambs, more often than not, needed some help to find the mother's teats. If the lambs were born in the pasture, then they sometimes became chilled before we had located them (although we checked on ewes likely to give birth many times during the evening and night).

Checking a lamb's temperature was easy: just insert a finger into the lamb's mouth and, if it feels cold to the touch, then the lamb needs immediate attention.

Chilled lambs do not survive long, so it sometimes becomes necessary to warm them. This we did by placing them in large pots of warm, not hot, water to give them warm baths. This worked well to warm them, but had the disadvantage that it often washed the individual smell from their bodies, and their mothers would not accept them as their own. Thus, lambs warmed in this way often had to be bottle-fed because their mothers rejected them when they came close.

One lamb that needed warming was named Barley. We brought him into the house and placed him in a pot of warm water. He warmed relatively fast, and we were lucky that he had a twin brother which had not become chilled, and who smelled to his mom like he was her newborn son. It may have been the smell of his brother that satisfied his mother that the pair were her own, and she accepted both lambs and allowed them to drink. We named him Barley because he soaked in the pot of warm water just like the barley grain that Cathy used to make our favorite barley soup. We named his twin brother Souper. Both grew well into fine big lambs.

THE ROOSTER WHO RULED THE ROOST

If our hens were going to be able to raise their own brood, we had to keep a rooster around to be the daddy. Roosters can be docile, or roosters can be belligerent. When we kept chickens we tried not to keep the feisty ones; they could be trouble. In addition to their confrontational personalities, they had bony spurs on the backs of their feet that could, if they so wished, inflict pain and injury on those victims being attacked. This type of rooster challenged all potential rivals, including humans. Sometimes, foxes would solve our rooster problems, but there were those roosters who were not to be victimized as some animal's dinner. This is the story of the rise and fall of one such bully of a rooster.

We had bought this rooster as a baby chick from a mail order hatchery with which we frequently dealt. At the time, there was no indication that this chick would grow up any different from any of the others. Over time, though, this is the one rooster from that batch of chicks that survived the rigors of being a chicken on our farm. Whether he had anything to do with the disappearance of his male chickmates or not, he alone remained.

He was a proud son-of-a-gun, as white as snow, but much more of a menace. He was not afraid of confronting people and terrifying them in the process. We once hired young Robert Knight Jr. to paint our barn for us. While Robert was on the ladder, he was safe from the rooster, but there were several times when this rooster would not let Robert climb down. Robert would stay marooned up the ladder until he could catch the attention of either Art or Cathy, who would grab a stick and chase the rooster away. Needless to say, Robert did not want to continue with his painting job.

The rooster finally met his match in our daughter Jodi, who was a preteen at the time. Jodi was very fond of animals, and usually fawned all over them. She could often spend her time walking around with a cat in her arms, or sitting next to our dog and petting it, or playing with baby ducks when we had them. But Jodi also had determination, and this rooster brought it out.

The mistake that the rooster made was threatening Jodi when she went into one of our sheds. The rooster could see her inside, and patrolled in front of the shed to make sure that she did not come out. Jodi was familiar enough with him that she knew that the rooster would not be above using his spurs on her if she confronted him; and, by confrontation, the rooster meant to show the he was boss by controlling where she could go.

Art and Cathy had left the farm for a few minutes while all this was happening. So, Jodi had no recourse but to solve the rooster menace problem by herself. She may have been threatened, but she wasn't terrified. Somehow, she managed to sneak out of the shed without the rooster taking note. Once outside, the rooster saw her and began chasing her. When being chased by the rooster, Jodi could flee quite rapidly. She ducked into the house.

At that point, she knew what she had to do. She grabbed the only weapon that she saw in the back room: it was a BB gun that could be pumped for a more powerful shot; she pumped the handle many times.

When she opened the door to exit the house, she did not have to search far for the terrifying rooster that had threatened her. He was close by. So, BB gun in hand, she walked up to the rooster. It was not in his nature to back away, so he stood there, tall and straight while she approached. She got within a gun's distance from him, pointed the gun at his head, and fired. When he fell down, she fired again, and again, and again. She put many holes in his head; that rooster would terrify no one again.

Art and Cathy returned home some time later to find the rooster lying where he had fallen. They shed no tears over his passing, especially after they heard the story from Jodi. And Jodi had found a new confidence in her ability to protect herself. From that point on, she added a new swagger to her step.

FAILURE TO SECURE LOAD

The pickup truck that we had at the time was an old 1972 Ford F100 that showed the cumulative effects of carrying cows and sheep between pastures, hay in from the field, fruit to the farmers' market, and loads of treasure from various farm auctions. It was a good old truck that served us well until the motor mounts failed and the front wheels started shimmying uncontrollably whenever the truck hit a bump in the road. At that point, it was time for a new truck.

Needless to say, a truck that had been with us for so many years would have tales to tell if it could. It would tell of hard work, maybe even mistreatment, but if it were given enough alcohol in its radiator so that it loosened up, it might remember some interesting times.

Once, Art was taking a load of garbage to the dump; the garbage was all bundled neatly in plastic bags or it was contained in barrels. The back of the truck was stacked full. There was no sense going to the landfill with half a load.

Art normally drove slowly on back roads to the landfill, but, on this occasion unfortunately he took US Route 1. And, on Route 1, you have to keep up with the speed of the other traffic.

It wasn't long before the wind blew a bag of garbage off the truck. Art saw it go in his rear-view mirror, and immediately pulled to the side of the road. He intended to retrieve the bag.

It was just his luck that the car following him, and the one in front of which the bag landed on the road, belonged to a State Trooper. He avoided hitting the bag and pulled in behind Art on the shoulder of the road. Just to be sure that Art didn't mistake this as a social call, he switched on his red and blue lights.

It soon became apparent that they were both at cross purposes. Art wanted to retrieve the bag from the middle of the road quickly, before a car came along and hit it. That could either do some damage or scatter garbage all over the road, and that would really have been hard to clean up. The Trooper wanted to see Art's license and registration, and didn't want to wait while Art ran down the road and back.

After a brief discussion won by the Trooper, Art handed him what he required, then went back to retrieve the lost bag. The Trooper disappeared inside his car for a relatively long time.

The rest of this incident was only revealed later when Art returned home. Cathy had been listening to her fire and police monitor and had heard the conversation between the officer and headquarters. As she described it, the conversation went something like this:

"So, what can I write this ticket for?"
"I'm not sure."
"Well, I have to charge him with something now that I stopped him."
"I suppose so."
"So, what will it be?"
"I don't know. Give us a couple of minutes, and we'll look up something."
"OK, but try to make it quick."
(pause)
"I've talked to everyone around here, and the only thing we can come up with is 'failure to secure load'."
"Will that do it?"
"It should."
"10-4."

And, that's what was on the ticket: "Failure to secure load."

THE OLD JOHN DEERE MODEL A TRACTOR

The first tractor that we bought was a 2-cylinder John Deere Model "A", also called a "Johnny Put-Put" because of the way it sounded when running. This particular tractor was probably manufactured in the early 1940's, and had a number of features that made it unique at the time we bought it. First, it had no electric start. To start the tractor, one had to open petcocks to the two cylinders. This released some of the pressure built up inside as the cylinders moved forward during their compression strokes. This was made necessary because the means to start the tractor was to manually spin the heavy cast iron flywheel located on the side of the tractor. If the gasoline pulled into the cylinders on their intake strokes was ignited by the spark plugs, then the tractor engine would start, and all would be fine once the petcocks were closed so that the engine could develop its full power, about 18 horsepower.

There were problems sometimes with this method of starting. If the stars and the moon were all aligned correctly, and the tractor started right away, then all would be fine. However, it took a lot of strength to spin (actually, "spin" is not correct: a more correct phrase would be "rotate with a lot of effort") the flywheel. Starting this tractor was not for the weak.

If the tractor did not start right away, then it could quickly drain the energy from the person attempting to rotate the flywheel. So, Art, not particularly liking to work hard to start the old John Deere, was in the habit of parking the tractor on a hill. He would disengage the clutch, unlock the brakes, start the tractor rolling down the hill, and, when the tractor was going fast enough, he would pop the clutch, engaging the transmission; the momentum of the tractor would provide the power to turn the engine, and, most times, start the engine. However, if he forgot to open the petcocks first, then the back pressure on the cylinders could stop the tractor without the engine starting. Then, Art had to get off the tractor, open the petcocks, and rotate the heavy flywheel. If he was lucky, the engine would start with one or two spins. If he was not so lucky, then it might take 5 to 10 spins. At that point, there was a question about whether or not the tractor was worth the effort to start it.

There was a time or two that this scenario occurred. Once, the tractor was going through a period when it was very hard to start. It was during the heat of the summer, in the middle of the day, and the John Deere decided that it really did not want to start. Art rolled the tractor down the hill, to no avail. Once at the bottom of the hill, there was no way to get the tractor back up the hill again unless the tractor started. So, Art got off the tractor and started turning the flywheel. He turned, and he turned. Nothing happened, at least to the tractor. He turned that flywheel until he was so hot and exhausted, and then left the tractor alone to think about what it was doing, compared to what it was supposed to do. He came back renewed and optimistic the next morning, opened the petcocks, and turned the flywheel with his early-morning strength. After a couple of tries, the tractor started. Relief. Art got on the tractor and returned it to the top of the hill, but decided not to use the tractor for a few days, or, at least, to rest before he tried to start the tractor again.

Another feature of this tractor was that it had a magneto to generate and distribute the spark to the two spark plugs. Modern engines all have distributors that perform most of the same functions as magnetos, but magnetos could sometimes misbehave in hot weather. They might not provide enough spark for the plugs to ignite the gas in the cylinders. This is probably what happened when the tractor would not start in the heat of the day but did start the next morning. Magnetos were rare, and expensive when they could be found, so it was not until it was absolutely necessary that they were replaced.

Our next-door neighbor also had an old John Deere tractor, but his was a Model "B" with an electric starter. Art was so jealous.

A third feature of this tractor was that it had a hand clutch. There was a lever where the operator sat, and pushing the lever forward engaged the transmission. Pulling the lever back took the tractor out of gear.

Most people familiar with manual transmissions are used to a foot clutch. So, the manual clutch took some extra attention. This caused some problems on occasion.

Art was helping Bob Knight with haying, and using his tractor to transport hay back to the barn. Art had asked Bob to take over when he reached the barn and to back a four-wheel wagon loaded with hay to the door of our barn where the hay could be off-loaded. Art had deferred to Bob for this task because what must be done to back a four-wheel wagon is completely opposite from what had to be done to back a two-wheel wagon; it is tricky business under any circumstances; Bob had more experience with backing four-wheel wagons than had Art, so he took over the driving.

Bob, however, was not used the manual clutch. As he turned his head to watch where the wagon was headed, he forgot all about the lever. Needing to disengage the transmission, he stepped on a pedal in a location that ordinarily would be where the clutch pedal would be. Instead, the pedal that he stomped down on was one of the brakes-tractors have one brake pedal for each wheel so that the brakes can be engaged separately, if need be. Stopping the one wheel turned the tractor sharply to the left, but left the tractor in gear. Before he could correct for this error, the rear wheel had run over the wagon tongue and bent it to the ground. It took a lot of muscle to straighten that tongue, and it never was exactly right after that.

There was another story about Bob Knight and that John Deere tractor. Bob had borrowed the tractor to bring to his house and use it to power a saw and cut firewood logs into pieces. Running a belt from a pulley on the tractor to the saw worked as it should, transmitting enough power to do the job. The problem was that the flywheel had developed a crack, and that made it somewhat loose on the spline on which it was mounted. Bob started the tractor without any trouble, but, as he was operating the saw, the flywheel came loose and rolled right by him. If it had hit him, it would have killed him for sure, but he was lucky. Without the flywheel attached to the tractor, the engine began to run erratically, so he had to shut off the tractor and could not finish his job. It was not easy to find a replacement flywheel, so Art found instead a welder who agreed to patch the cast iron crack. With some heaving and lifting, the repaired flywheel was reattached, and served fine until the tractor was sold, years later.

Art was not sorry to see that tractor go. The next tractors that we would buy were a lot more modern, although still old, but they did have electric starters, distributors, and conventional foot clutches. They were not nearly as exciting to start and operate as that old John Deere Model A, but they were a lot more useful.

TOO MUCH HELP

Help is usually appreciated, but there are times when the help actually makes matters worse. One of those times came when we had brought two half-grown calves and an unrelated cow to their summer pasture a half a mile down the road. The reason that the calves were there without their moms was that we had wanted to wean the calves off their moms, but to be suddenly separated from mom is a traumatic experience for a calf. And, therein, is the cause for what happened next.

In a new environment without knowledge of the boundaries of the pasture, and anxious to be reunited with their mothers, the calves tested the pasture fence and found a weak spot. They escaped and took the cow with them. Still a half mile from where they had to this point grown up, they ran all over the place searching for their mothers. The cow was also anxious to be reunited with her familiar companions, and also ran around.

We got a phone call from a neighbor who not only told us that the cattle were loose, but that they had tried to catch them without success. Uh-oh! Strangers chasing the cow and calves in an unfamiliar location would only have made them more inclined to run wild.

When we arrived there, we found that the cattle had scattered in three different directions. There was also a woman in a car, several dogs, and more kids than we could count on one hand chasing one of them down the road. None of the volunteers knew anything about catching cows, but they were trying really hard to help! The cattle were even more rattled now.

Catching the cattle was the easier job. The harder job was to try to keep those well-meaning neighbors from helping.

We managed to corner the cow within an hour, and tied her back in the pasture in case that would draw the two calves back to her. But, there was no such luck; they kept running. The two calves had split up and ran all over the place. The neighbors really thought they could help; we thought they couldn't.

The calves kept running and bawling to each other, trying to find their mothers, from distances as far apart from each other as a quarter mile. They ran up hills, through thickets, across streams, back and forth, up and down, through places that Art had never before been, or even imagined. By now, he was tiring, and evening was close at hand.

Finally, we were able to chase one calf back into the pasture in the company of the tied cow. The other calf, however, could still be heard across the hills. The neighbors had finally gone home, feeling good that they had done all they could to help with the cattle.

The other calf was very wild by this time; she ran through the woods and across farm fields, taking Art to places unfamiliar to him. This pursuit kept going for hours. Finally, as darkness was setting in, she found a hole in a neighbor's pasture fence and went through. Not wanting to follow her into the pasture, and afraid of spooking the neighbor's cows, Art retired from the chase.

He called the owner of the pasture in which our calf was now located, and told her what had happened; the extra calf in her pasture was ours. She listened in disbelief, because she had no idea that there was hole in her fence big enough for a calf to slip through. Her cows had not discovered the hole, or, if they had, they must have decided that life was good enough for them in their own pasture so that they had no reason to leave.

We caught the calf in her barn the next morning. It had calmed down and come inside with the rest of her cows. We took the calf back to our summer pasture and made sure that the fence was secure. Our cow and calves caused no more trouble after that. But, all this could have been so much easier if the cattle had not been chased by all the neighborly help that we had that day.

HORSERADISH FOR FUN AND PROFIT?

Soon after we bought our 15-acre parcel of land just down the road from our original five acre farm, we were looking for a crop to grow on the land. We had visions of pick-your-own strawberries, some hay, and some pasture. However, because the property was separated from our house by one half mile, the strawberries were a bit impractical. It was about then that we heard about Tulkoff's, a Baltimore condiment preparation company, wanting to expand and needing new growers of horseradish roots.

They invited interested farmers to attend an informational meeting, and, at the meeting, they made growing horseradish sound so easy. Growers would begin with buying horseradish roots from Tulkoff's. Farmers would plant the roots in the spring, grow them, and dig them in the fall. They would then take the crop to Tulkoff's processing plant, and take home about $5000 an acre. It sounded too good to be true. And, as it turned out, it was.

So, we bought 500 pounds of horseradish roots and cut them into pieces. We plowed furrows in the ground that was new to us and planted the roots by hand. There were now only two things standing between us and the promised riches: weed control and digging the horseradish in the fall.

About this time, Jodi was curious about how horseradish roots tasted. She asked for a bite of one to try. We tried to talk her out of it, but she persisted. We let her have a taste, and she never again wanted a taste of horseradish root. She also found out that it took a lot of water to rinse the burning sensation from her mouth.

A little while later, after the roots had grown a bit, we dug up a couple and intended to make some freshly ground horseradish for our own use in our house. We cleaned the roots, and carefully cut them into pieces while wearing gloves so that the caustic juices would not get on our hands. They were put into our blender with some water and white vinegar. When we started the blender, and the roots began to be pulverized, horseradish fumes filled the entire house. There was no place to escape the fumes, and everyone was soon tearing and blowing noses. These effects did not stop us from making ground horseradish again, because the condiment was really powerful and very good when used sparingly. However, the next times we processed horseradish roots, we warned everyone except the blender operator to leave the house or risk being assaulted by horseradish fumes.

Back in the field, we had mechanical cultivators for our old John Deere "A" tractor, and Art tried using them to control the weeds. That was not very effective, so he tried using herbicides. He purchased a wick applicator, which was a four foot long piece of plastic pipe into which the weed killer Roundup was poured. Ropes on the bottom of the pipe wicked the herbicide from inside the pipe. When the applicator was dragged over the weeds, they would be coated with Roundup and die. The horseradish plants, still smaller than the weeds, would remain.

Art tried attaching the applicator to the tractor, but could not control the height well enough to make it effective. Next, he and Cathy each held an end of the applicator and walked across the field, adjusting the height of the applicator to the height of the weeds. Walking this way through a weedy field several acres in area was not easy to do. But, the worst part was that Art was taller than was Cathy, and held his end of the applicator somewhat higher than she did. The Roundup herbicide flowed to her end and soaked her arms and hands. We quickly stopped using this method, but at least she would not sprout any live weeds for a while.

So, that didn't work. Another method was needed. A neighbor's boy was hired to rid the field of weeds. Art contracted with the boy to pay him an amount of money for weeding the entire field. The amount was enough that he could buy a car with the money, and he was motivated to start.

But, the weeding was more work than he had thought, and he wasn't as willing to continue as he thought he would be. He had started counting his money before he earned it. He wanted the money, but not the work, which apparently made the dream of a car suddenly not as attractive.

The weeds grew, but horseradish is a hardy plant that can grow in even the worst of conditions, and it grew well enough.

To harvest the horseradish, Art bought an old Iron Age potato digger at a farm auction. The digger lifted the top layer of soil and its contents and shook the soil loose from the potatoes, which were delivered at the far end. The digger had to be modified to dig deeper than it was designed to do with potatoes. We had that done by some mechanics, and were ready to go.

When the fall came, Art found out that his John Deere tractor would not pull the digger when it dug as deeply as it was supposed to. The tractor wheels slipped rather than pulled.

Art was talking about his problem when a neighbor, Henry Holloway, became intrigued by the challenge of pulling the digger and harvesting the horseradish. He came over with his much larger and newer tractor to try to see if his equipment was able to do what our old John Deere could not. As it turned out, it could.

But, once he had proven to himself that harvesting the horseradish with his tractor would work, he disappeared, and was unwilling to spend any more of his busy time on a neighbor's horseradish. So, Art was back to square one.

An even bigger problem was the many large rocks, boulders even, that were buried in the field. They stopped all harvesting operations. Tulkoff's hadn't said anything about rocks.

Art now had no idea what he was going to do to get that horseradish out of the ground and delivered to Tulkoff's facility. Without a harvest, all the money spent on the seed roots, payment for weeding, and gas for his tractor would have been lost. Worse, there would be no return for all the time spent. He began considering harvesting with dynamite.

And then an angel appeared in the form of a Columbia Gas Company pipeline representative. He knocked on our door and announced that they were going to lay a new gas pipe across my fields. They were willing to pay for lost crops.

Although he hadn't been able to bring any horseradish to Tulkoff's, Art knew how much it would have been worth; Tulkoff's had told him at the outset.

The gas company was willing to pay what Art was asking. After all, they had no prior experience paying for a field of horseradish. We were saved by a gas pipeline, and were handsomely rewarded for all of our troubles.

There were some very valuable lessons learned from this experience. The first of these is this: with ground as rocky as this, do not raise any crops that require plowing, planting in loose soil, or digging to harvest. After that, we stuck strictly to hay, pasture, and fruit trees.

The second lesson learned is that gas pipelines can be a blessing sometimes.

The third lesson is that cut and dried horseradish leaves make excellent hay.

BEWARE OF THE RAM II

One evening Cathy came in from feeding the animals that we had at the time, and she was half laughing, half crying. When Art asked what was wrong, she told him that everything hurt. It seems that she had gone into the pasture to feed the ducks, geese, sheep, and cows, and was chasing some ducks into the barn, quite oblivious to where the other animals were. Without warning, the ram that we had at the time, named Blunderbuss, hit her in the back of her legs so hard that it knocked her down, head over teacup. On the way down, she had also stepped on her foot, and that hurt, too. She dragged herself up, and was inching her way backwards away from the ram, when she stumbled over one of our John Deere cultivators and fell again. This time she was so angry that, when she picked herself up, she went over to Blunderbuss and whacked him hard over the head with a big stick that she was carrying. But the shock of hitting him was transmitted back down the stick and hurt her hand. By then, she sure didn't know whether to laugh or to cry.

TOO MUCH LIME

Old farm machinery can be challenging at times, and that's all we had to work with for the first fifteen or so years of our farm. At the time we had two tractors: an old Allis Chalmers model "C" tractor with an electric starter and an even older John Deere model "A" without the convenience of an electric starter. Quite often, one of these tractors was in good working condition when the other wasn't, and then, after the broken one was fixed, they often switched places.

All of our other pieces of machinery were purchased at least second hand, and some had very long histories. Most pieces were bought for the bargain prices that we could afford, and then restored to working order with a good deal of sweat, frustration, and parts that seemed to be as expensive as gold.

Sometimes, our machinery troubles could not be blamed on the equipment. There was the time when we needed lime to be spread on one particular field located a half mile down the road from our homestead. Access to the field was limited by a severely-eroded, muddy entrance from the road.

The most logical solution to bring the lime to the field was by arranging to have a lime-spreader truck carry the lime and spread it, as many farmers did. When a call was made to the lime spreader company, the man on the other end of the phone kept emphasizing that we would be responsible for towing him out of the field, should the truck get stuck. Towing a truck filled with 12 tons of lime stuck to its axles in the mud would have been impossible with either the Allis Chalmers or John Deere tractor. So, we decided to spread the lime ourselves with an old lime spreader that we had bought used. We would use one of our tractors and trailer to transport the lime to the field, and transfer it to the spreader once we got it there.

Our second-hand trailer had two wheels and was made from an old Ford pickup truck bed with a tongue made from a piece of galvanized iron pipe. Until then, the trailer was adequate to carry anything that we had asked of it. We hitched the trailer to the John Deere, and loaded it with the lime.

We bought bagged lime, which was the only way we could handle it. Bags of lime weigh 80 pounds apiece, and can accumulate a lot of weight in a small space. We were careful to keep most of the weight of the lime to the front of the trailer rather than over the old tires that we were afraid might go flat with all that weight.

We left our driveway and headed up the road, but within about 200 feet of leaving the driveway, the trailer tongue began to bend in the middle. Soon, it was dragging along the road, and starting to gouge a groove in the asphalt.

When it became apparent that it was no use to continue, we stopped. Cathy was in our pickup truck following behind, but what to do? The trailer could not be backed or turned while still loaded, and we couldn't stay there and block traffic. So, we backed the truck to the trailer and transferred every bag of lime from the trailer to the truck. The truck tires looked like they could go flat at any time.

It probably took no more than 30 minutes to move the lime, but seemed like forever. Fortunately, it was early Saturday morning, there was little traffic, it was cool, and we were fresh. Otherwise, we would have been blamed for a traffic tie-up in the neighborhood.

Cathy slowly made it back home with the truck, and Art managed to get the tractor and trailer home. It wasn't until then that we calculated that the load on the trailer, with that little galvanized pipe as a tongue, to have been 8000 pounds.

WHEN WE BALED HAY

We used to bale our own hay, but don't any more. When we had both sheep and cows, they ate a lot of hay. We didn't need that much hay when we had only sheep. Haying is a lot of work, and, when we started harvesting a significant amount of fruit, we could not afford to take the time away from the fruit to devote to haying.

We soon found out that our old haying equipment broke often, and needed expensive parts for repair. It probably would have been less expensive to buy the hay that we needed, but finding a supplier was not easy.

We used the have two slogans when we made hay: "make hay while the moon shines", and "cured in the bale". It seemed that every time we cut hay, no matter what the weather forecast, it always rained. We have baled in the rain before just to get the job done. But that's another story of checking stacked bales in the middle of the night to make sure that they did not heat up to the point of spontaneous combustion.

Suffice it to say that we consider the anniversary of the day we sold our haying machinery to be a day of continued celebration.

ATTEMPT AT A GOOD DEED

We were approached one week at the farmers' market by a homeless person living in a local shelter who was looking for work. She was going from vender to vender with the same request, anxious to get some work to give her an income. With a little extra money, she said, she could leave the shelter and get a place of her own. She said that she was strong, and was willing to do almost any kind of work.

Our first inclination was to say that we had nothing for her to do. We normally don't hire any help, but she seemed to be in need, so we decided to give it a try. Hiring her part-time seemed like it could help her toward her goal and could help us at the same time.

We decided that thinning peaches would be something that would help us and not be too strenuous for her to handle. So, we contacted her and she came over the next afternoon to learn about the proposed job. She and Art walked out to the peach trees, and he explained how to thin peaches. Just remove all the extra small fruits and leave a peach every six inches along the branch. Most of the work could be done by standing on the ground, but she may have to climb a couple of steps on a ladder to remove the higher fruits.

It was late in the afternoon on one of those hot summer days; and she started to sweat. It was too hot, she said, to do that kind of work.

Then she looked around at all the surrounding tall grass "Are there snakes around here?" she asked. Art told her that there could be, but he didn't know for sure. "I really don't like snakes," she said.

She left. Perhaps she was expecting a job in the shade, or one where she did not have to work too hard. Maybe she found a cooler job. But she wasn't quite as motivated as she had seemed when she first contacted us.

BEING RICH

"I'm just a country boy, money have I none.
But I've got silver in the stars,
And gold in the mornin' sun,
And gold in the mornin' sun."

These lyrics from a song sung by Harry Belafonte are poetic, but don't tell quite the whole story. It's just that star silver or morning sun gold are not legal tender, so we can't pay the bills with them. However, we at SweetAire Farm still think of ourselves as rich. Why? Because we have:

1. our health
2. enough good food to eat.
3. a safe and comfortable (but modest) home to live in.
4. true friends.
5. a reason to live.

Every time we look outside and see the fruit hanging from the branches, we feel very blessed that we have this opportunity to be productive and to help others in the process. That is our motivation to spend our days outside in all kinds of weather.

With these things, most, if not all, of us can consider ourselves to be among the richest people who have ever lived.

DRINKING FROM MY SAUCER

The John Paul Moore poem "Drinking from my Saucer" was printed in an issue of the *Lancaster Farming* newspaper, and expresses a grateful sentiment that we share: A few lines from the poem are all that is needed to get the idea:

> I've never made a fortune,
> And I'll never make one now,
> But it really doesn't matter,
> Cause I'm happy anyhow.
>
> As I go along my journey,
> I'm reaping better than I've sowed.
> I'm drinking from my saucer,
> 'Cause my cup has overflowed.
>
> I thank God for the blessings
> That His mercy has bestowed,
> I'm drinking from the saucer,
> 'Cause my cup has overflowed.

Living and working on SweetAire farm can be a chore sometimes; there are days that are too hot, too cold, too rainy, or too sunny to inspire us to do the things that we need to do. But, when we see the results from our efforts, we can certainly appreciate the goodness that follows.

First of all, there is the excitement of watching things grow and thrive. Then, there is the appreciation for the abundant harvests that ensue. Finally, there are the people who we see at the Farmers' Market who we know are going to enjoy what we have brought for them and who will be healthier because of the means we have used to grow the produce they have purchased.

One cannot ask for a better life than one that has meaning, is a healthy lifestyle, and serves others in ways that they are not able to do for themselves. Our cups certainly overflow.

OUT IN THE COLD

We are amused by media responses to Arctic cold air that moves into our area during the winter. They act like it was going to be the end of the world, with wind-chill temperatures of -20° to -30°. It can be cold, we are aware of that, but not as bad as the radio, TV, and papers make it out to be. In particular, there have been pictures in the *Baltimore Sun* newspaper of people bundled up so much they hardly had any bare skin showing. Those pictures were taken on the day when temperatures were relatively mild and Art was outside pruning apple trees. How would people cope another day, when it really got cold, we asked each other.

Our sheep are free to wander out into the fields or stay in their sheds. They do not stay long in the sheds. They carry their own wool blankets with them wherever they go, and they acclimate to the cold. When the daily temperatures soar into the 50s, the sheep do as they always do, and seek out a nice shady cool spot in which to lie. Animals that have gotten used to the cold are fine outside, despite all the pronouncements urging people to bring their pets in during cold weather.

Our sheep act very bored when the snow and weather limit their activities. They wander around, if possible, but don't stay long in any one place. They act as if they don't know what to do with themselves. Our ram becomes more belligerent when the snow confines the sheep to a small area around the barn. Without the snow, he pretty much minds his own business, eating and paying attention to his flock. When the snow prevents him and his ewes from visiting the back orchard, he cannot be trusted behind us.

The sheep can get used to the snow. Adult sheep learn to paw through the snow to reach the grass underneath, although it may take them at least one snow storm before they learn how to do that. We have watched as one of young twin lambs, as small as she was, pawed through the snow, dipped her head into the snow to the point that her head was totally obscured by the deep snow, and chewed a mouthful of grass. Snow then becomes nothing special to the sheep after they learn to do that.

While shoveling the driveway one day, Art observed a ewe high-stepping through the snow toward the stream to get a drink. She was obviously thirsty. But, she didn't want to go to the stream alone, so she would "bah" every few steps to let the others know that she wanted them to join her. No other ewe came, so, she eventually started eating snow. After a while, another ewe joined the first, and they both proceeded to the stream. Sheep are funny that way; they don't usually want to be alone.

When they can, the sheep blaze a trail part of the way out to the orchard. If we wait to follow their pathway, it might seem to make our walk out to the orchard easier, except for two things: first of all, the sheep wait for us to break the trail through the deep snow first before they go out there, and, second, their path is only about six inches wide, much too narrow for comfortable human walking. How the sheep can always track so closely behind each other that their path is no more than six inches wide is a mystery to us, but it happens all the time.

TRUCK RUNAWAY RAMPS IN THE MOUNTAINS

On the way to and from West Virginia, Art passed a number of truck runaway ramps located on the downhill sides of the highway. While he never had seen a truck needing to use one of these ramps, his curiosity was aroused when he noticed at the top of one of these ramps was a sign. He was too soon past the ramp to see what the sign would have said, but can only imagine its message. Would it say "Welcome"? "Whew, glad you could make it"? "Now how do you get back down out of here"? "Why would you want to"? "Are you still in complete control of your bodily functions"? "Prayers accepted – God"?

We can only speculate.

LISTENING FOR LAMBS

Cathy was always good at predicting which ewes were close to term and when they would likely deliver their lambs. She could not predict the exact hour, however, and so there were many a night when one of us would have to make nighttime trips to the barn or the pasture to check on the conditions of ewes ready to lamb. If she was sure that a ewe would lamb that night, then we might lock the ewe inside either the barn or the sheep shed, but that was not always the case, so sometimes we had to check a lot further out in the pasture to see what was going on. These trips outside were often made in total darkness except for our flashlight to guide us, and the flashlight was not always up to the task. It was often very cold on these winter nights, and there might be snow to trudge through. At the very least, these trips could be an unpleasant excursion, coming from a nice warm, well-lit house into the cold, dark winter night.

There is some lore that indicates that sheep could be induced to lamb at certain times by feeding them on particular schedules. Feeding grain in the early evening was supposed to result in lambs born in the daytime, but our grain feeding time for the sheep was in the early morning before other farm activities took place and while the sheep were most likely to be resting near the barn, so that probably destined us to experience a series of nighttime births.

The Radio Shack electronics store made our lambing operation a lot easier. We purchased some baby monitors from the store and plugged sending units into the electrical outlets in the barn and sheep shed. A monitor in our kitchen allowed us to listen to the sounds that sheep made at night while inside. If we heard the weak bleating of a newborn lamb, we were sure to make a trip to the barn to move the ewe and lamb inside, if they weren't already. Sometimes a mother in the process of birthing made soft cooing sounds; that also meant a trip to the barn. Otherwise, if all was quiet, we did not usually go out to check on them.

The monitors also came in handy when the one of us who had gone to the barn needed some help. All that was necessary was to call over the monitor to the other person in the house, and help would come as quickly as getting all bundled up would allow.

There were a few times when the sounds from the monitor spelled trouble. There were times, fortunately only a few, when the barking of a dog or dogs could be heard over the monitor. Strange dogs in with sheep can only mean bad news. Dogs kill sheep. When dog barking was heard, the time to get out to the pasture was immediate, and no time could be taken to bundle up, and the flashlight had better work this time.

The monitors eventually stopped working in the dusty and damp environments of the barn and sheep shed. When that occurred, there were no replacements to be had in Radio Shack. Soon, there was no Radio Shack either.

A RAM CALLED STOLZFUS

We bought Stolzfus the ram at a dispersal auction held a farm in Lancaster County, Pennsylvania, owned by an Amish family named Stolzfus. The ram was old and somewhat pot-bellied, and had seen better days, but he represented different genetics than we had in our somewhat in-bred sheep flock at the time, so he would be the ram of choice for as long as he could perform his breeding functions. Young rams can be quite rambunctious during breeding season in the fall, but Stolzfus was old, so he was one of the most gentle of our rams; he bothered no one at any time of the year.

Because he was trustworthy and not inclined to butt anyone near him, we felt confident enough to transport him to Bob Knight's back field in the middle of Darlington. During the summer, when our pastures were low on grass, Bob's field had a lot of grass, all of which needed mowing; sheep grazing in his back yard would be a help to us and to him, as well.

Bob also had an in-ground swimming pool in the same field where the sheep roamed free.

The pool was not fenced in. This had not been a problem in the past, but Stolzfus may not have recognized the danger of that open pool of water. And, he did not know how to swim. We found Stolzfus one morning floating in the water where he had fallen. With his full coat of water-soaked wool, he was difficult to pull out of the pool, but we managed. Stolzfus did not survive. Bob had to run his filter extra hours to remove all the wool fibers from the pool water before he was willing to take his next dip in the pool.

JOE

There is a reputation widely-held around here that all Amish people are industrious and hard workers. We found the exception.

About the time that the girls had grown and before the boys came to our farm, Art and Cathy decided that they would try hiring some part-time help. There are not a lot of people who are willing to do the work of a farm, because it is largely physical, can be hard, and must be done in the hot sun, at times, or rain or humidity at others. There may have been some local teenagers who were available to work, but those who wanted to work were already working on other farms. Living on the edge of Amish country in Lancaster County, Pennsylvania, we naturally turned to thinking of contacting an Amish man for possible employment at SweetAire Farm.

The person who told us about Joe was probably Amos Stoltzfus, an Amish man himself. When Art asked him for the name of someone he knew who needed employment, Amos recommended Joe. An Amish man currently without a job? Art should have been wary at that point, but he went ahead and drove to Joe's house.

Joe lived in a typical Amish house, simple, but adequate. He had a wife and at least two children, a son who was nearly an adult and a young daughter who still attended school. When he heard Art's proposal for part-time work, he said that he preferred full-time work. But Art could not promise enough work for full-time. However, Art said that he would see if the work could become full-time, depending on how the part-time work went for a while. Joe's wife, who was also part of the conversation, was much more enthusiastic about the work than was Joe.

Joe was hired to work on our farm for two or three days a week. He would be needed especially on Fridays, when we picked our fruit for the Saturday Farmers' Market.

Cathy's job on the designated days was to drive about a half hour to Joe's house, pick him up, and drive him back to our farm. She would also pay him and take him home at the end of his workday.

Joe usually came out of his house when Cathy drove up. However, Joe always seemed to have some errands to attend to before he was ready to come to our farm. He would ask Cathy if she would drive him to see somebody first, or to drive his daughter to school so that he would not have to harness the horses to his buggy. His errands usually took an additional half hour or so, and so Cathy would not get back to our farm to do her picking for at least an hour and a half after she left.

Joe would talk to Cathy as he rode in her van, but only about one subject: the weather. "Do you think it will rain today?" he would invariably ask. "I really would not like to get wet." If it looked like it might rain soon, he would ask to be brought back to his house, and he would not work that day. If he was already working at our farm, and rain threatened, he would ask to be brought home before it rained. This happened several times.

Joe also usually had somewhere to stop on the way home, and expected Cathy to take him there. Once, he stopped at a local roadside produce stand to buy something to bring home. Cathy accompanied him inside that time. "Oh", the proprietor said, "you must be Joe's driver." That remark revealed to Cathy the role she had been playing and what service she had been providing for Joe all this time.

There was one Friday when Joe could not come help pick fruit. Art inquired if his wife could come in his place, because she seemed a lot more ambitious than did Joe. She did not want to fill in for Joe, but suggested that his son come instead. That would probably be better than not having anybody help pick, so we agreed.

The simplest fruit that needed picking were the peaches, at least that's what Art thought, so he assigned the young man to pick peaches and fill peck baskets. He showed the man where the trees were, brought him the baskets, and pointed out where the ladder was that would be needed to reach the top of the trees. He then left to pick some fruit himself. When he came back a short time later to check to see if all the peaches were being picked correctly, he could not believe his eyes. The young man was on the ladder, picking peaches from the top of the tree, and dropping them from his hand into the basket sitting on the ground! All those peaches were bruised or smashed and definitely ruined. Art was angry, and reassigned the man to something closer to the ground until Cathy could interrupt whatever she was doing and take him home.

Cathy's patience with Joe was wearing thin by now. Joe provided the final straw one Friday when he was supposed to come help us pick fruit for the market the next day. As usual, Joe had a few places to go and things to do that morning when Cathy went to pick him up and drive him back to our farm. Cathy drove him to where he needed to go. When he had completed his stops, and was still close to his house, he asked Cathy if she thought it was going to rain that day. She had heard on the weather forecast that rain was supposed to fall a little later in the morning. Joe said that he really would not like to get wet. "But", Cathy explained, "the fruit has to be picked for the market tomorrow, no matter if it rains or not". Joe repeated the fact that he really did not want to get wet. After the third time he said that he did not want to get wet, Cathy asked him if he wanted to be brought back to his house. He said he did.

So, she brought him to his home, and as he exited the van, he told Cathy, "Maybe, if it looks better by noon, you can come back to get me then." This was all Cathy could stand. "No," she said, "we won't be needing you to come any more." And that's how she fired him, right on the spot.

When she got back home, she told Art what had happened. "I fired Joe today", she said. "Good", replied Art. And that's all that was said about the matter.

THE TROUBLE IS THAT THEY HAVE TO BE LOADED AFTER THEY GROW BIG

During the early years of our small farm, we thought it a good idea to raise pigs. We would buy a litter of them, feed and care for them while they grew big,, bring them to the local slaughter house, and sell cut and wrapped pork to friends and acquaintances. Each customer would pick up their meat at the butcher shop, pay the butcher for the slaughter, cutting, and wrapping, and pay us an agreed-upon price for the half or whole pig that they had bought from us. The idea was to do this for a profit, based mostly on the fact that the work that we put into raising the pigs cost us nothing and, consequently, was worth just as much.

When we started out, we bought baby pigs at livestock auctions located at that time either in Churchville, MD or Stewartstown, PA. Neither of these auction facilities is still in existence, which may be because we stopped spending our money there years ago.

We usually raised one batch of pigs each year. A litter of pigs was usually brought into the sale ring and were made to run around so that all potential bidders could see them well. The piglets were kept moving, prompted by the two floor workers in the ring. When we first started this enterprise, we learned to bid on animals we were interested in and to recognize when we had the highest bid at the time. If we kept our hand up too long, then it was likely that we could be bidding against ourselves as the price to pay went higher and higher the longer we kept our hand in the air. Once we learned that lesson, we were quite successful at buying the small pigs we wanted.

We usually went to the auction as a family crowded into the cab of our Ford pickup truck. We returned home the same way, which meant that the pigs had to ride back in the bed of the truck. If the air temperature was moderate, then they would be fine riding back there. Sometimes, however, we purchased baby pigs in the winter, when it was cold outside. We would then try to drive home slowly to keep the chilling wind to a minimum, but the pigs were not as sure of that as we were, and, when we arrived at home, they could be found snuggled together like pork sausages right behind the cab of the truck.

Once or twice, Art had something else of more importance than to spend his evening at the auction, so he sent Cathy and the girls to buy the pigs without him. Like a good farm wife, Cathy successfully took on the assigned responsibility, but, also like a good farm wife, she did not enjoy herself doing it. All three came back with the pigs we needed to raise for that year.

Diseases of pigs can be devastating. We once had an outbreak of erysipelas that hit our pigs especially hard. It took a lot of care and medicating to get the pigs over it; we did not lose any pigs to erysipelas, but we could have. Exposure to this disease probably happened at the auction where we had bought them, which was one reason that we searched for other sources besides the livestock auction for our baby pigs.

We found that we could do well by riding over to John Archer's farm on the other side of Darlington and buying small pigs from him. He bred his pigs in a sterile environment, which meant that, in order to go into his buildings to even look over his piglets, we had to swear to him that we had not recently visited any other swine facility, we had to disinfect our footwear and put plastic booties over our shoes or boots, and we had to doff our outer jackets and leave them outside. Stripping off all clothes was not required. John did not want to introduce any diseases into his swine breeding operation. Any such diseases could financially ruin him.

Raising pigs can be interesting, if not enlightening. Pigs are intelligent animals, and they get bored very easily. One symptom of this is that some tend to bite the curly tails off their siblings. Another is that they tend to fight each other when confined too closely. So, we had to make sure that we did not buy more than five or six piglets at a time for the space we had. At times, we would throw a plastic beach ball into their pen, and they would play with it for days, or until they bit it too hard and deflated it. At other times, the pigs would upset their feeder bin, and Art would have to then set it back upright.

Pigs can be clean animals, which, if given the chance, will choose only one corner of their pen as a bathroom. That's where they deposited their manure. If they are crowded too much, however, then they spread their feces all over the pen.

Cleaning pig manure is a stinky job. Almost invariably, some gets on the clothes and skin of the person doing the cleaning, and, not only does pig manure smell bad, but it is very persistent. The pen cleaner, usually Art unless the pigs were Jodi's for her 4H project, could take four or five showers, and the smell could still be detected on the skin. So, cleaning the pig pen had to be scheduled with enough days between the cleaning operation and other obligations for the smell to wear off before interacting with discerning other people. Smelling of pigs could only be associated with being a hick-farmer, and being shunned by polite society.

We grew the pigs until they were 180 to 200 pounds, 220 pounds at the most. That weight range was just right; they had by that time attained a desirable amount of meat, but had not yet added a thick layer of fat to their bodies. We were quite proud of the pork that resulted from pigs this size.

Loading the pigs on the back of our truck to carry them to the slaughterhouse was not an easy task, either. They had grown up in their pen; they were used to the pen and did not want to leave it. And, getting to the bed of the truck required climbing several feet above the floor of their pen. They did not like that, either. Adult pigs have necks larger than their heads, so putting a rope around their necks would result in a pig still in the pen and an empty rope in Art's hand. No, pulling a pig on to the truck would not be possible by putting a rope around its neck.

The next idea was to put the rope around one leg of the pig, and try to pull it on to the truck. Again, the idea was worth a try, but a stubborn pig can be immovable when one leg was being pulled in the direction that Art wanted the pig to go, but the other three legs were straining to go in the direction that the pig wanted to go.

Art had built a loading ramp on one side of the pen so that the pigs, if coaxed into the ramp, could be pushed, cajoled, or forced to walk up and into the bed of the truck. The problem was that no pig wanted to enter the ramp; getting them in the ramp was a circus in itself. Even if one pig was able to be pushed into the ramp, there was not another pig that wanted to be the second to do so. With five or six pigs in the pen, there were five or six struggles that had to occur.

There was a downward slope between the pen and the truck when it was parked in the driveway. Pushing pigs into the loading ramp could be avoided if a path could be constructed between the pen and the truck, with only the last step being the open tailgate. So, Art set up a temporary wire fence to channel the pigs down the slope into the truck bed.

Good idea, but the pigs were not going to have any part of it. They were used to their pen, and they stubbornly did not want to leave it. So, it took a lot of pushing and shoving just to get the pigs to leave the confines of their home and into the fenced-in channel. Once inside the fence, they had only two choices: either be pushed into the truck bed, or try to escape from the fence. The second choice seemed to be the most popular one chosen by the pigs, and there were times when they were successful at jumping over the fence, tunneling under the fence, or just knocking down the fence. Once they were out, then it became a matter of escaping all this mess by running all over the farm with Art close on their heels. This scenario happened often enough that the neighbors would inquire ahead of time from us about the day that we planned to load pigs. When they were told the date, they would set up chairs at the edge of their property on the other side of the hedgerow dividing our two properties to watch us scramble to catch those loose pigs and try to drag them back to the truck. They did not just do this once, they did it many times and enjoyed it immensely each time. Art threatened them that he would have to charge them for the entertaining shows they were witnessing.

Stiffening the temporary fence finally solved the loose pig problem, but now the problem of persuading the pigs to go on the truck still remained. The last time Art loaded the pigs was a telling experience. Art had to drag each of the very reluctant pigs down the slope and on the truck by brute force. All the while that they were being dragged, they struggled to return to the pen that they knew held security for them. If only they could overcome this guy who was causing them so much trouble. Art and each pig weighed just about the same amount, so it was a matter of determination as to who might win the struggle. To make the loading process just a little more possible, Art tried to flip the pigs over on to their backs, to keep their legs and feet in the air where they couldn't resist Art's pulling. Pigs do not like to be slid on their backs any more than they like to be pushed or pulled on the truck, so they resisted this with all their strength.

Art was fresh for the first pig, and, although there was a battle of wills, Art got the first pig on the truck and closed the gate on the truck's rack so that the pig that was already in the truck bed would not escape and undo his hard work. Cathy stood by to make sure that the pig stayed in the truck and to open the gate when Art was able to (literally) drag the next pig the thirty feet or so to the truck. She opened the gate, and the second pig was safely captured in the truck bed. Two down, four to go. By now, Art was tiring, but still determined. The third pig was able to put up a fight, and took just a little longer to drag on to the truck, but Cathy closed the gate behind it, and there were only three more pigs to go. Each pig started its struggle afresh, but Art was tiring more and more. Four down, then five down, only one more pig to drag on to the truck. By now, Art was almost exhausted. These animals, which were as heavy as Art was, were strong, and not at all given to cooperating. The last pig was pulled by its hind leg a little at a time down the hill. The thirty-foot distance from the pen to the truck seemed to Art like three hundred feet. He was sure that the pig thought it could win the battle; the pig almost won and returned to the pen. But when it was over, and Art had dragged that very reluctant muscled machine of a pig to the truck, and then pulled it in behind him on to the truck, he was so tired that he knew that he could not let go of that pig, which would scamper back to its pen, and would be able to overcome Art's almost exhausted self if it ever got loose. Art shouted to Cathy to close the gate quickly, and don't worry about Art being locked into the back of that pickup truck with the rest of the pigs all of which seemed to be almost as exhausted as he was. He needed to lie there among the pigs and suck in air. And that was the last pig roundup that we ever had.

As an epilog, it took Art at least ten or fifteen minutes before he finally recovered enough to climb out of the back of the truck. When he drove the truck filled with exhausted pigs the few miles to the slaughterhouse, his arms were so lifeless that he had trouble turning the truck steering wheel to make the few turns on the way there. Cathy was along in the truck just in case he could not get there without help.

AS GOOD AS GOLD

When we first started with our farm, all of our farming equipment was bought well-used. We could not afford to buy new equipment, and, in addition, because of prior experiences when growing up, we were more familiar with the ways that older machines worked than with the ways of newer machinery. Our choices of the types and makers of the machinery that we bought at that time were limited and depended wholly on what was available. We attended many auctions, both near and far, where we bought most of our tractors. There were also used equipment dealers in Maryland and Pennsylvania, sometimes with bargain prices on pieces that they wanted to sell quickly. We knew all of these places, and kept our eyes out for machines that we thought would be better in our inventory than theirs.

In the early years of our farm, we had cows and we had sheep, among other animals. The biggest need for equipment was for making hay to feed them. We needed to make our own hay for two reasons: first, the cost of buying hay was more expensive than we wanted to afford, and second, as farmers, we had our sense of pride and independence that inclined us against depending on someone else to supply us with something we could produce ourselves.

So, as a consequence of these various factors, we ended up with John Deere, Allis-Chalmers, and Massey-Ferguson tractors, New Holland hay rake and baler, Bush Hog mower, and a mix of other manufacturers of other types of equipment we thought that we needed at the time. Most of these machines were originally built in the late 1940s through mid-1960s. We still have most of these machines, but some of them have not been used for years.

One issue with employing older, used equipment is that they are inclined to break at very inopportune times. What that means is that they break when being used, and, likely, under some kind of deadline to get the job done NOW.

Fortunately, each of these manufacturers has a dealership within driving distance of our farm, and we visited them for replacement parts whenever our machines were sitting idle out in the field where they had been operating before they broke. Time is of the essence under these circumstances, so Art drove as fast as he could to the proper dealership to buy replacement parts, but sometimes Cathy went to get the needed part while Art was able to do something else.

These circumstances happened often enough that we became familiar faces to the men who worked at the parts departments of these dealerships. We even knew some of them by first name, and they knew us, too. There was Paul at Ag-Industrial in Rising Sun, MD for New Holland parts. Our baler was always breaking needles, and he began keeping some in stock just for us. There was George at Grumelli's in Quarryville, PA for Allis-Chalmers parts. Getting parts from George was just like going back in time by 50 years. He had no microfiche to look up part numbers, but he had a memory. And, when he wrote up the receipt slip, he wrote it with a short stub of a pencil that had not been sharpened for weeks.

There were also the Spicer brothers at the Massy-Ferguson dealership that existed at that time in Hickory, MD, on old Rte 1 before the Bel Air bypass was built. When that dealership no longer existed, we started dealing with MM Weaver in Leola, PA, now transformed into Agrineer. When we needed John Deere parts, we went to Enfield Equipment, in Whiteford, MD. Enfield's has since morphed into Atlantic Tractor. For Bush Hog, there was a dealer in Cochranville, PA. Walter G. Coale in Churchville, MD could sometimes be able to supply parts, and had the advantage of being close to us.

None of these parts was cheap. It is questionable if we ever saved any money by doing the work ourselves because of the cost of the replacement parts. Even if farmers were having a bad year and not making any money, the farm equipment parts manufacturers sure did. And, there was no negotiating; when the parts are needed, there is no recourse. We could either buy the parts and fix the broken machine or be unable to finish the job that had been started.

Someone once said that "there is a lot of money to be made in agriculture, as long as you are not the farmer." Another observation is: "to end up with a million dollars as a farmer, you must start out with two million dollars." Those pieces of cast iron and steel may not have looked like gold, but they were just as expensive.

HOW WE TAUGHT OUR GIRLS TO READ

We never knew anything about the phonics method to teach how to read, but that's essentially the way we taught our young children how to read. And, it worked well.

It was just a short time after Art returned from his tour of duty in Vietnam, and our eldest daughter, Joy, was already three years old. Our second daughter, Jodi, was a year younger. Cathy and Art had been reading to the girls for a long time, and Joy, especially, was beginning to be curious about how reading those symbols on a page were translated into understandable words. She was eager to unlock the mysteries contained in the written word.

Language is acquired largely by hearing sounds and associating the sounds with meanings. Babies become attuned to the sounds of their mothers' voices even while still in the womb, and they learn to mimic sounds they hear from people around them soon after birth.

Reading is much different, because, when reading, meaning is sensed by sight. Somehow, there must be a translation between what one sees and the sounds that one understands. That's where phonics comes in. So, it seemed reasonable to us that the key to reading is to associate sounds with the different letters of the alphabet. Once those associations are made, then most simple words, the ones most likely encountered by early readers, can be sounded out from the way they are spelled.

The girls had already learned most of the alphabet from a child's dictionary of the letters and associated pictures illustrating things that began with those letters. So, the next step was to teach the girls the sounds that were possible for each letter of the alphabet.

This made a great activity for long rides in the car. Art would name a letter, and the girls would give associated sounds. We would do this over and over. We played this activity as a game to pass the time and keep the children occupied. We did this for each ride for which we had enough time to go through the entire alphabet.

There are some letters, for instance "a", that have several associated sounds. We would go over all of these. With enough repetition, the girls got to be good at reproducing the sounds made by each letter of the alphabet.

When Joy was ready, she picked up a book and began to sound each letter of a word. It took her a little practice to be able to elide the sounds of each letter together to form a word that she could recognize. But, when she realized that she could be successful at this process, she was much encouraged. She began reading in earnest.

Soon, it was impressive to watch her sit in a church pew while Cathy and Art were practicing in the choir; she was reading the unabridged version of "The Wizard of Oz", the large book, not a small one, and she was not yet in school. And, she understood what she was reading.

There were occasional words that she had trouble sounding out. She asked us to help, but that was not very often. She was good at what she had learned.

OUR OLD KITCHEN TABLE

There is comfort in familiar things, and that includes furniture. There may be some people who would suggest that we replace our old kitchen table, and, if truth be told, we have contemplated doing such a thing a time or two. But, it never happened. Although it is not a piece of fine furniture, our table continues to serve its purpose well.

Our kitchen table is the center piece of most of our inside-the-house activities. We eat all of our meals at the table: breakfast, lunch, and dinner. We drink cups of tea at the table. When we sometimes snack, it happens there at the table. When we entertain guests in our house, we all sit around the table. Lively conversations occur there. Laughter and good times happen there. We have decided business deals there. We have made important decisions while sitting at our kitchen table. We have listened to music while sitting around the table. We read newspapers, catalogs, books, and our daily mail at the table. We have studied and learned at the table. We have spent many good hours around this table. Although our living room has comfortable chairs, sofa, and love seat, we don't use it for life as we do our kitchen table. It is the center-piece of our whole house.

One thing our kitchen table is not is fashionable. It shows signs of wear from years of use. But it was good use, not abuse. Our kitchen table has a metal frame and a wood composition top with a fake wood grain laminated hard surface. The tabletop surface is a little dull with a few nicks from years of work and play that happened there.. Around the metal edges of the table, the black paint has worn off in spots, exposing silvery metal underneath.

The size of our kitchen table is about five feet by two and a half feet, so it is not large by any means, but it fits very well into one side of our kitchen. It can be shortened by removing a leaf in the center, and we used to move the leaf in and out depending on what activities were going to happen at that time, but the leaf has been installed as a nearly permanent fixture for probably thirty or more years now.

Cathy bought this table from a second-hand furniture store in Edgewood when we had just moved out of Army housing after Art returned from Vietnam. We were on a limited budget, and this table served the purpose at the time. With the table came four kitchen chairs, which have long since been ruined and have been replaced with newer ones. The table moved with us when we moved from Edgewood to our present house in Darlington. It has remained in our kitchen ever since.

When we first bought the table, we had two little girls who needed someplace to eat their meals, cut out paper dolls, glue pieces of craft paper together, affix stickers to kids' books, and a place to eat oatmeal cookies or chocolate chip cookies or to celebrate birthdays. When they baked goodies to submit to the county 4-H fair, the cakes and other goods rested on the table until they cooled enough to package up. The table was useful just being there.

We eventually raised four children around our old kitchen table. We ate, sang, played games, talked and just relaxed around our table. The kids did their homework on the table. Art and Cathy wrote letters on the table. Sometimes the only flat surface free of clutter is located on the table, and that makes it prime territory for any of these activities. Sometimes there is clutter even there, but it can be shoved out of the way for a game of checkers or connect four or monopoly or cards.

Our old kitchen table has been the surface for many a card game. We don't need much room for dealing out the cards, and the table works fine for this purpose. Art likes to win his games, but he never blames the table the few times when he doesn't.

There were many luscious Thanksgiving and Christmas meals eaten at the table, and we celebrated many birthdays while sitting around it. Holidays usually meant that guests would come over to join us and eat, drink cups of tea, talk, and play games. Who cares what the table looks like if we are all enjoying each other's company.

The table has lately accumulated some things that need to be kept handy, such as bills to be paid, a jar of pens to play Sudoku games and crossword puzzles, cups for tea, and a few medicines that are supposed to be taken every day. When Cathy collects the daily mail from our postal mailbox, the pieces of mail end up on our table until they can be sorted into pieces to keep and those to be recycled. Cathy pays our bills at the table, and Art sometimes replaces the chain on his chain saw there, with a layer of newspapers on the table for protection, of course.

Our old kitchen table will probably be with us until the end. It continues to serve its purpose well. It is the site of many happy memories for the whole family. It endures.

BACK RUBS

When someone's back itches, there is nothing quite as satisfying as a rub. Even without being aware of an itch, a back rub feels so good that there are hardly any sensations any better. In fact, neonatal nurses have found that rubbing the backs of newborn babies under some distress calms their tiny patients like no other intervention. Back rubs, for many, are good therapy.

A thorough back scratch or rub is almost impossible for a single person to administer by one's self. A person's entire back is not normally accessible to the person with the need. Even if a few locations on the back are able to be reached and scratched or rubbed, there remain those inaccessible locations that still drive the imperative for total satisfaction. The person with an itchy back must either recruit a helper to reach all the spots, or must find a surface with just the right configuration to rub against to fulfill the urgent need.

Back rubs are not only extremely pleasurable for humans, but we have had livestock animals that also sought back rubs. When we raised pigs, they often needed to rub their backs on anything they could find that reached just the right spots. They had a large box made from flakeboard in which we poured their feed so that they could eat whenever they desired. The box had vertical sides that were popular with the pigs to rub against, moving their bodies up and down and shimmying against the board to satisfy their itchy spots. They also rubbed against other wood or concrete surfaces as well. In time, the flakeboard sides of their feed box showed significant erosion from the many times they used it for rubbing.

Cows like to rub their backs, as well. The motive for their back-rubbing activity may be the fact that flies can bite cows on their backs in places that the cows cannot reach with their swinging tails or by flinging their heads around with their long tongues hanging out to be able to reach farther on their backs. During a bad fly season, cows are often bothered very much by biting flies, and the cows may go off their feed if they are disturbed enough. Cows, like pigs, seek out surfaces to rub against to rub their backs, and, when they find the places that meet their needs, they rub their bodies against those surfaces. Tree limbs, branches, and brush are the often-preferred back scratchers. And, when one cow finishes her rubbing activities, other cows are likely to take turns at the same places. Often, the cows take turns following their cow pecking order when using these rare ideal surfaces that satisfy their needs.

It was, at least when we were keeping cows, popular to build a special frame for cows to rid their backs of flies and itches. These frames were built of two upright posts with a crossbar. From the crossbar was hung a pipe suspended by a piece of chain or rope at each end. The pipe was positioned slightly lower than the height of a cow, and the cow would voluntarily walk underneath the pipe and let it skid across her back, chasing flies away and, probably, partially relieving back itches. Some farmers added a burlap bag wrapped around the pipe. Oil would be poured on the bag, so that the cow's back would also be oiled when she used to device. The oil prevented flies from landing on, and biting, the cow's back.

Despite having heavy wool coats, sheep also required occasional back rubs. They were more likely to seek out places to rub their backs after they were just sheared. If a sheep engaged in rubbing with a thick layer of wool, this might be a symptom of parasites or of a condition called scrapie, a serious, transmissible disease related to mad-cow disease. Sheep with one of these disorders may rub so much that they pull handsfull of wool from their skins.

So, itchy backs requiring rubs are not confined only to humans. But, with a good scratch or rub, it feels so, so good. Don't stop. Don't stop. Don't stop……..ahhhhh!

DUNGAREES

Pants made with blue cotton twill denim cloth are very popular with people of all ages, all circumstances, and all walks of life. Everyone, it seems, wears them everywhere. Almost everyone calls these pants "jeans". While we were growing up on farms, where we wore them as work pants, we used to call them "dungarees".

To us, jeans were pants worn by sophisticates, people without calluses on their hands or dirt beneath their fingernails. Jeans were worn by people who hosted soirées or who made good salaries and lived easy lives. Jeans were neat and clean, and sometimes even creased. They were laundered often, whether they needed cleaning or not.

Dungarees, on the other hand, were caked with dirt, grease, and grime. They were honest-to-goodness work clothes needed to keep the legs inside isolated from dirt, thorns, poison ivy, cow manure, and sheep grease. They were worn every day for all types of farm work until they were so soiled that they could stand up by themselves. They might have been washed once a week, as long as there was an alternate pair of dungarees to wear while the first pair was in the laundry pile. Sometimes, that second pair of dungarees was too expensive to buy right now, until some money could be saved to afford them, although each pair of dungarees cost no more to buy than did a pair of jeans.

Dungarees are humble and honest; jeans can be ostentatious. Dungarees are ready for work; jeans are ready to show off.

Despite our family being financially challenged, Art's mother would never let her children wear clean dungarees to school. This, despite the fact that classmates in school wore them occasionally. "Dungarees", she said, "were only for poor people. Now go and put on that pair of dress pants that you have in your room." She had her pride, and wanted to be sure that we were never labeled as needy. These days, on the contrary, jeans are worn almost everywhere: restaurants, church, school. Jeans are sometimes even paired with sports jackets for more formal wear. Art's mother would have had conniptions.

Art's dungarees have stained knees from hours of hand and knee weeding of our berries and other fruiting plants. Although he usually wears knee pads to keep his pants dry and clean, his dungarees develop permanent smudges in the knee areas that usually are not completely removed when laundered.

We are astonished that there are some pairs of jeans bought new with holes purposely ripped in the knees. Art has dungarees in a similar condition, but his are worn and threadbare. The holes in the knees of his pants resulted from honest wear-and-tear, mostly tear. He wore those pants for hard work until they could resist no more. He would no more think of buying new jeans with exposed knees than he would think of buying a new car with a piston thrust through the side of its engine block.

Dungarees without knee protection (holes) expose knees to sunlight, dirt, fluids, and perilous plants (like poison ivy). So, one might think that a pair of pants with no knees might be useless for farm work and be a candidate for the trash pile. That is not the case, however. We have a large pile of dungarees with holes in the knees and with rips in other locations that still find use on extremely hot days, which are becoming more common every year. Art calls these pants his "air-conditioned" pants, because they allow air movement through the pants that is usually blocked by the intact heavy cloth barrier. He wears these pants when the forecast temperature is 90°F or more. He will put up with the exposure as long as he can be somewhat cooler.

Nonetheless, we do have dungarees that are so tattered that they cannot be worn at all. Are these finally thrown in the trash? No. If there is any possible use for any item on our farm, use of that item is redirected to a new application. We have a use for these very, very worn out pants. They can be used to plug woodchuck holes in and around our yard so that the holes cannot be used to access underground dens. Woodchucks find these pants stuffed into their holes to be nearly impossible to remove. This is the final application for worn-out dungarees. Once one pair is pounded into a woodchuck hole, we never see that pair of pants again. Nor do we see the woodchucks.

STUCK WITHOUT FUNDS

The Roots livestock auction just up the road in Manheim, Pennsylvania was a reliable source of young ducks, geese, turkeys, and chickens, as well as other small animals not usually seen at livestock auctions. These animals were brought to the auction by local Amish and other small farmers who raised small animals as sources of income. Not only were there poultry hatchlings, but, on any given evening, there might be Guinea Pigs, rabbits, and other small animals. It was always interesting to see what animals were being sold, even if we had no plans to purchase anything. Our children loved to go to the auction to see the small animals in their cages. They fawned over cute little chicks, ducklings, or goslings. They loved the rabbits and Guinea Pigs. Besides, the auction was also an opportunity to connect with other families who lived on and operated small farms in the area.

Often, if we wanted to acquire new poultry animals, we went to the Roots auction to do so. The advantage of going to that auction was that we could see the animals before we bought them, as contrasted with buying from hatcheries or from ads many miles away, where we always hoped that what was delivered was what we had wanted.

The auction was held on Tuesdays at all times of the year. The small animal auction was held in the evening on Tuesday. We discovered that we could drive the approximately forty-minutes through Lancaster to get to Manheim in time to catch all the action if we left as soon as possible after Art and Cathy came home from work. Cathy worked locally at the Darlington Library, so her work posed no problem to leave on time if she had to work that day. Art worked a lot farther away in College Park, so he had to plan to leave work early and hope that traffic would not slow him down on the way home if he wanted to go to the Manheim auction.

Once at the auction, bidders were required to register at the main office before they participated. A small card with a number was given to the registrant; if that person made a winning bid on a batch of animals, then the winner would show his or her card so that the auction staff could record who it was that needed to pay latter at the office. Once a person was registered, the same card could be used week after week.

With his card in hand, Art would bid and take possession of his newly-acquired property, and then pay later when he was ready to leave for home. All worked the way it was supposed to, except for once when we had not brought sufficient cash to pay for his unintended purchases. We offered to write a check for the amount owed, but the people in the office would not accept an out-of-state check. The clerk at the office window suggested that a local ATM might be able to supply the needed cash. Where was there an ATM? The clerk gave a few suggestions, none of which were on the auction grounds.

So, Cathy took the children in the car and searched the surrounding area for an ATM. Art had to stay at the auction to safeguard possession of the animals he had successfully bid on. Cathy found several ATMs in the area, but none would accept her credit card. After about a half hour she returned with the bad news. Art pleaded with the clerk, but there was no recourse: either pay in cash or go home without the animals he had come to the auction to buy.

So, without any alternative, Cathy again got into the car, drove all the way home, and drove back again with enough cash in hand to pay the bill. By now, it was getting late, most other people at the auction had left, and the clerk was becoming anxious to leave as soon as she could. Art, without much to do while he waited, was becoming drowsy. But, just as in those old Western movies, where the Cavalry comes over the hill just at the right time to save the day, Cathy came back to rescue Art.

With cash in hand, the debt was paid, the animals were loaded into the car, our children fell asleep in the back seat, and we made our way back to our home and farm in Darlington. With the care that we gave them, the animals grew and thrived. And we never again left for the Roots auction without extra cash in our pockets.

This is the young family in 1971 before they moved to SweetAire Farm, and just after Art had returned from a tour in Viet Nam. Pictured are Cathy and Art, and children Joy and Jodi.

The young family visited Bel Air, MD, in 1971, when Bel Air was a small town in the mostly rural Harford County. There were many stores of all kinds on Main Street, and this photo was shot while Joy and Jodi were peering in a store window at some stuffed toys. Main Street changed considerably after other shopping malls and plazas opened on the outskirts of town.

Uh oh! The girls got in trouble after playing in the mud puddle at the end of the driveway, and now must face the wrath of their stern mother. All messy clothes have to be removed outside before the girls go inside to clean up.

Art carries one of our first sheep to the pasture after having just brought it home. Because we had no good fences in 1972 when this picture was taken, the sheep would be staked out in the grass with a rope and collar around its neck, and moved to new grass every day. In the background are the girls and our Ford truck. Art grew his beard in 1972 while working for a month at Guantanamo Bay, in Cuba.

Here is Jodi in 1973 holding a kitten in our kitchen. Both girls loved to hold animals, especially small, cuddly animals.

Joy asleep in her favorite tree in 1973, cuddled with her favorite kitten at the time. She took naps in the branch of that apple tree almost every day when the weather allowed it.

Jodi and our dog, Timin, liked each other. Timin was a good dog around the girls and also liked to hunt woodchucks with Art.

This 1974 aerial photo of our farm was taken with the help of a pilot friend of Art's. We had already begun to make improvements in the farm, as shown by the brown and red paint on the barn and sheds, and by the large garden behind the sheds. The apple orchard in the front, next to the road, had not yet been planted.

Cathy and the girls are giving small, furry, baby rabbits a lot of attention. Joy is holding one in her hand, while Cathy was trying to figure out how to feed one with an eye dropper.

Here are the two lovelies in 1975 while standing in our lawn. Joy was seven and Jodi was six years old at the time.

GREETINGS FROM SWEETAIRE FARM

Who says calves don't like strawberries? Here, Cathy indulges one of the new calves that we bought at the auction with a treat that this calf would surely not have had if someone else had bought it.

Here is a view of our house and driveway, looking out toward the road in the fall of 1976. Art had added a narrow deck to the house by this time, and had planted flowers in the front of the house. Trim on the house, which was originally white when we first bought the house, was painted red and brown, the color scheme to match the barn and sheds.

We made grass silage from lawn clippings and stored it in metal 55-gallon barrels. This used grass from the summer that would have been wasted, and provided nutritious feed for our sheep and cows during the winter. The animals loved the silage. With the cover removed and the barrels tipped on their sides, the animals eagerly stuck their heads inside and ate the silage. Sometimes they fought over who would get to the barrel first.

This is Jodi in 1978 scrubbing her pigs in the back of our pickup truck to get them ready for showing at the local 4H fair. She ended up as wet and clean as the pigs.

Joy kept Dutch Blue rabbits as one of her 4H projects, and won ribbons at the 4H fair. Both girls also sewed clothes and baked goods to compete at the fair, also winning prizes for their entries.

Jodi continued raising and showing pigs for 4H projects for many years. This is her in the show ring in 1982, keeping the pig moving and under control. Pigs sometimes tried to fight with other pigs while being shown. When that happened, 4H monitors separated the pigs by thrusting a plywood shield between them.

The Middle Years

INTRODUCTION

The girls had mostly grown when Cathy and Art adopted two young boys, Paul and Eric, from Korea. A few years later, Jodi gave birth to their first grandson, Gregory, and he came to live with them for the first six years of his life. Cathy took a job as the librarian of the Darlington Library. It was during this time that we began participating in the Bel Air, Maryland Farmers' Market, selling fruits from our little farm. We soon realized that our fruit production was not able to supply all the needs of our customers at the market, and we needed to expand. We added additional acreage adjacent to our original farm and began to turn that unused land into a productive holding, with more fruit trees and plants, and pasture for cows and sheep. We stopped having cows when it became difficult to care for the fruits at the same time of the year that we had to make hay for the cows.

A GOOD MOM

We had a lamb born one Sunday morning. The mom was one of our young ewes from the previous year. Cathy discovered the lamb when she went out to feed the sheep and she put both mom and her lamb into a pen in the barn. We used to have ewes that often had trouble giving birth. There were times when we had to assist in the birth or encourage the ewe to clean off her newborns or to help the lambs find where to drink their first swallows of colostrum (milk). We had a baby monitor out in the barn, and when we heard noises that sounded like something was going on, we would hurry out to the barn to do what we could to make the birth a success. But over the course of years, we have selected ewes that can have their lambs without any help from us. So, we don't usually have to assist in the process. Now, the mothers can have the lambs by themselves, wherever they are, either inside or in the field, and they know how to care for them, and the lambs are smart enough to find a teat by themselves.

We lock the mothers and lambs into the barn for several days so that they can concentrate on each other without the lambs becoming confused with all the other sheep around. After about three days, the lambs can be docked, and get their vaccinations and anything else they need before they are released again to the outside.

It is typical with the mothers that they stamp their front feet warning others to stay away from their lambs. So, when Cathy went into the barn to give the ewe some hay, grain, and water, this mother stamped her feet at Cathy. That is a good sign that the mom has taken possession of her baby and is willing to protect her against threats.

There was another indication of the dedication of this ewe to her baby. The young lamb was small enough to be able to fit through some of the small openings in the sides of the metal pen where they both were located, and it apparently wandered off into the rest of the barn. This separated the mother from her lamb. When Cathy went into the barn to care for the two of them, she did not see them in the pen where they were supposed to be. Instead, they were in a different pen. The mother had apparently been upset by the absence of her baby, and somehow must have jumped over the walls of the pen. Note that the pen walls were made of metal grates about three and a half feet tall with nothing to climb on, so it wasn't easy for her to escape. But escape she did. This was a good mom.

CATHY GETS HER GATOR

Cathy had enough walking all the way to the blueberry patch, picking the blueberries, and walking uphill all the way back to the house. In addition, she had to take a wheelbarrow or wagon with her to transport the berries or other fruits that she had picked. She began looking for a better way.

So, she started looking at ads for vehicles that she could purchase so that she could ride there and back and haul her load of fruits. A friend of ours owned a golf cart that he used to ride around his property, so she first looked at golf carts. But, they were powered by batteries, and also didn't seem to be rugged enough for use on our farm.

It was then that she saw ads for John Deere Gator utility vehicles. The more she looked into getting a Gator, the better she liked the idea. So, she made up her mind: she would buy a Gator the first chance she could.

Her sister, Carolyn, happened to come from near Binghamton, NY for a visit just about the time that Cathy had decided to shop for a Gator. The two of them took off during the day to see what they could find. With some inherited money from her mother's estate, she had the cash to make it happen. All she needed to do was to be sure that the used Gator that she had bought could be delivered to our farm.

Imagine Art's surprise when Cathy announced to him that she had completely transacted to purchase a used Gator without him suspecting a thing.

When the Gator arrived in a day or two, Cathy had the time of her life, driving her new (to her) Gator all over our farm, taking everybody who dared to ride with her on exciting trips to the orchards and back. Hold on! Cathy's Gator can go fast.

Since then, Cathy and her Gator are nearly inseparable. She uses it daily to carry her to wherever she needs to go to do her work for the day. Once, she even drove it several miles on the road to the middle of Darlington to Tommy McCurry's Garage to have its oil changed. That trip scared her enough that she never considered repeating it.

Art was also impressed enough to buy a Gator of his own years later and to forego using his Allis Chalmers C tractor for transportation on the farm.

But, for Cathy, her Gator is the love of her life.

AFTERMATH OF A STORM

Wednesday of one summer week began as another of those hot, oppressively sticky days when we would come in from working outside with clothes wringing wet with sweat. By early evening, however, the sky turned dark and threatening. Our electricity went off even before the storm hit, so we decided to sit out on the porch to watch the thunderstorm lightning, listen to the booms of thunder, and feel the spray of wind-blown rain. It was impressive. The heavy rain was needed and the cool wind was welcome. Toward the end of the storm, sun shone on the very top of some of the tall trees to our east, and then we had a visit from ROY G. BIV. Yes, we had a beautiful rainbow, with occasional lightning streaking through it. After the storm had blown over, we watched as two mother deer and their half-grown fawns emerged from near the stream and browsed on the lush grass at the bottom of the pasture near the house. This was one of the joys of living on our farm.

AIRCRAFT SIGHTINGS

We often have aircraft fly over our farm, in addition to the many jetliners flying on their glide paths into and from Baltimore and Philadelphia airports. One flyover that we spotted was a small, fixed-wing aircraft that kept flying in a traversing pattern, back and forth, back and forth. We don't know for sure, but we suspect that this was an airplane with a Google Earth camera, taking pictures to post to the internet. Somehow, Google has to update its photos, and we guess that this is the method to do so.

Just over the hill is the Conowingo Lake sequestered behind the Conowingo Dam. Several times a week sometimes, A10 fighter aircraft flown by Air National Guard pilots based in Middle River fly over the lake and down the Susquehanna to return to their home field. A10 jets are noisy and not to be ignored. These flights remind us of the servicemen who guard our country, and we are so very thankful that these planes belong to the USA rather than to some foreign country.

There is an old open-cockpit biplane or two that may fly over the lake, as well. We usually notice them in the summer or on beautiful spring or fall weekends. Old biplanes make a very loud distinctive engine sound that is hard to miss. They used to perform acrobatic maneuvers, climbing, diving, turning, and spinning, but they don't seem to be doing tricks anymore. They must think that the lake makes a relatively prudent place to practice stunts, in case they would crash; they wouldn't take anyone else with them. We used to hear them and watch them do their tricks as they performed.

An additional recurring sighting involves a helicopter flying back and forth over our farm and surrounding area. Helicopters flying over our farm are not unusual; there are military, police, and power company helicopters in the air almost all the time. The helicopter that visits us almost annually, however, doesn't just fly straight from one end of our farm to the other, but circles around a few times. We know what this is: the helicopter occupants look for illegal marijuana growing in the area. This helicopter has a sensor wand protruding from its side to sniff for some telltale chemical emissions. They check around us every year, and, of course, never find anything. They usually show a lot of interest in our netted blueberries; it must look suspicious.

Many years ago, during a time when we were not at home, our neighbors told us later that a helicopter had hovered for quite a while above our herb garden, probably for the same purpose. We can only imagine the readings that were recorded on their sensors with the many different volatile emanations from the collection of herbs that we were growing at that time. We imagine the conversation in the helicopter went something like:

"There's something down there, but it doesn't quite seem like marijuana."

"What could it be? Should we get a search warrant?"

"The sensors tell me that it's something like oregano mixed with basil and bergamot. Can you see anything?"

"I'll go closer. Nope, all I see is oregano and basil and bergamot and some other strange things."

"That makes me hungry. It's time for lunch isn't it? Let's go eat. Your treat today."

FENCE POSTS FOR CASTLETON

Each of the three parcels of land that we purchased, and were eventually united into what is now SweetAire Farm, were badly in need of improvements. Among those that were needed were good fences to surround pastures and contain the livestock animals that we had at the time. Our original five-acre plot did have a few old and dilapidated barbed-wire fences, but they would have given no challenge for animals determined to break through. So, we began our fence building projects right there, close to home.

When we purchased our second land parcel, a half mile from our house and called by us "Castleton" after the name of the crossroads nearby, there were no fences that had ever been erected on that site. We needed more summer pasture land to for our cows and sheep, so we needed to get busy with fence-building.

Pasture fences require posts at a spacing of eight feet between them, and the fence was to be several hundred feet long, so a lot of posts had to be found. There were mature locust trees on the land, and locust posts last a long time, so that was to be the source of the fence posts. That would save the money that otherwise would have been needed to purchase that many posts,

Art had asked friend Jim Caldwell to bring his chain saw and help with felling the trees and cutting the posts. Jim agreed without hesitation.

The trees that we chose to cut had to be mature enough to have enough old wood because new locust wood does not last long in the ground. The trees that were cut were at least eight inches in diameter and as large as twelve inches in diameter. They were at least 50 feet tall or taller.

The posts had to be six feet in length. This would allow them to be sunk about two feet into the ground with four feet sticking up above ground for the fence wire to be nailed to. The woven wire stock fence that was to be used was four feet in height.

In order to cut the trees into six-foot lengths, Art used himself as a measure by briefly lying down beside the fallen tree and marking where the top of his head was located. This gave the necessary six foot length. Jim then cut the log at the mark, after Art had moved out of the way, of course.

Once they were cut, the new posts had to be moved to a pile uphill from where they had been cut, and close to where they would be used later to build the fence. Newly cut posts of this size are not even close to lightweight. It took a good deal of strength and energy to move them from where they were cut to where they had to be piled. Both Jim and Art did the carrying.

The day in which all of this was done was a cold, blustery day with occasional snow squalls all day long. The two of them hardly noticed the temperature, however, because all that heavy work generated lots of extra body heat.

Over the course of the day, the pile of posts grew, but energy levels of both Art and Jim began to flag. Toward the end of the day, they both found it harder and harder to move the new posts. They tired.

It was after dark that they finished their work. By then, the snow squalls had ceased, and the sky had cleared, displaying many stars and a beautifully bright full moon. The two men were too tired to move. So they remained there until they could muster enough energy to leave and go to their homes to eat supper.

Back home, Cathy began to be concerned about the welfare of the two of them when they did not return at the end of daylight. She had waited supper, but they still did not show up at home. So, worried that something really bad had happened to them, she got into her vehicle and drove to our Castleton land. She got out of her car, and walked the length of two fields to see if she could find them, and to give help if needed. She was apprehensive about what she would find. And there she found them, two exhausted middle-aged men slumped down on the cold, hard ground with no more energy reserves to move even a muscle.

CRICKET WARS I

There was one year when we had more crickets than usual visit us in late summer and early fall. At least one cricket sneaked into our kitchen while we were visiting family in upstate New York. It is not easy to reach our kitchen, because it would have had to go across the porch and through the back room first. Chirping crickets can be very loud and annoying. This cricket was somewhat subdued for a few days, but soon increased its decibel level past the threshold of bothersome. Either there were several crickets in the house or the chirping echoes made it seem that way. When we were in the front room, the chirping seemed to be localized there; when we were in the kitchen, the sound seemed to come from all directions; when we were in the back room, it seemed as if the cricket was there. We had a hard time trying to place where the cricket was located. And, it never came out of hiding to show itself to us. So, we had little hope of putting an end to the cricket disturbance.

We returned home one Sunday evening after visiting our daughter Jodi, and, when Cathy turned on the kitchen light, there was the cricket, in the middle of the kitchen floor. It had finally come out of hiding, and was now vulnerable to Art's cricket-hunting prowess. He (Art, that is, not the cricket) dropped to his knees in front of the interloper; it didn't move. Carefully cupping his hand to be able to trap the cricket without harming it, Art quickly brought his hand down over his prey. The cricket escaped through a hole between Art's thumb and fingers, and jumped away. Art jumped, too, quickly following the cricket towards the side of the kitchen. If the cricket reached a hiding spot, there would be no other chances to capture it. It took two more tries, but Art had it in his grasp. He took it outside, and unceremoniously threw it across the driveway, where it could mingle with others of its kind and swap stories about amazing adventures in alternative dimensions.

That should have ended it, but there was a second cricket near one kitchen wall. It was barely visible. Art chased it from its hiding place, but the cricket was able to find a better hideout. Art had had only one chance to capture it, and he had blown it. His self-esteem suffered a hit.

Since then, the kitchen was mostly quiet, but, every now and again, we heard loud cricket noises to remind us of nature displaced to where it should not be. The hunt continued.

The next Sunday, just before we were to leave for church, a cricket crawled out from under the dishwasher and sat exposed and a prime candidate to be caught. Art was dressed in his Sunday best, with suit pants, black shirt, a Maryland flag tie, and dark sports jacket, making him, as he intended to be, the "grandest tiger in the jungle". Thus, he was not exactly dressed as a cricket hunter. Nevertheless, he rushed over near the cricket, dropped to his knees, cupped his hand, and, after two quick tries, had the cricket in his hand. Out it went, with a hearty "Bon Voyage".

Later that day, Cathy took the plastic bag containing ears of corn that she had bought the day before at the Farmers' Market and went out to the porch to shuck the ears before cooking them for Sunday dinner. When she reached the bottom of the bag, there sat a big, fat cricket, probably thinking that he had a nice, comfortable place to rest for a while before he was brought into the house. That cricket, too, was sent into exile.

On Monday, Art came in from a morning of weeding to eat lunch, and, feeling cooler in the kitchen compared to the outside, put on a long-sleeved shirt and sat down. A small cricket had somehow gotten into his shirt, although the shirt had been hanging off the floor on the back of his chair. The cricket popped out of the shirt and onto his chest. Without any wasted effort, he grabbed the insect and took it outside to be with its compatriots.

Three crickets removed in two days! That made our kitchen nearly quiet again, and ready for the next cohort of chirping troubadours to make its appearance. That didn't take too long. We came into the kitchen from the back room on Monday evening, and there it was, a cricket right in front of us inside the kitchen door. Art reached down to capture it, but he was tired and not as fast as he should have been (half fast?). He missed it, and the cricket jumped away to an undetermined place. Now we again had cricket music in the kitchen. The quiet had not lasted long. There were at least two crickets in our kitchen, and they sang to each other from opposite sides of the room. Stereo crickets.

On Tuesday evening, after Art had come home from being away all day, he sat down in the kitchen to talk to Cathy and Greg, who had come over earlier. For some reason, Art was suffering an extended bout of sneezing and blowing, and reached inside his pants pocket for his handkerchief. As he pulled it out, a handful of coins came out with it, and all those coins scattered noisily all over the floor. "Doggone", he said, "I was hoping to bomb some crickets with at least some of that change."

The cricket war continued. We then had at least two crickets in our kitchen and one in the back room all week, serenading us with loud chirping. The melodies they offered were monotonic, and only interesting to other crickets, but they were loud and annoying to us non-crickets. The crickets hid their little chirping selves behind the dishwasher and other appliances. One cricket did crawl out twice that week. The first time, Art was not fast enough, and the little critter escaped to its hiding spot. The second time it wasn't so lucky, and, although it struggled to escape once Art had it in his hand, it was subsequently tossed from our house into its natural milieu outside. On another day, Art captured a cricket at the top of the stairs to the second floor of our house. How could it have gotten there? Are crickets capable of flight (other than the flight that they take when tossed into the grass outside)? The next morning, Art was able to catch one more cricket in the corner of the kitchen and remove it. Then, Cathy caught one that had shown itself near the pantry door. In this way, she passed her cricket-catching merit badge practicum.

Not long after, Cathy came into the kitchen and exclaimed, "It sounds like the whole Mormon Tabernacle Choir!" And so it did. There were crickets chirping in the soprano register, some singing alto, and a few tenors (any cricket that is large enough to chirp in bass is too big for us to mess with). We had crickets in every corner of the kitchen, but no time to deal with them. And it got worse. In midweek, Cathy declared that it now sounded like "two Mormon Tabernacle Choirs". It was time for action. Over the course of the week, Cathy caught at least a dozen of the songsters, and Art caught nearly as many. Without ceremony, each of these was promptly evicted. Most of these trespassers were small in size, likely juvenile sopranos, so perhaps instead of the Mormon Tabernacle Choir, we had a youthful Vienna Boys Choir. Now, there were just a few soloists left in the kitchen singing their siren songs enticing others outside to come on in. We couldn't wait.

We continued to catch a few crickets in our kitchen, one or two every couple of days or so, but we sometimes had an hour, or even an evening, without the annoyance of cricket songs. With the coming of cool weather, it would soon be over. But, until then, there was an occasional cricket serenade going on in our house: that's our house, not theirs.

Still later, Cathy reported that she found two such little interlopers in the downstairs bathroom. In order to get there, they had to come into the house, go through the kitchen and living room, down a short hall, and into the bathroom. In other words, they had to move a long way. Cathy said that she had to catch one cricket in one hand and the second cricket in her other hand, and then to turn doorknobs and open the doors to the outside without letting the critters escape. This she accomplished with some degree of difficulty, but she was successful. Proudly, she announced her feat to Art, although her feet had very little to do with it. She has developed into a country cricket catcher extraordinaire. If she were a girl scout, she could easily have earned a merit badge for cricket hunting.

CATHY'S BEST EVER CHILI

This chili is so delicious that it is in demand when she makes it for church. We love it especially when the weather turns cool in the fall, but it is also good at other times of the year when we have been working hard outside on the farm.

Ingredients:

1 pound lean ground beef
1 cup chopped onions
1 cup chopped green peppers
3 quarts canned tomatoes
3 bay leaves
Salt and pepper to taste
1 40.5 ounce can kidney beans
1 18 ounce can tomato paste
5-6 tablespoons chili powder (more or less, according to taste)

Brown ground beef in a large pot with onions and peppers. Season with salt and pepper. Add tomatoes, kidney beans, bay leaves, and chili powder. Simmer for an hour or so, stirring occasionally. Add tomato paste and mix well. Continue to simmer until hot and thick (30 minutes, or so). Taste and adjust seasoning if needed. Enjoy!

ANIMALS LOVE TO EAT APPLE PRUNINGS

The sheep really love to eat the prunings, especially in the winter when their diet consists largely of dry hay. They treat the apple prunings as salad. They chew the small ends off larger branches and consume entire small twigs.

This means that pruning apple trees does double duty: the trees need to be thinned to keep light falling on the inner branches, and the sheep need the vitamins. When we used to have cows, they also loved the branchesl, and all of the animals prefer apple branches to any other kind of tree prunings.

We load the prunings on a trailer behind the Allis Chalmers C tractor or on the cargo compartments of our John Deere Gators as we prune, and offload them in the pasture. The animals spend all their time for the next day or two hanging around the piles of prunings. By the time they are done with them, the prunings are almost gone.

APPLE PIE MIX

There is an inverse relationship between the crispness of an apple and its flavor; apples don't usually develop their full flavor until they are dead ripe, and that usually means that they also become softer. Many of the apple eaters that we know would rather have crisp apples than softer, but fully ripe, apples. In many cases they are missing out on the full flavor that the apple could deliver. That is customer choice, but it is one thing of which you should be aware. That is one reason why we advocate for our mix of apples for apple pie. When customers ask for an apple pie mix, we include a mélange (a word one of our customers used) of different flavors and textures. That way, your apple pie filling will be full flavored, yet not overly mushy.

ALMOST A WETHER

A wether is the technical term for a castrated male sheep. Most of our male lambs were castrated so that they: 1) were not so belligerent when they matured, 2) made better meat when butchered, 3) couldn't breed our ewes as they grew, and 4) were easier to sell when they grew to size. They were castrated when only a couple of days old by encircling their scrotum with thick rubber bands, specially made for the purpose, that cut off the blood supply to that area; deprived of blood circulation, it falls off in a few weeks. As long as the testicles had descended into the scrotum, the castration was successful. Testicle descending does not occur until a few days after birth, however, so castration has to wait until that time.

There were a few instances when we did not castrate our male lambs, and that usually happened when we needed a replacement ram to breed our ewes. We tried as much as possible not to raise our own rams in order not to interbreed our sheep. When interbred, the progeny may not be as healthy as crossbred lambs, and they seemed to have problems when birthing their own lambs. There were a couple of times, however, when our older ram died when finding another ram to buy from some other shepherd was not convenient or possible. One such instance happened in 1989.

Our close friend Jim Caldwell wanted to buy a lamb from us that year, and the only one that we had available to sell to him was a lamb that had somehow avoided being castrated. The lamb was brought over to Jim, with the message that he probably should castrate that lamb before having it butchered.

Jim tried. He tried using the rubber bands, but could not stretch them over the scrotum, which by now had grown larger as the lamb had grown almost to adult size. He tried many times to band the scrotum, and he even contemplated cutting the testicles out, but, upon further examination, decided that he was not up to such a thing. This turned out good for us, because our older ram died abruptly, and we needed a quick replacement. Without other prospects for finding another ram, we needed a ram for breeding soon if we were to have lambs the next spring, and so we asked Jim if we could buy back the lamb, now an almost full-grown sheep.

Jim agreed, and we brought the lamb back. When it was discussed how close that lamb had come to being castrated, Jim went over the many times that he had attempted castration without success. "But," said Jim with a chuckle in his voice, "I think the lamb liked the attention."

ART'S NEW GATOR

Art bought a second John Deere Gator utility vehicle. Gators are very useful around SweetAire Farm for transportation and light hauling, but the Gator that he already had was dedicated to the 40-gallon sprayer tank that he used mostly for the grapes. This sprayer occupied the entire rear cargo section of the Gator, and this took up so much room that he could not carry tools, supplies, or fruit in his Gator. So, he had to do something.

He hesitantly asked Cathy for her blessing to purchase another Gator. He had prepared one or two impassioned pleas complete with Power-Point slides if he needed to make his case. Cathy ruined his state of anticipatory readiness by saying "yes" almost immediately.

He didn't waste much time going to the dealer and ordering the first Gator he looked at, just in case Cathy would be tempted to reconsider her permission.

The Gator was delivered in three days, and put into service almost immediately. This Gator, unlike the other one with the sprayer loaded on, was much more responsive, even to the point where just the weight of his foot on the accelerator made it go too fast. He gave Cathy a ride, and she turned white with fear. Now, he says, he will have to tie a helium-filled balloon to his right shoe to keep within the farm speed limit.

LAMB IN TROUBLE

One Monday in the late spring, a new lamb got into trouble twice and needed rescuing both times. For the first time, he had trapped himself on one side of the wire fence and his mother was on the other side. He kept bawling and she kept answering. Although they could touch noses through the fence, he could not drink or follow his mom to the shade. Neither of them knew enough to walk the fifty feet or so to go through the opening in the fence to join the other. He was stuck in the sun, and, being black, he was very hot. Art heard all the fuss, and, when he came over to pick him up and over the fence, the lamb was panting like mad, but happy to be reunited with his mom.

The second time that day, the lamb managed to get himself stuck between and behind the watering tubs. The lamb had feet and legs going in all directions, but no two able to help him extricate himself. Again, loud noises from the sheep pasture drew Art's attention while he was picking strawberries, and he again rescued the lamb. It was good that this all happened while he was close. If he hadn't been there, the lamb probably would not have survived either of these emergencies. Since then, if the lamb did get into any more predicaments, he found his own way out.

BEES IN THE AIR

We kept honeybees at SweetAire Farm for quite a number of years. They are very fascinating creatures and worthy of admiration for their hard work. Because of this feature, they are the insects identified with Utah, the Beehive State. Bees make sweet honey seemingly from nothing, and they share their honey with their keepers without too much protest. On a warm and sunny day with flowers everywhere, the bees are in particularly good moods – very businesslike – and they are not bothered by handling. It was on days like that it was a pleasure to work with the bees.

A few puffs of cool smoke from the beekeeper's smoker could quiet the bees. On particularly beautiful sunny and warm days, almost no smoke was necessary to allow the beekeeper to lift the frames of honey-filled waxy hexagonal cells from the hive and watch the workings of the bees as they moved here and there, filling empty cells with nectar, concentrating it into honey by moving air across it with their wings, and capping the concentrated honey with wax. It was easy to watch them for hours on days like that, and rarely get stung while wearing no more protection than a tee shirt.

Rainy, dark, or cold days, when the bees cannot fly to forage for nectar, are days when it is difficult to inspect the hives. The bees display their bad moods by threatening and stinging anyone entering their hive. It takes quite a lot of smoke on such days to quiet them, and the beekeeper must be prepared to be stung a few times. It was on just such a day that the trouble occurred.

Our bees were at one time conveniently kept in the pasture next to the fence, and the cows and sheep could move around and between the hives at will. They often grazed the lush grass that grew right next to the hives. There were, at that time, two hives located close to one another, and one of the hives housed a particularly mean colony of bees.

The evidence gathered later pointed to a piece of honeysuckle vine that was snagged on one of the animals and caught on the mean bee hive. What Art saw after that were two upset hives, one on the other, and thousands of angry bees flying around looking for revenge.

Art knew that there was not enough smoke in the world on that occasion to quiet the bees. Even if he had burned every blade of grass in the pasture, there would still not be enough smoke. The bees were looking for someone to blame for the upset of their tranquil homes, and they would not be satisfied very easily. Art also knew that he had to set the hives upright before he or anyone else could go near the area before the bees either left the area or died. The menacing sight of all those angry bees in the air was bone chilling.

Perhaps, he thought, if he could just put on many layers of clothing, then they couldn't sting him too badly while he restored the hives to their proper orientations. So, he put on several pairs of pants, coveralls, his heavy Army field jacket, canvas gloves, boots, and his bee veil with hat underneath. He was dressed like it was the coldest day of winter.

With determination to do what needed to be done, he advanced into the midst of the thick cloud of bees. Real terror is walking through thousands of bees flying everywhere, with hundreds of them diving and attacking at once.

Most landed, tried to sting through his thick layers of clothes, but did not affect his mission. Some stung his head through the top of his veil, hat, and hair. He had expected a few stings, however, so he continued toward the hives. The other hive had toppled on to the mean hive, so the hardest hive had to be set upright last; he couldn't correct his major problem until the other hive had been dealt with first.

When dealing with bees, one usually tries finesse, gentleness, and slow movements. In this case, he had to be quick, using brute methods, and hoping that any bees trapped between hive sections would not be crushed or made any angrier when the sections were crudely and quickly placed on top of each other.

He was doing fine setting up the first hive, and had but one section to put on top when something caused him to stop in his tracks.

After bees land, they tend to crawl upwards. That is why the beekeeper should tie the bottom of his pant legs; if he doesn't, then bees that land on his shoes will walk up his pant leg and cause considerable consternation and unease.

Several bees had landed on his jacket and started crawling upward underneath his veil. Now, he thought, he could tolerate stings on his hands, arms, and legs, but bees walking around his face were not tolerable. He somehow had to remove his veil and brush the bees off before they reached his face. But, he couldn't remove his veil where he was because that would expose his face to hundreds of kamikaze bees. Walking away didn't help either, because, by then the bees had blamed him for their troubles and were bound to get him for it. Try as he might, he couldn't explain to them that he was only trying to help.

The animals got him into that situation, and he decided that the animals were going to help get him out of it. There was a group of sheep over in the corner of the pasture, and he walked over to them. The bees followed. The sheep stood there, watching as this funny-looking, bundled-up human with his thousands of buzzing escorts came toward them. They stood for a while longer, even as they were enveloped by the cloud of bees. They ran as soon as they realized the bees were for real. Being stung a few times in their most sensitive places not covered by thick wool probably helped their realization.

It worked. About half of the bees went with the sheep as they headed down the hill toward the swamp.

Now, where were the cows? Oh, yes! They were relaxing and peacefully chewing their cuds, over by the barn. Art went over to say "hi". The cows didn't know what hit them! They kicked up their heels and ran as fast as cows can run, down the hill and toward the swamp with bees trailing behind.

There weren't too many bees left with Art, and he was able to duck into the house and leave behind the few remaining companions. His immediate problem was to remove the bees from beneath his veil, and that was accomplished relatively easily once the veil was removed. There were only three more problems to overcome: 1) the remaining overturned hive, the mean one, had to be restored to its proper position, 2) the swarm of bees guarding it, and 3) the fact that he could no longer use the house as sanctuary because the bees that he had removed from his clothing were flying around inside.

Again donning his veil and securing the strings that fastened it, he ventured outside again. All was quiet. The animals were keeping their distance. It was then that Art noticed all the bee stingers in his clothing. They hadn't hurt him, but he was glad that he had worn so many layers of clothes.

He walked back to the hives, wanting very much to run the other way. But there was no one else to do the job, and what must be done must be done.

He worked quickly to right the remaining hive, not caring whether the bees were made angrier by his lack of carefulness. Now, he had more bees than before circling everywhere around him. Everything was done, but the bees had to be removed again.

It worked before, and it would work again! Art trudged down the hill, followed closely by his entourage of bees, to where the livestock had set up their defensive perimeter. Instead of watching him approach, as they had before, when their eyes caught sight of the many flying fiends that accompanied him, the animals ran. Fortunately, the bees split up, probably seeking revenge on anything that seemed as cowardly as those sheep and cows appeared to be. A few more passes, and Art had lost most of his escorts. There were only several hundred left.

Down in that part of the pasture, a lamb was grazing that had required bottle feeding Bottle-fed lambs can become a big nuisance because they come running whenever they see a person and they follow that person around while bleating to let the person know that they would sure like a snack. This lamb caught sight of Art and didn't seem to mind that Art looked like an overdressed Martian. Art walked like the guy who fed her.

Art didn't want the lamb to get hurt, so he entreated with something like, "No, don't come, little lamb!" But it was too late. The bees had seen the lamb, and began landing. Now, the lamb had a dilemma: she wanted to come closer to try to persuade Art to feed her, but the closer she came, the more it hurt. She stood still for what seemed like a very long time, with a puzzled look on her face. Then, she turned tail and ran, taking a hundred or so bees with her.

Art then walked leisurely out of the pasture with about fifty bees still around him. Without noticing our dog, Timin, he walked by the place where she was peacefully sleeping on the lawn. He may not have noticed her, but the bees did. Within an instant, she was up and running through the underbrush, crashing through leaves, branches, thorns, and thickets.

There were only two bees left with Art.

By this time, Art was enjoying himself, laughing out loud and feeling warm deep within that he could share his good fortune with his animals. And then he spied the cat.

We've had many cats, but this was perhaps the most staid and composed cat of all. He was a male in his prime, and nothing bothered him.

Art walked over to the cat, and the two remaining bees caught sight of him. They both transferred their attention to him, and both landed on his side, and, presumably, started stinging. With purpose, he arose and walked slowly away with no sign of acknowledgement that the bees were injecting him with venom, except for a slight tremor in his skin on his side. He walked slowly and stately straight into the swamp.

All the bees gone, hives set upright again, animals licking their wounds, Art sat down and laughed as hard as he had ever laughed before or since.

CIDER-MAKING AND APPLE POMACE

When October rolls around, and we have a lot of apples to sell, we load a hand-operated cider press on the truck and bring it to the Farmers' Market, where we unload the press and offer to our customers the opportunity to make fresh, no-pesticide apple cider from apples chosen to have a mix of varieties with different flavors. Our customers look forward to October for just this reason. We require them to bring their own containers, and we sell apples for a discounted price. Some, but not all, of these apples are very misshapen and would not be good enough to sell otherwise, but they are good enough to press for cider.

During a normal year, about one gallon of juice can be pressed from a half bushel of apples. Some apples are juicier, and some are less juicy, so we sell the apples by the quantity before pressing rather than by the amount of juice produced.

There was no preservative in this juice, and no pesticides to kill natural yeasts that were present on the skins of the apples, so, left alone for a few days, the juice would begin to ferment.

We always thought that the cider tasted better after it fermented a slight bit, but not to an extreme. Some of our customers were especially attracted to our cider for its ability to turn hard after a couple of weeks or so.

Many of our customers pressed their own juice, but we did offer to help them or press it for them if they were incapable or unwilling to press it themselves. Grinding the apples by hand before pressing them requires a good bit of work.

We have had young adults, older adults, and youngsters as young as 7 or 8 provide the muscle power to grind and press the apples. When the press is in operation, others crowd around to watch, and apple-pressing season becomes one of the main draws of our particular Farmers' Market.

There have been a few customers who have brought many containers for us to fill. They drop off the containers and, usually, come back later to pick them up and take them away. One customer used to give gallons of fresh-pressed juice to others as gifts; he thought that highly of the finished product. One customer once forgot to come back, and we had to track him down later. After that, he always left his car keys with us when he dropped off his container so that he could not leave without returning to pick up his cider.

Left over from making apple cider is the apple pomace, or the apple solids that have had the juice squeezed out of them. We keep the pomace. People often ask us what we do with it, and we answer that we give it to our sheep. Our customers are satisfied that this is a good use for it.

Our sheep just love the pomace. They really like apple left-overs much better than grain, and beg for anything apple-related (pomace, peelings, or picked apples not good enough to keep) any time during apple season that a human appears within eyesight. They keep a close watch on the area even when they are eating grass hundreds of feet away from where they are fed. All it takes is one alert sheep spotting someone walking by, even if that person has no intention to feed them, and they hurry en masse as fast as they can to see if there has been anything appetizing dumped over the fence for them to eat. If apple pomace has been dumped there, then they scarf it up as fast as they can. If no apple pomace was left for them to eat, then they reluctantly return to eating whatever it was that they had been eating before, but continue to be watchful and full of hope that they next time they run to the fence there will be a treat for them to gobble up.

CRICKET WARS II

Late summer is cricket time, and is when we play unwilling hosts to crickets in our house. It's not that easy for crickets to jump onto the porch, go under two doors into our back room, and then under another door into our kitchen, but some are able to negotiate this obstacle course and visit us where we live. Once inside, they tend to hide and make lots of cricket noises to taunt us. At that point, it becomes a challenge on our part to catch them and exile them back to their original outdoor home that nature provides, and, on their part, to avoid capture. This isn't just a cat and mouse routine, although one might say so if one saw how the game is played. First, the cricket has to be found. Sometimes, that is easy, as when a cricket ventures out of its hiding spot and exposes itself in the middle of the floor. At that point, Art positions himself on his hands and knees close to the offending little critter, raise his cupped hand, and try to bring his hand down on top of the cricket to capture it. He is not allowed to harm the cricket in this maneuver. If he succeeds in this attempt, then the cricket is carried in his closed hand to the outside where it belongs. If Art has not succeeded, then the real game begins, where the cricket heads for the hills, or, rather, the safety of the underside of an appliance or cabinet, with Art crawling on his hands and knees as quickly as he can to try to cut off the cricket before it reaches its haven. If he is able to stop the cricket before it reaches safety, then the game goes back to the first step, where Art again raises his cupped hand. If the cricket has won the race, then the game is suspended until a later time.

RENEE'S RHUBARB CAKE

This is a delicious cake that contrasts the tartness of rhubarb with the sweetness of the cake. We make it several times during the rhubarb season, which lasts for us from May to October. This recipe came to us from, and is named for, our relative, Renee.

Ingredients:

Cake:
1 ½ cups firmly packed brown sugar
½ cup shortening
1 egg
1 tsp vanilla
1 cup sour milk
2 cups flour
1 tsp baking soda
2 cups rhubarb, cut into 1-inch pieces

Topping:
½ cup sugar
1 tsp cinnamon

Preheat oven to 350 degrees. Mix together all of the cake ingredients except the rhubarb until well blended. Stir in rhubarb. Pour into well-greased 9 by 13-inch baking pan. Sprinkle with topping after combining sugar and cinnamon. Bake at 350 degrees for 30-40 minutes.

DON'T TRY THIS YOURSELF

All's well that ends well. Art decided one Sunday afternoon to resume cutting up the trees that fell on our machinery shed during a recent storm, so he got out his chain saw, climbed the orchard ladder that he was using to reach the downed tree limbs, and sawed a large chunk off one 20-inch diameter limb. The piece fell down and jarred the ladder. He was holding the chain saw with both hands, so couldn't steady himself. When the limb hit the ladder, he dropped the saw. The saw stopped running, but Art's foot caught in the upper rung of the ladder. He was hanging upside down from the ladder by his stuck foot without being able to reach anything useful. He flailed a while, but couldn't extricate himself. He called for help, but no one heard him. Neighbors were not far away, but they were mowing and trimming their lawn, so they could not hear Art's calls. He was very afraid that he would either break his caught foot or twist his ankle. Desperate by now, he finally managed to stretch beyond comfort to a place where he could push himself up just enough to free his foot. He came down hard, but relieved, and suffering only some minor scrapes and bruises on his lower shin. He decided to wait until another day (and when others could help him) to complete the job.

FARMERS' MARKETS

The Farmers' Market is a truly magical place. Like other magical places, there are crowds of happy, cheerful people, many smiling and visiting with other pleasantly cheerful people. It's the best of the city mixing with the abundance of the country to form the very best amalgam of both. It's a place to greet old friends and make new ones. It's the backyard fence without the fence. It's the social event of the week for some. Friends and families greet each other to catch up on the latest happenings and rumors of happenings. There is an air of excitement that only a crowd of this type can provide. It is so special that teenagers have even been seen in attendance long before they really wanted to arise out of bed on a Saturday morning. And sometimes they even walk around with their moms and dads. And sometimes they even smile. It is a safe place to be; little tots, who would never be able to leave the sides of their parents anywhere else, run free. Their parents know that they cannot get into trouble, unless they stumble and fall on the hard surface. Even then, there are numerous others who, as surrogate parents, come to their aid and console them until their parents catch up. It is a place of freedom, yet with a willing sense of decorum. People gladly wait in long lines for their favorite items, yet, if they buy the last remaining item, offer to let the next person in line have it so they won't be disappointed. At the very least, they apologize for taking the last one. They are all there to provide for themselves and their families in the hope of fresh, tasty, and healthful products, some of which cannot be found anywhere else.

And the bounty displayed! The beautiful fruits and vegetables, the luscious baked goods, the jams, jellies, and condiments, the wines, and the colorful flowers! There may also be crafts and other homemade items skillfully made by the sellers.

Everyone at the market is usually on his or her very best behavior. People who would otherwise be competitive in other environments become friendly and cooperative at the Farmers' Market. And the vendors are the salt of the Earth: practical, hard-working, and proud of the wares they have brought for their customers to see. They have big hearts in their chests and calluses on their hands. If they had no optimism, they wouldn't be here. When misfortune or accident happens to one or more of these wonderful people, all are concerned and offer to help, if possible. There may be competition among vendors of the same types of items, but there is no animosity; there are enough buyers for everybody. Perishable food items returned to a vendor's home after the market are not wasted. They are used as much as possible by the vendor or the vendor's family or friends: this is the farmer's share, that which is unsellable or of questionable quality. The best items are always the ones offered to the buyers.

We also have dogs greeting other dogs, tails wagging, happy to be there to meet others of their kind. Having these representatives of man's and woman's best friends present add to the festive nature of the market.

Like a circus, the Farmers' Market forms in the early hours of the morning, as each vendor busily concentrates on setting up his or her showy canopy, tables, and wares displayed in the most attractive ways. Some even decorate with extra embellishments to make their locations even more festive. Soon the people will come, a few at first, but then filling the space. They add the air of anticipation and fulfillment. Food at its best, always beckoningly alluring, appeals to the inner hungers of those in attendance. These things they purchase with thoughts of scrumptious gratifications in the minutes, hours, and days to come. Some cannot wait for the gratification, and eagerly consume their purchases right there for instant enjoyment.

All too soon, closing time arrives, and the magic gradually diminishes as the happy crowd thins and disappears. The time for meeting and greeting has come and gone. All of a sudden, customers-to-be have to attend to their business of purchasing the last remaining items on their lists. They rush around the market, with no time for small talk, and only a cursory "hello" to the vendors they visit. They turn, and are gone to the next stall, knowing that their time window of opportunity is limited. Soon, the vendors rush to store their canopies and other paraphernalia so that they can return home to the many other chores that await them once they get there. Yes, just like magic, Farmers' Markets are ephemeral; the magic quickly gone until the appointed hour next week.

A YEAR (ALMOST) WITHOUT PEACHES

When, in 1987, we bought the 22 acres next to our original farmstead, we had in mind to expand all of our farming projects, including more pasture for our animals and more trees for our orchard. So, we built pasture fence and ordered many more fruit trees; there was room for both. While we were planting (by hand) our new peach trees, one of our a new neighbors hailed to us across the fence separating his property from ours and, after introducing himself, asked what we were up to. We said that we were putting in a peach orchard. He suggested that we might be better with growing beef cattle rather than fruit trees. "You ought to stick with something you know, like cattle," he suggested. But, we continued planting trees anyway, and they were soon growing well in the new orchard.

Peaches are one of the most difficult, if not the most difficult, tree fruits to grow in the humid northeastern U.S. Peaches are very susceptible to many diseases that thrive in the wetness, and require sprays to protect them from rotting on the tree as soon as they begin to ripen. So, many years before we decided to transition from chemical agriculture to organic, we used as many and as potent sprays as were necessary to produce a crop.

And, we were successful. We had about 300 peach trees in that orchard, and harvested many bushels of peaches to sell at the Farmers' Market, to other sellers, and to many individual buyers. Fridays before the Saturday Farmers' Market were very busy days, picking all the ripe fruit, especially peaches, for that week. We were so successful that Art became known to our customers at the market as "the peach man". We had nice looking, wonderful tasting, fully ripened peaches that were a customer favorite.

There was a year in the early days of our participation in the market when we had a particularly bad spell of weather. It was not unusual that we would get a light snowfall on our opened peach blossoms. This happened so often that we came to expect it every year. But, a light snowfall at that stage did not really affect the crop. The temperature during a light snowfall rarely went below freezing, so the peaches did not suffer.

Contrarily, a freeze, especially a freeze on a clear spring night, can kill the blossoms. In the year in question, we had not one, but a series of nightly freezes that killed the opened blossoms. Unopened blossoms are a bit more hardy than opened blossoms, and trees do not open all their blossoms at once. So, if a set of opened blossoms is killed, then there is usually another set that opens later and can set fruit. This one year, however, we had a freeze one night, and then two days later another freeze, and then another, and another, for a total of five or six freezes spaced just right to kill all the blossoms that opened that spring.

Consequently, out of a total of 300 peach trees, we picked a total of two bushels of fruit that year. This compares with a usual harvest of one or two hundred bushels of peaches in a normal year. It clearly wiped out any peaches that were to be brought to the Farmers' Market.

We were not the only vendor without peaches that year. All the fruit growers participating in the market had suffered the same fate. Peaches were not to be had, except from another vendor who brought in peaches that he had bought elsewhere for resale. Because the Bel Air Farmers' Market is a grower-only market, we confronted this cheating vendor, and he stopped selling peaches immediately.

The same set of freezes had affected all orchards in the northeast, so there were no local peaches to be had, anywhere close to Maryland. The first law of economics states that if the supply of anything declines, then the price of that product should increase. But the price of peaches in the local area did not increase, because there happened to be a bumper crop that year of peaches in Georgia, South Carolina, and other southern states. The fact that the price of fresh peaches in Maryland did not rise to absurd levels attests to the efficiency of our transportation system and our global economy. Whatever is not available locally can usually be had from some other place where the supply is adequate or better.

Years later, when Art made the decision against using chemical pesticides that could cause him harm and required him to wear personal protective equipment, such as an extra coverall suit, respirator helmet, and gloves, he discontinued the use of those harmful chemicals. This decision was disastrous for our peach production, because, without those chemicals, peach trees and peach fruits suffer from a series of diseases that are difficult to control with organic sprays.

Much depends on the weather; organic sprays are not very persistent or effective, and a spell of rainy or very humid days can cause the loss of a crop. Without much guidance from fruit experts about growing peaches organically, we have had to experiment to find effective ways to control peach diseases, and each experiment consumes another year. The experience of a year without peaches has been repeated several times since then, although not due to repeated freezing nights in the early spring.

WHEN SHEEP GOT LOOSE

We have had many days in the early springtime when the grass growing in the neighbors' lawns was much greener than the grass in our pastures or orchards. Our sheep could always find a hole in their fence and go visiting. We dreaded hearing the telephone ring early in the morning, because it often would be from a neighbor reporting that they were hosting our entire flock. That meant getting dressed before we were ready and trying to figure out some way to get them back home without chasing them down the street. Of course, if we knew how they got out, then we could have herded them back that way, but we usually had no clue about where they had found their way out. Sometimes we had extra help in the form of other adults, children, and dogs. That always made the process much harder; sheep get used to some people, and run from others. They tend to stay together if not pressed too much, but will scatter if chased vigorously. So, if possible, the easiest solution to getting them back home is to allow them to come back by themselves; they always seemed to know the route they took to start their adventure, and they could always retrace their path. If we were lucky enough to have the luxury of time, so that they would reappear on our property when they had had their fill of the contraband grass, then we would spend hours trying to find the place where they had escaped. Many times there would be telltale signs of wool fibers stuck near the hole in the fence, but that didn't always happen. One time, the place where they had escaped was so subtle that we couldn't find it for a long time, no matter how hard we looked. It was frustrating us that the sheep kept getting out and we couldn't stop them from doing so. Finally, there was enough snow that fell that we could follow their tracks to a secluded spot where the sheep could sneak under the fence and off our property.

Cathy had to crawl under the fence in that spot to prove that was the path that the sheep took to go visit the neighbors. We think we have now shut off all of their escape routes, because we haven't had our sheep wander onto the neighbors' yards in several years. But, if they ever do again abscond, it won't be hard for the neighbors to know who to call at daybreak.

To add to everything else we had to do, the sheep still jumped fences. They jumped the fence at the lower end of the summer pasture and spent the afternoon browsing in the adjacent woods. Art went to feed the sheep on Sunday afternoon and discovered most of them missing from where they should have been. When he found out where they had gone, he really didn't know how he was going to get them back. There was no opening in the fence to drive them through unless he would cut the fence wire, and the way the land sloped it was easier for the sheep to jump out than to jump back in. So, when all else fails with the sheep, ignore them and hope that they come back all by themselves. He had some weeding and fertilizing to do near the pasture fence, and watched all afternoon. Soon, three sheep came back, but the others were still marooned on the other side of the fence and "bah-ed" to the three. So, the three went back and joined the others by jumping the fence again. One more time, three sheep came home, and, again, went back with the others. Just about when Art was finishing his job several hours after he had begun, and he was more seriously considering his options for getting them back, ten sheep came running to the top of the pasture. Problem solved, at least for the present. We didn't know what we would do to keep the sheep from jumping the fence, but scolding them didn't seem to help.

FARMER'S SHARE

As you probably have guessed by now, we at SweetAire Farm are not the most hip, do not use a lot of the newest technology, or are not inclined to do things the most commercially-acceptable way. Indeed, what we pride ourselves in is the good, wholesome food that we provide for our friends and customers. This is one of the drivers for what we do. And, as a beneficial side effect for us, we exercise and get to eat some of the same fruit that we bring for you at the market. The only difference for us is that the fruit that we get to eat is only that which we cannot sell. We call that the "farmer's share". If it's not good enough for our customers, it's still good enough for us.

CRICKET WARS III

The annual in-house cricket safari and hunt is almost a tradition at SweetAire Farm. There had been a cricket in our house for a few weeks, but with all the other things going on, we had mostly ignored this cricket for several weeks. Yes, it chirped all night, and could be somewhat annoying, but its chirps were not so loud that they interfered with television or radio audio. But, good times for all house crickets must end sometime, and its time was now. We had seen the cricket last week. It was just a little guy, barely ¾ inch long. Art went looking for the cricket on Sunday, and moved some furnishings away from the walls and corner, where the chirping sound appeared to be coming from. There it was, but before Art could drop to his hands and knees, it quickly hopped into one of our baseboard heater elements. Short of taking off the element cover or turning the electric heat up high, the cricket was safe; there was no way to reach it.

The cricket sound began to move around, and, by Wednesday, the sound was coming from the downstairs bathroom. The cricket had gone through the living room and front room to get there. Art turned on the light, and there was the little guy, right in front of his eyes, in the midst of the floor mat. Art quickly dropped to his pounce position, and, aided greatly by the extreme difficulty for a cricket to hop when enmeshed by the cozy soft fibers of a bathroom floor mat, put his cupped hand over the cricket and captured it. He is a mighty hunter, indeed. The cricket was released in the early morning twilight outside of the house that it had called its home for the past few weeks. So ended another attempt by members of the cricket cabal to infiltrate our peaceful inner sanctum.

FAVORITE APPLE CHOICES

Customers at the Farmers' Market used to ask Art and friend and helper Bernie about their favorite apples. This happened all the time, because we would sometimes bring 20-30 different varieties of apples to the market in the fall. Bernie usually answered that his favorite was Snow, a rather small, sweet apple that is a parent of Macintosh and gets its name from its white flesh. Art invariably answered the question with the name of the Spartan variety, also related to Macintosh, but with a slightly different flavor and a little more crispness.

A few years ago, these two would ply customers with samples of one after another of these two kinds of apples until the customer, reeling from eating too many apple slices as samples, and under pressure from both Art and Bernie, had to choose one or the other as the variety to purchase. Then, depending on the choice, either Bernie or Art would gloat over the other until the next customer came and asked the same question.

Since then, customers have become wiser and do not ask the question nearly as much.

FEEDING A LAMB WITH A PAIL

Cathy is the lamb midwife-if-need-be, but her midwifery is not needed for most of the births on our farm. She does, however, make the determination about the availability of milk from the mother, about the health of the young-'uns, and about their genders. Art is the mean old guy who gives them their shots at three days old and applies bands to castrate and dock them.

Occasionally, there is a ewe without enough milk for her lambs. In that case, Cathy makes up some lamb milk replacer and feeds them with a bottle. When the lambs are very young, they need to be fed every three or four hours, so this can be quite a chore, especially on cold, wintry nights when making the dark trip to the barn is not at all pleasant. If the mother sheep has abandoned the lamb, then Cathy sometimes brings the lamb into the house and keeps it in a box with tall sides, so that it can't escape and walk around the house looking for food. This makes feeding the lamb at all hours of the day and night a lot easier. However, the mother will not care for a lamb that has lost its unique smell, as happens when it is brought into the house for a while, so Cathy doesn't separate the lamb from the mom unless the mother shows no interest, or even rejects, the lamb.

When a bottle-fed lamb is old enough, Cathy can train it to drink *ad lib* from a nipple pail, which is a container, usually a pail, most times with a top, with a nipple protruding from its side at the bottom. The nipple pal can either be hung from a nail on the wall or placed on a stand so that it is the correct height for the lamb to drink. The milk replacer in the pail must be replaced each day, or even more frequently, to assure that its quality is maintained. The pail is also washed out at this time.

When the milk replacer is first mixed and poured into the pail, it is warm, but it cools to ambient temperature as the day goes on. If the outside temperature is enough below freezing, the milk may freeze and the lamb cannot drink solid milk from the nipple. Lambs especially like the warm milk, but tolerate cold milk if they are hungry enough.

Bottle-fed lambs soon associate the presence of a human being with fresh food, and, so they become very friendly, sometimes to the point of nuisance. Some lambs will learn to follow humans all around wherever they go, and some lambs do not discriminate any other human from the person who usually feeds it. This can become annoying to anybody who has chores to do without a lamb constantly underfoot.

There was a male lamb born to a ewe that seemed to have no milk, so Cathy bottle-fed it for a while, and then tiring of this routine, decided to train it to drink from the nipple pail, which she did. Soon it became apparent that the lamb must have been getting some milk from its mother, because it seemed to be doing fine despite not drinking from its nipple pail all day long. Most mornings, just after Cathy cleaned and refilled the pail, the lamb gorged on fresh, warm milk until its little tummy swelled to the point of exploding. One morning, after the milk in the pail had frozen the night before, the lamb was so eager when Cathy went out to renew the pail contents with warm milk that he kept getting in the way and knocking things over while she attempted to change the nipple and remove the old milk. If she didn't come right out and utter nasty words at him, she at least thought them very loudly.

Cathy went to the barn one morning, as she did each day, to clean the nipple pail and renew the milk for the lamb. She found the nipple chewed apart and ruined for further use. A raccoon had discovered the pail and availed him- or herself of the opportunity to partake of a pretty good free meal. Aside from the gall of losing another round to a raccoon, that nipple was one of only a few that we bought years ago that were the best for suckling lambs. We can't get any more, so the loss was more than just a round of an ongoing fight.

FOX AGAINST GOOSE

A few years ago, Art watched as a fox stalked a Canada goose behind our Bernie Barn. The fox pounced, grabbing the goose by the upper wing. They fought, the fox hanging on as tightly as it could and the goose furiously flapping its wings to pummel the fox. They made quite a commotion, these two. Within a few minutes, however, the fight was over, and the goose had won. The fox slunk away, bruised and defeated. Art had never seen anything like this before, and certainly didn't expect that the goose would triumph over the fox. We've lost a number of domestic geese to foxes over the years, but we guess they aren't as tough as wild Canada geese.

IT MUST HAVE BEEN GOOD FOR HIM

Our grandson Gregory lived with us for his first six years. When Art and the boys, Paul and Eric, went outside to do some farm work that needed to be done, very young Gregory would go with them as soon as he could walk. After all, it is never too early to learn about work that needs to be done on a farm.

So it was that all four of them were one fine day prepared to construct a trellis for our newly-planted grape vines, quite far from the house. They brought their tools with them: a clamshell posthole digger, shovels, and a tamping bar for setting up the posts, hammer and nails for the cross pieces, and staples and wires that were to run the length of the row. These were all brought to the designated location on the trailer pulled by the Allis-Chalmers "C" tractor. The boys also rode on the trailer, hanging on tightly as it went over a bump or two.

The rows were about 300 feet long, more or less, and the crew needed to place one post every 10 feet or so. Like much of farm work, there are few exact dimensions; almost every measurement is estimated by eye or by stepping or pacing. So it was this day.

Putting posts in the ground on SweetAire Farm is not usually too difficult. The ground is usually not too rocky so that a post hole can be dug relatively easily without obstruction. If an occasional rock is ever encountered in the hole, it can usually be removed with the help of the bar leveraged against the side of the hole. Once the rock has been removed, the posthole digger can then be used to continue removing the dirt.

Where Art grew up in upstate New York, the ground was little except shale rocks with a little soil mixed in. Fortunately, the soil in Maryland is more easily moved.

After digging the hole to the correct depth, more or less, the post was placed in the hole, a shovel was used to mound the removed soil against the post and it was tamped using the bar to firm the soil around the post. There is usually a little soil left over after a post has been planted, and this can remain behind in a little heap or it can be used elsewhere.

Gregory had a fascination with the soil. It was a rusty red color, meaning that it probably contained iron, and every time Art looked over, Gregory was filling his little fist with a handful of dirt and eating it. Now, many people might be upset by this, but when Art saw that Gregory was ingesting the dirt, he asked himself why Gregory was doing so, and what could possibly be the harm. He decided that there was nothing that he knew in the dirt that could cause harm; the dirt was newly dug and as clean as possible, if dirt can ever be called clean. He reasoned that the dirt must have tasted good to Gregory and that it contained something, probably iron, that Gregory's body was craving for. So, he did not interfere.

They continued to dig holes and planted all their fence posts; Gregory ate dirt from many of the holes as they went along. He has said later, as a healthy young man, that he remembers that day and that dirt, and how it tasted somewhat salty, but really good. He is still glad he had the opportunity to satisfy some nutritional need that he craved.

LAMBS AT PLAY

Lambs love to play with each other when they have had enough to eat, are feeling good, and the weather is nice. It is a delight to watch as they run around the pasture together, playing tag or just racing. They may hop off all four feet at times, appearing to be on pogo sticks, jumping around the pasture. They climb atop almost any high protuberance, whether it be a large rock, or platform, or any kind of pile. Once on top, they play as if to be the last lamb standing, trying to push each other off, and playing king or queen of the mountain. And then, tired after all this activity, they snuggle against each other and rest.

We use a lot of leaves for mulch on our berries and rhubarb plants. Several of our Farmers' Market customers rake and bag their leaves and save them for us to pick up and bring to our farm. Not all of these leaves can be spread right away, so we pile some bags of leaves waiting to be spread. There was a tarp over the bags to keep them dry. Cathy kept noticing that the tarp was coming off the pile, and ripping in the middle. She kept pulling the tarp back over the pile, until one time she observed that the lambs were playing king-of-the-mountain on the pile. It was their fault that the tarp was being pulled off and ripped. At that point, Cathy gave up. The lambs didn't.

We once had some tree workers cut some large trees that were threatening to collapse on our raspberry patch. Before they left, they dumped in the pasture a pile of wood chips that they had made that day from tree branches and small limbs. The sheep had been locked out of that portion of the pasture so that they wouldn't bother the men as they worked, and they were anxiously waiting on the other side of the gate to be let into the rest of the pasture. As soon as Cathy opened the gate, they ran to the pile of chips; it probably looked to them like a huge pile of food. As soon as they reached the pile, they realized that it wasn't going to taste good, and they lost interest. The lambs, however, saw the pile as another opportunity to climb, and soon began playing on the hill. After that, the lambs played on that pile early every morning. For some reason, the pile became shorter and the bottom seemed to spread out more than it was. Come to think of it, that could also describe a lot of people we know.

THORNS

Late spring and early summer is the time of the year for blood-letting on the farm. With the thorns on the gooseberry bushes, blackberry canes, and raspberry canes, Art comes back from picking these fruits with his arms and hands looking like he had just given a bath to a cat. His daily evening-time activity is attempting to dig out the thorns from his fingers and hands.

Gooseberries, especially, have formidable and treacherous thorns that cannot be avoided if the goal is to pick the fruit by hand. As careful as one can be when picking gooseberries, there is always a thorn lurking somewhere among the leaves and berries, just waiting to reach up and poke at the intruding hand. Fortunately, the gooseberry season is short, only a couple of weeks long, so the damage to Art's hands has few lasting effects. It is mostly his mind that develops a fear of gooseberry bushes rising out of the mire of a nightmare and attacking him from all directions, holding him and poking holes in every square inch of the skin on his hands and fingers. When he awakes from this hallucination, he can still feel the nagging pain of the thorn or two that stubbornly persist under his skin.

Blackberry canes are usually not nearly as bad to pick from as are gooseberries. There are some thornless blackberry plants that we have, but the earliest blackberries that we grow have thorns. The stickers on these blackberries can often be avoided, but, when the most beautiful, biggest, ripest berry is located way inside the mass of canes, then the threat of thorns becomes real if that beautiful berry is to be plucked from where it grows and placed in the picking container. Wearing a thick glove on one hand while holding the canes can protect against some blackberry thorns, but a similar glove is too clumsy to be worn on the hand that picks the berries.

Raspberry thorns are insidious. When raspberry thorns embed themselves in the skin of one's fingers, they are very difficult to see and are very hard to remove. They are soft and easily broken inside the skin, so can stay there for a long time, chronically reminding their victim of their continued presence each time any kind of pressure is applied to the surface of the fingers. And, that consequence becomes very common during normal daily activities.

We once grew Sea Buckthorn bushes that bear orange-colored clusters of berries ripening in late summer and early fall. They also bear thorns worthy of gooseberry bushes. Although the berries of these plants had an interesting citrus flavor, they were very difficult to pick without a lot of pain. We do not have them anymore.

By the late summer and early fall, the threat of thorns has been reduced to almost nothing. Over the winter, Art imagines his skin thickening, so that he can face the thorn threat anew next springtime.

LAMBS DOING WELL

You may feel sorry for our little lambs having to live outside in the cold temperatures, but they do well there, much better than they would inside. The cold cannot be overwhelming for them, because they act perfectly natural outside, following their mothers, prancing around, and lying down to sleep in the grass. As long as they are well fed and have enough milk to drink, they do fine (sheep milk is very high in fat, so its energy content is high). It takes just a few minutes after being let out of the barn for the first time with their moms for the new-born lambs to find out that all adult sheep do not welcome the lambs to feed from them, and that they had better pay attention to who their moms are. They learn this because unrelated ewes will butt them away when they try to drink. The mothers, too, must keep track of their lambs so that they do not separate by too far. It happens infrequently that a mother will wander off without checking to see if her lambs are following. This happens sometimes when the sheep return on the run from the back orchard to the Bernie Barn area in hopes that grain awaits them in their shed. They get so excited at this time, running and bah-ing, all racing to be the first to discover a treat. When that happens, and they find out that they don't get grain every time they return, the moms who lack their lambs begin to call for their missing offspring. Sometimes we can hear the moms bah-ing in the barnyard, and tiny voices from lost lambs coming from way off in the distance. More bah-ing and crying, and all eventually reunite.

MOWING WITH SWALLOWS

Anyone who has mowed tall grass or hay has seen the swallows that swoop and turn in front of the tractor during the cutting operation. They do this to catch and eat the many leafhopper insects that inhabit and feed on the grass, and are disturbed by the mowing. The leafhoppers fly into the air and are vulnerable to the hungry swallows. It is both fun and entertaining to watch the swallows as they fly acrobatically around the tractor as it moves forward through the tall grass. Swallows only appear in the morning or early afternoon. Later in the day, there are no swallows present to amuse and amaze as the grass is mown, but it is a real treat when they return the next morning.

FEED BAGS

They don't make them like they used to. We have all heard this statement about any number of different things. One thing they do differently these days is the way they sell bags of feed for livestock and pet animals. If someone goes into a Tractor Supply store these days to buy feed, that person would see piles of feed in strong paper bags in 25, 40, or 50-pound sizes. What a difference from the way it used to be sold.

In the days before the Occupational Health and Safety (OSH) Act limited allowable weights of packages people could lift without injury, livestock feed used to come in 100-pound bags. They were sold at what was known then as "Feed Stores", which later became known as "Farm Stores", and now are known more as home and garden stores, as they changed to serve a customer base much less agricultural than residential and suburban. With less than 2% of the U.S. population involved with production agriculture, catering to residential homeowners gave these stores a lot greater opportunity to reach an expanded clientele.

Feed Stores sold a variety of products for feeding animals. A farmer could buy a 100-pound bag of a single grain, such as field corn or oats, or a mixed feed for dairy or beef cows, or a mash (ground up grain) for chickens, ducks, or turkeys. Each of these came in 100-pound sacks. And feed was the main offering of the Feed Store, although some tools and other farming supplies and implements might be available in the store, as well. In the days before and immediately after World War II, when refrigerators were uncommon in American homes, Feed Stores also supplied blocks of ice for household ice boxes in which foods were kept cool before the ice melted completely.

Each person on a farm was expected to be able to handle those 100-pound bags of feed. The men were certainly expected to be able to lift them and move them around. Young boys learned to handle them as soon as they could. Farm wives had to be able to move them on occasion, and the young girls were not exempt. Some carried them in their arms; while others carried them over their shoulders, as would a fireman rescuing a victim. Some who had difficulty lifting 100 pounds might drag them. These days, 100-pound weights may only be found in a gym, but, years ago, they were everywhere that livestock animals were kept.

A single piece of cloth approximately 30 inches by 30 inches in size was folded and sewn at the bottom and the side to form a bag. During the lean years of the depression and post-World War II, the cloth was a medium weight cotton material. Later, the cotton was replaced by burlap, a coarse and rugged material that did not tear as easily as did the cotton. Burlap was itself replaced by a woven plastic material in the 1960s and 1970s. Empty, used plastic feed bags were not very useful for other uses around the farm, because they tended to fray and tear relatively easily. Used burlap bags were more robust, and could be used for storing things or as blankets for animals, or as root ball coverings for dug plants. Used cotton fabric was very useful. During the depression and beyond, the material could be cut into pieces needed for a sewing pattern and then made into shirts or dresses for family members. Some feed bags made from cotton material even had a print pattern on the fabric to favor their uses as material for homemade clothes. Such bags were highly sought-after, and difficult to find in the Feed Store.

Each bag was tied with a Miller's Knot, which was a means of tying a piece of string without actually knotting it, as in more conventional bows, square knots, or half hitches A Miller's Knot could be untied with a yank on one end of the string. This made it easy to open the bag of feed when dumping it into a barrel or in front of the animals for which the grain was intended.

A Miller's Knot is formed by holding a piece of strong string about 15-20 inches long in one hand while also holding the bag shut with the same hand. One end of the string is used to form a loop over the index finger of the holding hand, while the other hand wraps the rest of the string around the top of the bag and over the loose end of the loop around the index finger. After several wraps, the other end of the string would be tucked under the loop. Both ends are then pulled to tighten the wrap around the top of the bag.

When harvesting a crop of grain in the field with a machine called a combine, one person in the cab of the combine was the operator-driver, and another person in the cab bagged the harvested grain and tied the tops of the bags with Miller's Knots. That's how it used to be done. Nowadays, there is only one person in the combine cab, and the grain is discharged through a chute on the side of the combine to a truck being driven beside. The grain is then stored unbagged and in bulk in a storage bin. Even newer, are smart combines that run themselves and require no one in the cab.

Often the grain producer wanted a feed for his animals that consisted of more than just a single grain. If a mixed feed was needed, bags of grain were brought to the Feed Store for formulation. Other grains and nutritional supplements would be added at the store, and the mixed feed would be filled into the same bags that were brought to the store by the farmer, who then brought them home after paying the bill for the extra materials and the service.

Sometimes the farmer would want to use a grain to make mash for his poultry or for flour for baking in his household. Farms often had hammermills in which whole grain was beaten and pulverized into powder. These mills were run by wide belts from pulleys on the sides of tractors or by small internal-combustion engines that powered the driving belts.

A lot has changed since the days of grains in 100-pound feed bags. Large production agriculture farms can no longer find the help nor the time to be as labor-intensive as things used to be done. But, there are memories, nonetheless. Things were not always so badly done in those days. But, they certainly don't do them now like they used to.

LAMBS DON'T RECOGNIZE SHEARED MOMS

Sheep-shearing day usually happened on a Saturday in late May at SweetAire Farm. Grandson Greg came over to help, which meant that he got to wrestle sheep and sometimes win. Greg has been told that when he catches each sheep and wrestled it into the shearing pen that whoever ended up on the bottom would be the one who was sheared. So, he tried hard to stay out of that relative position, and, so far, has managed to avoid a haircut.

This is a very big job for both Greg and Art, so it is good to get it over with. The sheep agree. If cool temperatures are forecast for that day, then that is good because it minimizes stress on both the sheep and the shearers. Cool weather doesn't always happen, and there have been hot years when cold water had to be thrown on a newly-sheared ewe to cool her down before she overheated and expired.

For the lambs, shearing day is also a stressful time. When we finished with the ewes, their lambs often did not recognize their moms. They had gotten used to identifying their mothers by smell, and the smell comes off with the wool. So, mom and kids can be standing right next to each other, with the lambs bawling for "mom", and moms respond by saying "I'm standing right here next to you". When they all do this at the same time, it causes quite a racket. This miscommunication can go on for days at a time until they finally figure it all out.

MUSINGS FROM THE HAYFIELD

Cutting, raking, and baling hay the way we used to do it was a time-consuming, mind numbing, and sometimes tedious process. The work was done a little at a time, usually in hot weather, and the scenery did not change much or quickly. It was easy to become bored, and the mind wandered. And so, these are the kinds of thoughts that went through one's mind out there alone in the hayfield.

It's a beautiful day today, with blue sky and brilliant, early morning sunshine. Not a cloud in the sky. There's no prettier place to be than right here in this hayfield. I feel good. I'm glad I started early today, because it feels like it could get hot later. I hope my machinery works well and nothing breaks today. If I don't push it, then everything should be fine. Boy, it's a beautiful day.

The birds are singing. Well, it's not that I can actually hear them with my machinery going, but I heard them singing earlier before I started mowing. And, I can see them as they fly around through the sky. Boy, it's a beautiful day.

Hey! There are a few swallows swooping and diving around my mower as I'm cutting the hay down. They always come out this time of the day, and try to catch all the insects as they jump and fly off the hay as it falls. Those swallows sure are graceful. I could watch them all day, but I hope that mowing won't take that long. I'm making good progress, so I should be done soon. The sun feels nice. Boy, it's a beautiful day.

The machines are working perfectly. I'm thankful for that. I remember how it was before I bought these new machines. It hurts to think about it. I remember the mower-conditioner that used to break chains all the time, and when I tried to fix it, I had to take it halfway apart. I remember also the time that the needles on the baler broke and it took a day and a half to replace them. And right in the middle of Darlington, at that. It seemed like everyone in town was watching me fix that baler. I'm glad that I have better equipment now. Please God, it's such a beautiful day, keep my machinery from breaking and wasting this day.

This is good drying weather, and it's not supposed to rain for several days. With luck, the hay will dry nicely, and I won't have to push the equipment. Then the machinery won't break and haying won't be so bad this year. I hate it when there is pressure, and haying is OK when the pressure is off. So far, this is a great day. There's even more swallows now.

Haying really isn't bad. I wonder why I was dreading it so much? Just look at the blue sky and the warm sunshine. There are a few white, puffy clouds appearing over there. They sure are pretty.

I think I saw the grass ahead of me move in a straight line. It must be a rabbit was hiding there. They usually run ahead of the mower and stay in the unmown grass. It would be safer for them if they ran to the outside, where I have already mowed the grass, but no, they stay in the grass. I know that each time that I go around the field that the rabbit will run a little further toward the center of the unmown grass until it decides to make a break for the hedgerow at the edge of the field. Look behind the mower … there's where the rabbit had her nest and raised her family of young. That's an old nest and there were no little rabbits in it. That's because I'm mowing the hay so late this summer.

Over there is a little critter trying to run under the hay I've already mowed. It's a vole. Those things are all over the place. And there is that bird again. See, she is the one who keeps landing on twigs right in front of my mower. She's playing chicken. When I get very close, she flies off until she can get right in front of me again. She's a pretty bird, black head and gray body. I wonder what she's trying to do.

Around the field again, and there's that bird again. Maybe she has a nest nearby. It looks like she caught a grasshopper in her beak. Watching all this wildlife is making this job much more interesting. It's still a beautiful day. The sun is bright and there are fluffy clouds all over the place. The mower is working great. I'm glad for that. It's getting hot, though.

Run, little turtle, run. That's right, go in the direction of the grass I've already mowed. That way you won't get caught. You sure don't move very fast, Mr. Turtle.

There's that bird again, perched right in front of me. The swallows are still swooping and diving, but there's not as many as before. They must have each had their fill. It must be getting late. I'm doing fine, however. It may be hot, but I'm not thirsty or hungry. And the mower is still working well. It hasn't clogged up yet; must be the grass is dry enough. Just don't push it or do anything stupid, and this field will be done in no time. I've just noticed a few more clouds in the sky. It was supposed to be clear today.

There's a shadow moving across the ground. It must be the shadow from a hawk. I wonder where he is. I haven't spotted him yet.

There goes a snake. He slithered fast when he saw me coming, but he moved into the area that I haven't mowed yet. He'll have to move again the next time I come around. I don't see as many snakes as I used to. I wonder why. There's still a few swallows. I wonder how many leaf hoppers and grasshoppers they've caught. Not all of them. Some insects keep landing on me. Get off there.

Boy, it's getting hot. I'm starting to be thirsty, and maybe a little hungry. Don't do anything stupid, and the mower should keep working nicely until I finish. Don't push it, and I'll be done soon enough. I have to keep telling myself to stay careful, because I know that the more tired I get, the more likely it is that I'll do something wrong.

There's even more clouds in the sky now. Where are they coming from? I hope I can get this all mowed, dried, raked, and baled before it rains. There's only a few more times around the field before it's done.

Where have the swallows gone? Must be they ate their fills. Now, I'll have to finish the field alone. I like to have them around me. I wish I were done. Don't do anything stupid.

I'm getting close to finishing. Boy, am I hot and thirsty! Maybe I should have brought some water with me. There are a lot of clouds in the sky now, and it's becoming overcast. At least it won't be as hot without the sun beating down on me. Perhaps I ought to go a little faster, so I can finish sooner. No, that's stupid. I'll clog or break the mower, and then I'll be out here a lot longer. I wish I were finished. Just one more time around the field.

The end is near. Everything is still working; just don't do anything stupid. The sky seems to be a little less cloudy. That's good, but I don't care as long as I can finish soon. I really don't care. Just keep working, mower.

Ah, finished. Whew! I'm hot, tired, and thirsty, but I'm done. Now, I can go home and drink, and drink, and drink. I'll probably have something to eat, too, but not until I've drunk all the liquid there is in the world.

Hooray, I'm going home. Nothing broke, and I'll be fine as soon as I get a big, wet drink. Now, that wasn't so bad, was it?

THE RAM'S NEW TRICK

Art was weeding flower beds adjacent to the sheep pasture and threw the weeds over the fence into the pasture. Despite being quite far away, the sheep had seen Art do this, and wanted to get to those delectable morsels. But this was a section of the pasture on the other side of locked gates from where the sheep were, and the ram did not like that he couldn't get to those weeds, so he took his front leg, pressed it on one of the fence boards, and rocked the board back and forth, thus loosening the nails that held it in place. He would have removed the board completely if it hadn't been nailed to three posts. When Art went into the pasture with hammer and nails to secure the board, the ram objected to the undoing of his hard work. As Art turned to leave, the ram expressed his displeasure by butting Art in the back of his leg. At that time, however, the ram did not butt very hard, so Art was able to scold the ram, as he had done before, and the ram stopped his bad behavior. That time at least.

NAMING FIG TREES AFTER THOSE WHO GAVE THEM TO US

Some Italian figs plants were given to us many years ago by Benny the barber who used to work at Monte's barbershop on Pennsylvania Avenue in Bel Air. Benny brought those figs when he came many years ago from his native Italy and had them planted at his house for many years. Benny was a good man who could talk forever with his thick Italian accent to captive customers sitting in his barber chair. He gave Art some of the shoots that came from the roots, and Art kept them in 5-gallon buckets for years before he finally decided to plant them in the ground. In remembrance of the man who gave him the shoots, Art called plants derived from three different source trees Benny 1, Benny 2, and Benny 3.

Millie was a woman who attended the same church as Art did and who also lived in Bel Air. She frequently bragged to Art about the fig tree growing in her yard and the bumper fig crops yielded every year. Responding to his request, she gave him several shoots that he again planted in 5-gallon pails until planting them in the ground years later. He named these fig trees Millie, after the women who gave them to him.

Other fig trees were named Ahmed in remembrance of the pleasant man who gave some fig shoots to him. Ahmed was a businessman originally from Iran and a customer at the Farmers' Market. With the names they bear, the people who generously gave us those plants will not be forgotten.

PAPERS USED FOR MULCH

Nearly every piece of paper or cardboard that comes into our house eventually becomes mulch for our berries and flower beds. That includes newspapers, flattened cereal boxes, old catalogs, cardboard fast food containers, and letters of all kinds … if it is made of paper or cardboard, then it is collected and used as mulch on our farm.

Papers and cardboard form a nearly impenetrable layer through which weeds cannot grow. When used as mulch, a bottom layer of paper forms the foundation for an effective weed barrier. A layer of bark, chips, or leaves on top of the paper hides the unsightliness of the disordered paper layer and also traps moisture so that the papers do not blow in the wind. When we had sheep to be sheared every year, the harvested wool was also used as the top layer.

When we formed new flower beds over grass and weeds, the first thing we did was to put down a layer of papers and top them with wood chipped from our tree prunings. The papers nearly always did their job in smothering the weeds hidden beneath. Often, the only weeds that survived were the wild onions growing everywhere in our lawn. They would sometimes have enough stored energy in their little bulbs to poke through the layer of papers where the layer might have been relatively thin. But, the grass and other weeds would not be a problem.

We mostly use papers in between our raspberry rows and rows of currants. For the raspberries, in particular, their roots wander out of their designated row spaces, and raspberry shoots can appear between the rows. If not prevented from doing this, the raspberries can eventually fill the spaces between the rows and make it difficult to care for them and pick them. Different rows contain different raspberry varieties, so they could all eventually intermingle, with the likely possibility that the most aggressive variety could dominate all others. That would not be good.

We have been using papers and cardboard as mulch for many, many years. Early on, the job of placing the papers was often given to one or both of our daughters, Joy and Jodi. They were instructed to place the papers carefully, because at that time we did not subscribe to as many newspapers and we did not receive as many catalogs in the mail as we do now. So, the papers had to be spread thinly enough to cover the entire required area.

Both girls did as they were told. They went outside for their daily chores usually by 8:30 in the morning, got their boxes of papers, and started placing them down at least semi-carefully. But, it invariably happened that Jodi would finish, at the latest, by lunch time, whereas Joy was nowhere near finished. She had to return to her job after eating, and she still took hours to complete her assignment.

Why was there such a large difference in completion times? It turns out that Joy was fascinated by what she saw written on the papers. She had to read every cartoon and every article that appeared on the papers before she carefully placed them down as mulch. It did not matter that these papers had already been seen weeks or months before; to her they were new and exciting. Sometimes, the allure of the written word can happen almost anywhere, even outside under the hot summer sun.

PAUL AND ERIC COME FROM KOREA

Our daughters, Joy and Jodi, were in their mid to late teenage years, and were at the ages where they would spend most of their time alone in their rooms. The house was very quiet. We missed having lively family interactions; we were sure that we needed to add some new children to our lives. We considered adoption.

After applying for an adoption of Korean children, two young boys from a Korean orphanage were assigned to us. They came by plane and landed at Baltimore-Washington International (BWI, now known as Thurgood Marshall) airport about midnight on the 10th of November, 1984. It was an emotional experience for us all.

We were both nervous, not knowing exactly what to expect, and wondering what we were about to do. We were tired and tense. We had seen pictures of the boys that had been sent to us, and the boys had been sent pictures of us, but this was more than just pictures; this was reality about to unfold.

Paul and Eric, with their escort, were the last off the plane. There they were, two little boys with black hair cut very short, and obviously scared. They reeked of kimchi, the national food of Korea made from fermented cabbage, and that just added to the surreal mix that evening.

I took Paul in my arms, but Paul didn't know what to expect. He was scared, and he was crying. I tried to console him as best as I could, but I was not having much success.

He was a couple of weeks shy of six years old, and the escort, Korean herself, was explaining to him in Korean what was happening. She kept talking to him, and he kept listening, but was still very frightened.

Eric was only three, and was scared because Paul was scared, but wasn't as aware of his new surroundings. Cathy held him, and he was so small. He seemed to have been undernourished, and his legs were so small and bent that he could hardly walk.

Somehow, we made it through that evening. The escort taught us a few Korean words and wished us well, then talked again to the boys, and left. All of a sudden, we had two small humans in our care, without the benefit of nine months of pregnancy as preparation. All of a sudden, we had doubled the numbers of our offspring, and these little guys looked and smelled differently from our other offspring. But, they obviously needed us and we needed them, so it wasn't hard to accept them that night.

We brought them home, and tried to make them comfortable enough to sleep. Fortunately, they had each other in bed, and, as was their custom, they held each other's ears as they slept.

PAUL'S AND ERIC'S FIRST DAY

The morning after we brought our new sons Paul and Eric home from the airport was much different from the night before. While they were still in Korea, we had sent to them pictures of us, the girls, our dog Timin, and our house. They had little albums with those pictures in their hands when they awoke the next morning. Paul's face lit up when he recognized Art as "Opa", the man in the picture, and Cathy as "Oma", the woman in the picture. The dog, the house, and now everything was making sense to him, and he was excited and happy.

Art took Eric in his arms and took Paul's hand and they toured the outside. Everything was exciting, and they jabbered together spiritedly in what we thought must have been Korean. Every now and then, Paul would look up at Art and say "Opa" with a smile on his face.

When they were taken to the front orchard, there were still a few apples on the trees. Art picked one and gave it to Paul. You would have thought he had been given something extremely rare and precious by his reaction. To have fresh fruit growing all around was apparently a luxury the boys had not had in Korea. By his reaction, it had become apparent that it was wonderful and that everything was now okay.

They continued to talk to each other in Korean. The English words that they knew were few, but included "Superman", "Mickey Mouse", and "tomato ketchup". Other than that, we were pretty much on our own to try to teach them English words and to gesture when the meaning of what we were saying was not clear. Paul would point to an object and we would give the English word. He would repeat the word and teach it to Eric.

Eric had a hard time walking. It was months before his little legs were strong enough to propel him to run, and even longer before he could climb gates. He was, however, good-natured and easy with a laugh, and we couldn't imagine not having him and his brother Paul in our family. They had certainly filled our home with the lovely noise of little children talking and playing and making lots of wonderful noise.

PAUL AND ERIC: THE EARLY YEARS

It was great having sons in a house that had, up until that time, only known daughters. The girls certainly used to help with chores and duties outside, but the boys helped with a different enthusiasm. The girls used to go with Art to farm auctions, but it seemed that they mostly went because they thought it was their duty; the boys really liked going. Better, the girls would reluctantly accompany Art to the Lancaster, PA Central Tractor farm supply store, but the boys were eager to go. The boys had interests different from those of the girls, and that made those outings and experiences more fun for Art.

They made those trips to the Central Tractor store as often as Art needed some supplies for the farm, and the boys usually returned from the forays each with a small toy of some kind. Paul's toy made it home; Eric's toy was almost always in pieces by the time they reached home. Eric had a talent for taking off the wheels or otherwise disassembling his toy as soon as it was opened.

Later, when the boys grew a little bigger, they were able to help cut boards, repair machinery, or do other jobs around the farm. They were a lot of help. They could change the oil in tractors, or take apart an engine to find out what was wrong, or install a part, or help build a shed, or nail metal roofing, or be helpful in many other ways. All of this was when they were not all that old, certainly preteen. They were a big help, and Art loved the company.

Paul had a specific knack with machinery, and could usually figure out how something was supposed to work, and how to fix it if it wasn't working. Eric was good at climbing and could work in high places without fear. He helped to install the cap on metal roofing of a barn extension that we were building.

The boys used Art's tools for these jobs, and Art began to notice the absence of some tools, and others that were broken. When asked who lost a tool or broke one, the typical response from both of them was "Not me". This became so much a stock answer, that, when they once went to Central Tractor to buy a replacement tool, Art introduced the boys to the check-out clerk as "not me", and "not me Jr." She got a big kick out of that. Art knew that he would have to wait until Paul and Eric were grown and had boys of their own before he got total satisfaction for his lost or broken tools.

SHEEP ARE SOCIAL ANIMALS

Sheep are social animals, led by the females. Whenever the dominant female decides to move, as to the pasture to graze, she starts to bleat. The others answer, and they all go together. If no one follows right away, then the dominant female waits until the others are ready. If one sheep becomes separated from the rest, for some reason, she panics, making lots of noise and running around until she finds the others. So, sheep normally stay together, where they are most comfortable. The ram eventually ambles out with them. The ram is usually last in line when a herd of sheep move anywhere on their own. The only exception to this rule is when they are being fed grain or other good food.

Sheep do not like to eat tall grass; instead, they will continue to graze short forage plants that they have eaten before, even to the point of eating them to the ground. The tall grass and other weeds sometimes get so tall that the sheep cannot be seen in the pasture. Not being able to see each other disrupts the social structure of the sheep herd, because they like to know where the others are at all times. If they are not all together and cannot see the others, they must call to the others to find out where the others are. So, when they can't see each other unless they are side-by-side, they make long-distance calls. When we stand out there near the pasture, every now again we hear them calling each other like ghosts in the ether. It's funny and a little weird.

When sheep graze, they usually graze together with their heads down in the grass and they cannot see things going on in the distance. One sheep looks up often as a lookout to watch for predators and to spot other novel or tempting things in the environment. If the sentry sheep eyes something of importance, she (always a she) calls to the others, and they all come running on the double. It is hard to sneak up on sheep because the sentry sheep always alerts the others. Nonetheless, we sometimes treated it as a game to give them their grain before they were aware while they were grazing far off.

A few years ago we had a ewe which demonstrated an altruistic attitude toward the other sheep in the flock. On occasion we would put something out for them to eat and sometimes this particular ewe would be the only one who noticed us doing it. She could have come over and eaten it all, or at least had a large portion, but, instead, she would call the others before she came to eat. One time she even ran out to get the others when they were too far away to hear. We sometimes think that sheep are just dumb animals, but they surprise us on occasion.

Sometimes they lie in the pasture, and wait for us to come out of the back door of the house. When they spot us, or even when they hear the door open, one of them alerts the others with a series of "baas", and then they expect some goodies to be given to them. Even if they don't get any grain, or grapefruit peels, or apples, most of the time, they still expect something good to come their way. They are optimistic that way.

They have many human qualities. We have seen love, cooperation, care, and concern in our animals. We have also seen jealousy, hatred, meanness, and competition. We have even seen homosexual behavior, both male and female, on occasion. We are not so different, really, from the animals in our care.

Like many other animals, sheep have a pecking order, and dominance is sometimes challenged by subordinates. Whether that is the reason or not, disagreements among ewes are usually settled by two of them butting heads, and sometimes a third would butt one of the two others in the rear end. That ewe would turn to face her backside attacker, and then it seemed that there were two against one. This could go on nearly all morning sometimes. Occasionally, the ewes would each grab a quick bite of grass and then go back to the melée. Whether anything was settled or not was not clear, but all three would eventually return to the others lying near the fences.

Hot weather makes the sheep uncomfortable. Their tendency on these days is just to lie around together in the shade, usually up against a fence, if possible. If the dominant female doesn't move to graze, the others tend not to graze, either. They don't eat much during this time of the year and malnutrition can become a problem. In years past, some of them would succumb to parasites and die. We learned to give them a little grain every day just to get them up and moving. It seems to have worked; we may only occasionally lose a sheep in the summertime, but it has gotten to be a much rarer event, Nevertheless, we still hold our breath about survival of the lambs until cooler weather comes in September.

SHEEP NAMES

You may wonder if we call our sheep by individual names. The answer is "yes", and "no". When we first came to our farm in 1972, and bought our first sheep from Jerry Watson, we used to name all of our sheep. The first ewe was named "Tammy" by Jerry before we acquired her from him. The first ram was named "Rambo", also before he was ours. Over the years, we named the lambs appropriate names. The lamb that required a bath in hot water to warm him up when he was first born was named "Souper". A lamb born unexpectedly, and seemingly instantaneously, was named "Polaroid". One particularly large lamb was named "Jupiter", and the ewe that bore him was named "Jupiter's Mom". Cathy once taught as a substitute teacher at Darlington Elementary School, and several times at Dublin Elementary. On one occasion she asked her second-grade students for suggested names for a new lamb that had just been born and required to be bottle fed. The student suggested a name and misspelled the word "Girl". That is how we named that lamb "Grilnippy", a very unusual name, indeed. However, after a while we couldn't keep up this creative exercise; the ewes were relegated to identities based on ear tag numbers. The rams, on the other hand, continued to have names, for two reasons: first, several of them had been named by previous owners, and we just assumed these as we changed ownership. Second, our rams are recognized as individuals as contrasted with our relatively many ewes. Rams' names, in rough chronological order were: Rambo, Blunderbuss, Stolzfus, Roscoe, Burpee, Temporary, Virgil, Rhett Butler, Brick, Peter, and Jack. Jack was the last. No more rams, no more names.

PAUL AND ERIC TEAM UP

They made a good team: our sons, Paul and Eric. Together, they could do a lot of things. Paul was the boss, and Eric was expected (by Paul) to do a lot of the grunt work. If Eric did not do it right, then Paul hollered loudly at Eric.

Wherever they were, anybody within earshot could know their location exactly just by listening to where the shouting was coming from. And, they were loud enough that the earshot distance extended throughout the entire neighborhood.

If they were building a fence, you could tell exactly where they were just by listening for the shouting. If they were spreading manure, then you could tell where they were by listening for the shouting. If they were pruning trees, the shouting gave them away. Neighbors knew this and often remarked about it. Everyone knew it was Paul and Eric. Once, when Art was standing at the barn near the house and the boys were working in the apple orchard nearly a quarter mile away, he heard them arguing loudly and knew because of that sound that they were still doing okay.

No matter how unreasonable the demand, Paul would tell Eric to do something, and Eric would do it. As an example, Eric one time rode his bicycle from the far field to the house. But that left Paul without a ride back to the house (his had flat tires). So, he shouted to Eric to bring the bike back to him so that he could then ride it to the house. Eric did as Paul demanded, even though that meant that he was stranded out there without his own bike to ride back. Paul rode; Eric walked.

STANLEY THE YOUNG SHEEP

When Kate Umbarger (now Dallum) was a young teen active in her 4H club, she used to raise sheep and show them at the annual 4H Fair in the county. She did well, as we recall, and won her share of ribbons.

Our daughters were also in 4H at the time, and also had entries in the fair. As parents, we attended whenever our girls showed.

So it was, that one year when Kate showed a market lamb, we were looking to expand our sheep flock and bring some outside genetics into our breeding stock. Art was interested in this fine-looking sheep that Kate had brought, and was selling at the 4H market lamb sale at the conclusion of the fair.

He had the winning bid, and purchased the lamb. It was a fine-looking Suffolk ewe lamb, and, he was looking forward to adding this female lamb to his flock. Ewe lambs on our farm often bred the first year, and he would expose the lamb to the same ram that was breeding the rest of our stock.

After buying the lamb, he asked Kate if the sheep had been given a name. "Stanley", she answered. He thought that this was a curious name to give to a ewe lamb, but perhaps she had some reason to like the name. Anyway, he took the sheep home and turned it out into the pasture with the other sheep. This was late summer, and the sheep were just beginning to breed. The ram was running with the ewes at this time, and Art fully expected that the ram would be interested in this new female.

However, the ram did not pay much attention to the new ewe lamb. This actually continued throughout the fall. The ram should have paid attention to the lamb, but he showed no signs of interest. This was curious behavior.

This went on for several months. No interest by the ram in breeding the new female. Perhaps we would not get any offspring from this ewe the next spring, as we had expected.

The question of why the ram paid no attention to the lamb was a topic that occupied many of our conversations that fall and winter. We made a special effort to observe the behaviors of the ram and Stanley, but were never able to see that the ram showed any special interest. It was a curious situation; he should have had some romantic thoughts, but seemed to have none.

It wasn't until sometime in late winter that Cathy noticed Stanley standing and urinating from underneath rather than squatting and peeing from the back, as ewes do. Omigosh! Stanley was not a female; she was a male! We had been wrong about her sex for all this time. We had assumed that he was a female because he had a full coat of wool that obscured his body configuration, and we had not checked for sure what sex he was. We had just assumed that he was a she.

This revelation became quite an amusing embarrassment for us as veteran sheep producers. We did not own up to our faux pas for quite a while afterward. Now, we chuckle at our ineptitude whenever we think about this episode in our life.

SUSPICIOUS BALLOON

An amusing thing happened the other day with our sheep. A helium-filled shiny birthday balloon had come down just inside the entrance to their pasture. There are always balloons coming down somewhere on our farm, but this one landed in the sheeps' domain where they could view it with suspicion. The balloon was floating about a foot above the grass, still tethered to its attached string, and swaying in the soft breeze that we had at that time. The sheep did not know what to make of it. They all stood there, all bunched together, silently staring at the interloper in their pasture. They moved not a muscle. When Art saw this, he retrieved the balloon, but it was still a while before the sheep dared venture into their pasture to eat.

THE PARABLE OF THE LOST CONTACT LENS

There once was an old curmudgeon who lived on the land and spent his waking hours in agricultural pursuits. One day not long ago, this old curmudgeon was pulling weeds from his blueberry bushes, when an unruly branch smote him in the eye in a very untimely fashion. Out popped his contact lens, and it fell uncontrollably upon the Earth. Without his lens, he had little useful vision, so he fell upon his hands and knees to search for the errant lens. He searched here and he searched there, but it was not to be found. A pall fell upon the land and darkness descended upon his thoughts. He muttered oaths. Too soon, it became time for his noontime meal, so the old curmudgeon reluctantly abandoned the search. There was silence during the repast, as he contemplated what could be his fate. How could he recover from this terrible tragedy? He gnashed his teeth.

After partaking of the noontime sustenance, and his hope renewed like the eagle's, he journeyed back to the site of his scourge. He searched the Earth again, holding out hope that he could find the lost lens. After what seemed to be an eternity, the lens was made apparent, glistening in the afternoon sun. The old curmudgeon rejoiced, for what was once lost was now found. His vision could now be restored, and he had saved many a Denarius, equivalent to about three hundred smackeroos. And he said, let us all rejoice and be glad, for what was done has now been undone, and what was unseeable has now been seen, and what could have been gone forever has now been recovered. So, let us all celebrate, he said. I shall kill the fatted lamb and bid all people on the street to join together, and we shall revel in my good fortune. I shall shower the people with gifts, and party into the night.

And do think that is what he actually did? Of course not, he was, after all, still an old curmudgeon.

The End

THE 23RD PSALM

Sheep and shepherds are quite often mentioned in the Bible and also in sermons delivered by several of our pastors. One pastor was from the Baltimore city area, and not very knowledgeable about sheep, but he was learning. He served two churches, and, in each one, there was someone who raised sheep. Now, when he had a question or two about how sheep act, he deferred to us. For instance, the part in the 23rd psalm, where it talks about leading me beside the still waters ... sheep are very suspicious of rapid movements. They spook very easily. They prefer still water to water that moves rapidly; still water doesn't scare them the way that fast-moving water would. That is why they can be attacked by dogs. Dogs come upon sheep by running. That scares the sheep, and they run. The dogs chase them and try to bite them. What they get is a mouth full of wool pulled out from the sheep's skin. It has a little blood with it. The dogs taste or smell the blood, and then they go for the kill. We know this because we have had problems with dogs in our sheep in years past. One year we lost 22 sheep to dogs.

We like to listen to Handel's *Messiah* at the holiday time of the year, but we have noticed that George Frederick Handel did not know much about sheep. In the *All We Like Sheep Have Gone Astray* portion of the oratorio, the words go on to say "for each to his own way". Sheep, it is true, can go astray, and we suppose that applies to us as well. But sheep do not go each to his own way. They stay together. When one goes astray, they all do. We have had our sheep go astray, especially in the spring, when the grass always looks more luscious on the other side of the fence. Usually, one of the lambs will be first to find a weak spot in the fence. Then mom follows, and, after her, all the rest if they can. This used to happen a lot with our sheep, as they wandered around the neighborhood looking for the best grass to munch on. Our sheep used to know the neighbors better than we did. Having sheep that wander was a good way to start a conversation with neighbors near and far. It was also good for promoting a feeling of anxiety in the shepherds, especially early in the morning when a phone call usually meant nothing but trouble.

After we had made that observation, we were corrected in that Handel copied his Messiah words straight from the book of Isaiah, so he wasn't at fault for saying that sheep go astray each in his own way. So, either biblical sheep were different from Darlington sheep, or Isaiah himself was not familiar with sheep habits.

THE ROAD ANGEL

We probably have all had occasion to have something happen to us while driving and, if we were fortunate enough, have someone come along to give us roadside assistance and help us with our predicament. We have had several such occasions, but the one about to be related could have had dire consequences.

Our grandson, Greg, was in the truck along with Art making another trip to Modern Mushroom Farms (MMF) in Avondale, PA. There, they were to load as many used polypropylene nets as they could fit on the back of the truck. MMF uses the nets in the process to make compost for their mushroom-growing operation. The nets are at least 150 feet long and woven with polypropylene cords. Air is blown through them while the compost-to-be sits on top of them. When they begin to wear, they are removed and replaced by new nets.

Disposition of the used nets was a problem for MMF. They had sent the used nets to a local landfill, with some expense and effort, but Art had seen them and asked if he could have them for free, with the intention to use the nets as mats around orchard trees to suppress weed growth without the use of herbicides. An MMF supervisor agreed to Art's request. So, they stockpiled the nets awaiting Art's trips to load them on his truck and bring them home.

The nets were each very heavy, and it usually took a lot of effort by several people to load them. If they were wet, they were even heavier. Loading began by tugging one end of the net, and then pulling it and dragging it onto the truck bed by hand. Once on the truck, someone had to stomp them to pack them down so that more nets could fit on the truck. It also made sure that they were less likely to be caught by the wind and blown off the back of the truck on the way home. We were usually able to carry 5, 6, or 7 nets home that way.

By now, this procedure had been repeated enough times that it had become routine. Sometimes MMF people could help load the nets, but there were times when nobody was available. On those occasions, Art had to do most of the work himself. Greg, as young as he was, could help pack the nets down.

Soon after acquiring a full load of nets, we were on our way on US Rte 1 back to Darlington. Art never drove too fast on the way home because the load on the truck was considerable, and he did not want to risk a flat tire. Also, going faster meant more wind to catch the undersides of the nets and blow them off the truck. The nets were tied on as best as possible, but there was no reason to take a chance.

The highway in this part of Pennsylvania is dual lanes in each direction, divided with a grassy median strip, so he could drive in the right hand lane without causing all the fast Pennsylvania drivers to pay unwelcome attention to his slow speed.

Unfortunately, this one time, the wind caught the nets and blew several of them off the truck. They were trailing the truck for several hundred feet, and lying across both lanes of southbound US Rte 1. If there had been a lot of traffic at that time, it would have had to come to a complete standstill until the nets were removed from the highway. As it was, there were only a couple of cars, and they stopped. There was no time to lose; the nets had to be removed from the roadway.

This particular incident happened in the early 1990's, when Greg was only a few years old, so he was going to be of little help. He was told to stay in the truck, especially because removing the nets from the roadway would require someone actually standing in the middle of the road to move the nets.

Art pulled the truck onto the shoulder of the median strip and then got out and started pulling the nets onto the median. Fortunately, there wasn't too much net blocking the right hand lane, and with considerable effort energized by a dose of adrenaline, he was able to open up one lane of the road within a minute or two. The time seemed to be a lot longer than that, but it could not have been too long because the drivers of the stopped cars were not visibly upset as they passed on the right hand lane.

It would take a lot more effort to pull the nets from the left lane to the median, and Art was beginning to prepare to drag the nets the rest of the way off the road. But, it was going to be a really big problem. Also, how was he going to be able to load them back on the truck? That was more than he could handle at that point.

Just then, a roadway angel appeared in the form of a driver of a truck loaded with panes of glass. He was driving on the other side of the divided highway, going in the opposite direction, but had noticed Art's huge predicament. He stopped. First, he helped drag the nets off the roadway. Then he helped load the nets back on Art's truck, and gave Art some of the ropes that he was carrying on his truck so that Art could tie the nets down better than before.

He didn't have to stop, and he didn't have to pull and tug those nets back off the road and on the truck, but he did both of those things. And then, he helped to tie the nets down. When all this was done, he hopped back into his truck, and continued on his way. Art never got his name, but he remembers him and his good deed with gratitude to this day.

What could have been reported as a traffic incident where southbound US Rte 1 was shut down for a long time, involving Pennsylvania State Police, upset drivers, court appearances, and who knows what else, had turned into a minor incident remembered only by the very few who were involved. But, that other truck driver came along at just the right time. He was truly an angel.

THE TWELVE DAYS OF CHRISTMAS, REVISITED

Years ago in the middle of the town of Darlington, there were several peacocks owned by two families, one on Main Street and one on Shuresville Road. Peacocks are noteworthy not only for their colorful iridescent blue plumage, but also for their calls. To hear a peacock call is like hearing someone yell "Help!" at the top of their lungs. "Help!", "Help!" They certainly were loud and they certainly attracted attention. When new visitors to Darlington would hear these peacocks for the first time, they didn't know what to think, but they were sure that there was trouble brewing.

The peacocks were also prone to wandering around the small town and sometimes even walking in the middle of the street. Peacocks are big birds, so they can't be missed when they are strolling down the road, and they are big enough to cause damage to a vehicle when hit. They didn't get hit, however, because drivers who knew enough to look out for them slowed or stopped to avoid that unpleasantness. Imagine having to go to someone's house, knock on the door, and inform the occupant that his or her peacock had just been run over. How much are peacocks worth, anyway? And also imagine filling out the car insurance forms, and in the space provided for a description of the accident, jotting "Hit a peacock in broad daylight." No, that is something no one wanted to have to do.

These peacocks would fly up into trees at night and roost there until the crack of dawn. When the first peacock awoke, he would let out a loud, blood-curdling "Help!" to start the day. That woke the others, and they returned the greeting "Help!". It also woke every human within earshot, which is to say everyone in town.

It was the tradition in Darlington for a Christmas caroling group to form, walking up one side of the town and down the other, looking in windows to see if anyone was inside, then knocking on doors, and singing several carols to the household. We had quite a repertoire, being able to sing twenty or thirty Christmas songs, some even with two verses. Of course, we didn't sing all of them at each house, but usually sang a carol or two of our choosing to start the impromptu concert and then asking the house occupant if they had a favorite Christmas song that they would like to have us murder. Sometimes we proceeded to do just that, but most times it was lovely, even if we had to say so ourselves.

One of those years, we made our way to Chuck and Debbie Gradys' house on the corner of Main Street and Shuresville Road. Among the songs that we started to sing was the Twelve Days of Christmas. You know that The Twelve Days of Christmas is a long song to sing, and it is very redundant. By the time we would have gotten to twelve drummers drumming, we would have been over quite a few verses. But, we didn't get that far. Just above our heads, in the evergreen tree in Gradys' yard was perched one of the remaining peacocks in town. And, our singing must have awakened it somewhat. It stirred. Now, when a large peacock stirs, everyone knows about it. Some of the singers quickly moved out from under that tree. Others looked up and saw what it was, recognizing the darkened shape of a peacock. Nearly instantly, the first verse of The Twelve Days of Christmas was changed from "A partridge in a pear tree" to "A peacock in a pine tree". And we have sung it that way ever since.

LINZERTORTE

Whenever Cathy is asked to make a special Christmas dessert, she makes a Linzertorte, which not only looks pretty, but also is very rich and delicious.

Ingredients:

1-½ cups all-purpose flour
⅛ teaspoon ground cloves
¼ teaspoon cinnamon
1 cup finely ground unblanched almonds
½ cup sugar
1 teaspoon grated lemon peel
2 hard-cooked egg yolks, mashed
1 cup butter (2 quarter-pound sticks), softened
1 teaspoon vanilla extract
1-½ cups thick raspberry jam
1 egg, lightly beaten
2 tablespoons light cream
Confectioners' sugar

Sift the flour, cloves, and cinnamon together into a deep mixing bowl, then add the almonds, sugar, lemon peel, and mashed egg yolks. With a wooden spoon, beat in the butter, raw egg yolks, and vanilla extract. Continue to beat until the mixture is smooth and doughy. Form the dough into a ball, wrap it in wax paper or plastic wrap and refrigerate it for at least 1 hour, or until it is firm.

Remove about three-fourths of the dough and return the rest to the refrigerator.

With a paper towel or pastry brush, lightly butter a round 9×1 or 9×1-½ inch false-bottomed cake pan. Add the dough (if it is too firm, let it soften a bit) and, with your fingers, press and push it out so that it covers the bottom and sides of the pan, making a shell about ¼ inch thick. Spoon in the raspberry jam, and spread it evenly over the bottom of the shell with a spatula. On a floured surface with a floured rolling pin, roll out the rest of the dough into a 6×9 inch rectangle ¼ inch thick.

With a pastry cutter, or sharp knife, cut the dough into strips ½ inch wide, two of them 9 inches long, and the rest 8 inches long. Lay one of the 9 inch strips across the center of the jam and flank that strip on each side with one of the 8-inch strips placed halfway between the center and sides of the pan. Rotate the pan about one-quarter of the way to your left and repeat the pattern with the other three strips, so that they create Xs with the first three in a lattice-like effect.

Run a sharp knife around the top of the pan to loosen the part of the bottom dough that extends above the strips Press this down with your fingers into a border about ¼ inch thick. Lightly beat the whole egg with the cream and, with a pastry brush, coat all the exposed pastry. Re-refrigerate for one half hour. Meanwhile, preheat the oven to 350°F.

Bake the torte in the middle of the oven for 45 to 50 minutes, or until it is lightly browned. Set the pan on a large jar or coffee can and slip down the outside rim. Let the torte cool for 5 minutes on the bottom of the pan, then sprinkle it with confectioners' sugar. Cool to room temperature before serving.

ARTHUR T. JOHNSON

USE FOR WOOL

Shearing sheep is not an easy job. The sheep being sheared doesn't want to be there, and the shearer doesn't either. Given that both parties would rather be doing something else anywhere but where the shearing is taking place, it's never going to be a pleasant experience. When we shear sheep, we have to do it in a small pen with gates closed so that, if the sheep manages to wriggle out of the grasp of the shearer, there is nowhere else for it to go. And wriggle it does. The shearer, in this case Art, has to control the sheep as best he can, bend over more than he would like, and try to use the sharp electric shears carefully so as to cut only the wool and not the sheep's skin. If the sheep is old and has wrinkled skin, then it takes extra care not to run right down a wrinkle and remove it by cutting it off. So, the head of the shears must be kept at a certain angle or else blood oozes all over the place. If a cut is made, then it must be sprayed with BluCote disinfectant to help it heal and protect it against the flies that take every opportunity to lay their eggs where they will hatch and hungrily consume sheep flesh.

Once the wool is off the sheep, then we must deal with it. If the wool is to be sold as fleeces, then they must be kept clean and wrapped a certain way to allow potential buyers to assess whether the fleeces meet their standards. The price of wool used to be good enough to make it worthwhile to sell it at the Maryland wool pool, a central location where many small producers bring their fleeces to be seen by buyers. In the 1980s, however, the price of wool plummeted, and we began storing the wool.

Until you've had to store wool, you probably would not realize that wool makes a great home for mice or, especially, bumblebees. It's not wise to try to move stored wool in the summer because of the possibility of being stung by bumblebees. So, there had to be a better use.

Wool is made of protein, an organic form of nitrogen, and nitrogen is needed for all plants to grow and thrive. Wool can decompose to supply nitrogen for our plants. Wool, in its raw form, can also provide a thick layer on the soil to retain moisture and smother weeds. We soon decided to use the wool as mulch in our strawberry patch, and, later, between the rows of raspberries. This is an excellent use for wool, which has some additional side benefits: first, long-stranded wool is preferred by buyers who use it to weave clothing; wool used as mulch can have short strands that result from second and third cuts when the sheep is being sheared. Second, buyers prefer clean wool, free of manure, weed seeds, and other organic matter (such as skin or blood); the horticultural nutritional value of wool used as mulch actually benefits from foreign matter. So, mulch is the perfect use for our wool.

DEER EVER SO CLOSE

We've had close encounters of the deer kind. One Friday afternoon in the late summer, as Cathy was in the shed packaging the berries we had picked earlier for the Farmers' Market the next day, she looked out to see one of the fawns that we have been seeing and its mother in one of the flower beds in front of the our house. Cathy walked outside, and explained quietly to both of them that they were not authorized to stay there. The mother must have believed her, because she immediately jumped over the fence into the adjacent pasture. The fawn must not have understood her admonition, because it started walking toward her, and got within about fifteen feet of her before it stopped, thought better of what it was doing, turned, and walked calmly through the open gate into the pasture to join his or her mom. Our deer are pretty and not usually a problem unless they start eating the plants that we really care about.

Then Tuesday evening the two fawns were back in the pasture near the house, eating merrily away. Actually, we couldn't tell exactly whether it was merrily or not, but they didn't seem to be bothered by our presence.

Wednesday evening, Art was mowing in the apple orchard and chased a couple of deer, a young buck and a doe, out of the orchard. He had some trouble with the mower, and walked back to get another tractor. As he did so, the deer pair ran from him in the peach orchard. Then, later, as he was bringing the second tractor back, the deer were over a couple of rows, warily watching what he was doing. The deer probably think the farm belongs to them when we are not there to claim it.

EUROPEAN FRUIT HORNETS

European Fruit Hornets (EFHs) are our nemeses in the apple orchard. They are several inches long, and look like yellow jackets on steroids. They love tree fruits, especially apples and pears, but they have been known to molest peaches, persimmons, and plums, too.

When the fruits are ripe enough for us to pick, the EFHs usually get there first. They chew through the skin and hollow out the inside pulp. An apple that has been eaten by a EFH can appear to be perfectly fine, but it collapses in the hand when picked. And, if a EFH happens to be in the fruit when a hand is put on it, watch out! They have a very powerful sting. Put your hand on an apple in the wrong way and you quickly find out how painful their stings can be.

EFHs are also aggressive. When there are several going after the fruits on a tree, then they will fly close and threaten the human picker. Occasionally, they sting even unprovoked. This can be frightful, especially when the picker is several rungs up on a ladder.

We have tried trapping these insects all summer to reduce their numbers, but have not eliminated them. For each one we trap, several more emerge from their in-ground nests. So it is that, as the number of apples remaining on the trees diminishes, the concentration of EFHs increases. We are very likely to run into an EFH when picking the last remaining apples. Luckily, cooler temperatures slow them and make them somewhat lethargic, so it is easier when temperatures are cool to kill them with our organic flying insect spray. However, they still damage a lot of apples, and these are the apples that Farmers' Market customers do not see because we do not bring them to the market. The sheep are given them to eat.

DID IT TASTE AS GOOD AS STEW?

Our dog, Ouija (pronounced "Weejee") was at the time in need of a little TLC, and was lying in our back room, not feeling well. Instead of the dry dog food that we normally fed to her, we had bought several cans of nutritious canned dog food to ease her condition and help her return to health. She waited patiently each day for her once-a-day treat that would come at the prescribed hour.

Growing young boys, especially ones who work hard on a farm, are known for their appetites. They always seem to be hungry, and will devour any food placed in front of them with little, if anything, left over. That is, all except Paul. He did not like string beans or Brussels sprouts. He could not stand to eat either one without complaining. We required him to eat anything that was served, at least a spoonful, so his remedy was to slather anything he didn't particularly care for with a generous helping of salsa from a jar. So, we always kept a jar of salsa in our refrigerator.

The boys were particularly fond of Dinty Moore beef stew, and cans of it were piled high in our pantry. That stew was easy to heat: all that was required was to open the can, place it in a pan, heat it on the stove, and it was ready to eat in no time. And, there was no need for salsa, which was good, because the stew was gobbled up faster than the time the trip to the refrigerator would take.

Each week Cathy went grocery shopping to renew our supply of Dinty Moore beef stew. And, each week the pile of cans rapidly disappeared, as if by some huge swarm of stew-loving locusts.

For whatever reason, Paul did not look closely at the can of stew that he grabbed for lunch that day. He was hungry, and the only thing standing between him and a nice bowl of hot beef stew was the time it would take to open the can and heat its contents. He worked as fast as he could. Soon, the bowl of warm stew was in front of him and he eagerly dove into it with his full appetite driving him toward the first, luscious spoonful.

Into his mouth went the first full portion, and his demeanor changed rapidly from eager anticipation to horror. This wasn't stew; it was dog food, meant for Ouija. He spit out the part of the mouthful that he had not yet swallowed, and began complaining loudly to anyone within earshot. He tried rinsing the taste from his mouth with glasses of water, but the taste of that dog food lingered, and the memory remained much longer. He had learned an important lesson: he would never again grab a can of Dinty Moore beef stew without checking it first to confirm that its contents were fit for a human boy to consume.

And Ouija, having smelled the dog food as it heated on the stove, wondered disappointedly why she wasn't getting any.

THE MIRACLE EAR VAN

This is a tale that many people probably can relate to. It involves a van that passed quite often along the road in front of our farm. The driver of the van liked his music loud. It didn't seem to matter whether it was winter or summer, with the windows open or closed. We never heard whatever melody that was playing, but we always heard the bass beat. The driver sure did like his bass loud: BOOM…BOOM…BOOM…BOOM…

And, it didn't matter where on our farm that we were working when the van passed by; whether we were near the road or far from it, we could hear the BOOM, BOOM, BOOM wherever we were.

The boys labeled that vehicle the Miracle Ear Van, prompted by the hearing aid ads that were on television and radio at the time. We all agreed that the driver of the Miracle Ear Van, if he wasn't already, would soon be a candidate for a hearing aid all of his own.

When we heard it, we would stop whatever we were doing and remark to anyone around us that the Miracle Ear Van was going by. If we had no one around us, then we said it aloud to ourselves. It was that noticeable.

The Miracle Ear Van has, for years now, stopped using our road, or, at the very least, blown out his woofers.

CHECKMATE, OR LAST MAN STANDING?

When asked why he wanted to adopt two boys from Korea, Art explained that he wanted to have someone with which to play the game of croquet. At the time that we were considering adoption, the girls had grown into their teenage years, and they spent most of their free time alone in their rooms. Dad was largely ignored; he loved playing indoor and outdoor games with the girls when they were younger, but that had largely come to an end when they grew older. Having some young children around would liven up the household.

We wanted to adopt two children at the time because we thought that they could then each have a peer to help them grow in our household. Joy and Jodi were close enough in age that they related very well with each other; they sometimes fought over things, but usually got along quite well. We thought that two more children would be better than one.

We did not know at the outset whether we would get boys or girls from Korea. We thought it more likely that two girls would be assigned to us, because we had heard that girls were more likely than boys to be placed in orphanages. So, we were pleasantly surprised when it was made known to us that our new children would be boys.

After Paul and Eric arrived here, we became aware that little boys are, indeed, different from little girls. Their interests were different, for instance. When Art had gone to the Central Tractor store with the girls, they had gone, it seemed, just to go out with their dad; the boys relished going to Central Tractor, and to hardware stores, and to any store that their new Dad really liked to frequent. The boys were really interested.

There were other differences as well. The boys were much more competitive than the girls. Jodi had some competitiveness in her nature, but the boys had much more. They did not like to lose — anything (except, of course, Art's tools, but that's another story).

Paul and Eric loved to play games, be they physical sports games, such as basketball or lacrosse, board games, such as checkers, chess, or Sorry, or card games, such as King's Reverse (which will be explained later). They would play between the two of them, and shout at each other when they thought the other had cheated or disobeyed the rules. Paul loved to beat Eric, and often did, but he loved even more to beat his Dad. It was his passion to beat his Dad.

Art taught both of them the rules of chess, and they loved the game. They studied the game, and soon were more than a match for Art. Either of them could beat him at chess on most evenings when they sat down to play. They may have played round-robin sometimes, but, most often, they played so that the winner kept playing until he lost, and then the new winner played as many games as he could win.

Art tried to explain to them his first rule of playing games: that is, that he was always to win, at whatever game they chose to play that session. You see, Art had a competitive streak, also.

The boys would have no part of the first rule. They completely ignored it, and tried as hard as they could to beat Dad at the game being played. They were not going to concede anything to their Dad. "Something had to be done", thought Art. So, he declared that the winner of the last game played that evening would be the champion for that day, and would remain the champion until they played more games the next time. It didn't matter who had won the most games that night; the champion was crowned with the last victory.

The boys did not like that designation. They accepted the fact that their Dad could call the winner of the last game the champion; they could not dispute what he chose to call the winner, but they could dispute whether the last winner was, indeed, the champion. They protested loudly, because it was often that one or the other of the boys would have won everything but the last game; it was unfair to call the winner of the last game the champion, especially if the last winner was Dad.

Art, being the competitive guy that he was, would often keep the boys playing their games until he won, and then he would declare himself the champion and go to bed. This sometimes reached extremes. Sometimes he would keep playing long after the boys' bedtimes, until he could win at the last game of the evening. It was almost entirely voluntary on their parts that they stayed up late playing games, but they were so competitive that they would automatically accept the challenge of another game with their father, no matter how late it got to be. It got to the point that sometimes Art's opponent or opponents would purposely lose just so that they could go to sleep that evening, especially if they were really tired. This didn't happen too often, however, because the boys hated to have Dad call himself the champion, especially if they both had proven game-playing prowess superior to his.

To this day, Paul still hates to be reminded that Art had shot as many foul baskets as Paul had at the last time they competed with a basketball. Paul clearly had better basketball skills on all other occasions.

But, it didn't end there. We had another little boy in the house for several years, and then on weekends for many more: grandson Gregory. Greg wasn't much of a chess or checkers player; he liked to play the board game, Sorry, and he loved to play the card game, King's Reverse.

King's Reverse has the same rules as Uno, but it was played with a regular deck of cards. The important rules are these:

1. The person with the highest score loses the game.
2. Scores were based on counts of card values in the hands of those who still had cards when one person discarded all of his cards.
3. Cards were discarded on a central pile to match either the numeric value or the suit of the previously discarded card.
4. If one player could not discard during his turn, he had to pick another card from the deck, and either play or pass. If he could not play, then he added that card to the number of cards in his hand.
5. There were wild cards that could be played at any time, such as Jacks, and Jokers. When these were played, the person playing them could name the suit of the next card to be played.
6. There were penalty cards: playing an 8 would skip the turn of the next player, a 2 caused the next player to have to draw two cards and add them to his hand, and a Joker meant that the next person had to pick up five extra cards and skip a turn.
7. A King would reverse the direction of play.

Gregory soon invented cutthroat King's Reverse. He would save all his wild and penalty cards until the end of the game, when all he had in his hand were cards that he was able play one after the other and keep his opponent from discarding any cards. Instead, his opponent had to keep adding cards to his hand and increasing his score when Greg threw down his last card.

Greg and his Grandfather would often play King's Reverse one-on-one on Saturday afternoons after returning from the Farmers' Market and Cathy was still working at the Darlington Library. He loved to trounce Art at these games, and Art seethed whenever it happened. After a while, Art had to retaliate by playing cutthroat King's Reverse against Greg. It had to happen. But Greg probably did not take his losses as personally as Art did. At least he could sleep well later that night. He did not seem to be bothered by conscience over transforming a perfectly fun card game into a test of one's vocabulary.

LEFTOVERS? THERE AREN'T ANY

Cathy has been an excellent cook all her like. She learned early as a young girl from her mother, who was also an excellent cook. Cathy is not an adventurous cook, she doesn't experiment with food, spices, or herbs, but she certainly knows her way around a good recipe, and everything she makes is particularly appetizing.

She used to cook supper meals nearly every day. Even when she worked at the Darlington Library, she had a break in her work hours between afternoon and evening, and she would come home and prepare a good meal for our little family at the time.

When our family consisted of Cathy, Art and two daughters, there may have been some leftover food in the refrigerator. But it did not last too long because Art was used to working hard physically when he was home, and he was hungry enough to finish whatever food was left from the day before. He was used to eating a lot of food for his meals at that time; the girls did not eat all that much. Only when Cathy prepared a huge amount of food, such as for holidays like Thanksgiving and Christmas was there food that was not eaten right away.

Everything changed when we had three growing boys in the house, all leftover food was quickly eaten, and no extra food was ever present for long in our refrigerator unless it was hidden behind something larger in the front of the shelf. Even then, hungry boys would sometimes ransack our refrigerator looking for something, anything, to eat.

Cathy cooked and canned a lot in those days. Both Cathy and Art had come from families used to raising a lot of their own food and preserving it for later consumption. Cathy canned tomatoes, peaches, pickles, sauerkraut, jellies, and other foods all made at home. Our pantry shelves were stocked tightly with jars of food. Wherever we had room, we had stacks of boxes upon boxes of canning jars all full of preserved goodies. Our freezers (yes, we had more than one) were packed to the top with frozen vegetables and meat that we grew ourselves. All this preserved food was consumed when fresh produce was not available at home.

Now that Cathy and Art are the only two at home, there is hardly any more canning done. Cathy cooks a lot less; she cooks only on Sundays and special occasions. Greg usually comes over for Sunday dinner, and he still loves his grandmother's food. He can eat more than Art and Cathy together. However, Cathy is still used to cooking enough food at a time to feed a large family, so even Greg cannot eat it all. That makes Monday leftover day for Art, who looks forward to his lunchtime meal of food previewed the day before.

Since Cathy lost her sense of smell after her accident in 2009, she cannot appreciate the wonderful aromas that come from the meals that she prepares. That might make it less appealing for her to eat food left over from her Sunday or holiday endeavors. That leaves more good stuff for Art to eat.

PHILOSOPHIES FROM THE FIELD

During the many hours that we spend working on our farm, it is only natural that our minds wander. We have come up with some life lessons based on things that happen on our farm:

1. A garden without weeds is unnatural. Likewise, a life without problems cannot be expected.
2. There is always another weed. Despite our best efforts, ridding the garden of all weeds is nearly impossible. Likewise, we can always expect something to spoil our otherwise smooth and comfortable life.
3. Weeds sometimes hide among the plants you want to grow. Weeds are crafty that way. Likewise, there may be problems with each opportunity you encounter. Things are never quite as good as they seem on first glance. Nor are they as bad.
4. Where there is one thistle, there will be others. Thistles grow in clusters. Sometimes there is one person or situation causing a lot of trouble; look beyond that person or situation to be sure there are not others quietly supporting the troublemaker.
5. Prune trees in the winter, when they appear to be dead. What one does in the bad or hard times sets one up to prosper during the good times.

SOMETHING TO REMEMBER US BY

SweetAire Farm was formed from three pieces of property. The third piece was bought in late March of 1987, and it was immediately adjacent to the original five-acre homestead where we had lived and farmed for 15 years. One of the reasons that we had bought the new piece of property is that we were running out of room to realize our dreams. We had almost no place to plant another tree, and there were plenty more that we really wanted to grow. Our cows, too, needed more room to graze; the pastures behind the house had gotten to be too small as we expanded our small herd. We needed more room for cows and trees.

So it was that within weeks of our land purchase we planned a work party to build a fence to enclose several acres for a new cow pasture. The plan was to build the fence in one day, if possible, and that would require extra help. So, we invited friends and family to help us. Jim Caldwell could come for a few hours and bring his chain saw to cut trees; Jerry Watson could come and bring his tractor and brush mower to clear the fence line. Art's brother and Sister-in-Law, Don and Renee, would come south from their home in upstate New York to see if a whole pasture fence could really be constructed in one day. This many people would be enough help to do the job; they were all used to hard work.

The early spring Saturday that was scheduled dawned warm and clear. This was a good omen for a successful day and outcome. All went well that day, everybody worked together like parts of a well-oiled machine Jim cut locust trees on the property for fence posts. Locust posts would last for many years insofar as they were old wood and large enough. Jerry coaxed his old tractor to keep running and mowed the fence line. Art had bought a tractor PTO-driven auger just for this occasion, and he used it to drill holes in the ground to install the newly-cut fence posts. If a rock became an obstacle for the auger, then the post location could be moved slightly, or, in a pinch, there was always the clamshell digger and pry bar to be used to dig a hole by hand. It was up to Don and Renee to drive the posts from where they were cut to the open holes, and assist by holding the post while it was being tamped into the ground.

Many of these posts were big and heavy. Because they were newly cut, they had green wood, meaning not seasoned. The process of seasoning dries the wood and the lost weight of water can be considerable. However, these were still wet when they were to be used, and heavy enough that they sometimes had to be hugged to move them from place to place, and while they were being installed. This was hard work, and it was soon warm enough to strip down to light clothing with short sleeves as they manhandled the heavy posts.

It was still early spring, and there were no leaves on the trees when they were cut. And, nobody noticed the vines growing on the trees and still clinging when the trees were cut into the proper lengths. Nobody paid any attention to the vines as the posts were being held steady while being installed. Nobody noticed the juices that emanated from the vines and permeated the clothes worn by Don and Renee. Nobody noticed, however, until Don and Renee arrived back home the next day. It was then that they realized that they each been exposed to massive amounts of juices from poison ivy.

Over the course of the next week or two, they itched and scratched, itched and scratched, many times over, day and night, night and day. There wasn't enough calamine lotion in this world to satisfy their needs. They remember that day and they remember what happened to them afterward. They still remember and they remind us every so often about the worst cases of poison ivy that they had ever had. And, they have not ever since volunteered to help us put in another fence.

Incidentally, we did manage to finish the fence that day, including installing wire on the fence later in the afternoon. So, building a whole pasture fence in one day can be done, but it can come with some surprise outcomes.

WHEN WE RAISED OUR OWN TURKEYS

For many years while our boys were young, we raised our own turkeys for Thanksgiving, Christmas, and other occasions during the year. At first we tried breeding our own turkeys, keeping a tom or two and several hens, but they didn't cooperate so well, never hatching any young ones, and the upkeep on adult turkeys was a considerable expense. Besides, toms can be formidable foes on days when they disagreed with us, which were most days. So, we gave up that attempt. We don't exactly remember how they were dispatched, but it may just be that they contributed to the nutritional needs of the many foxes that we had in the neighborhood.

Consequently, every spring we ordered turkey poults from a hatchery in Pennsylvania and raised them until they were grown. They were sent to us through the mail, which, along with the 3-pound packages of honeybees that passed annually through the post office on their way to our farm, soon conferred on us a reputation of sorts. We were known as THOSE people. In a small town like Darlington, everyone knew what that meant.

The minimum number of young turkeys to order was usually 25, which was a lot more turkeys than we could eat in a year. And maybe a lot longer than that. So, we would feed and water them all for several weeks, or until they were past their most critical young lives and starting to grow their first set of feathers. If the young turkeys survived these first few weeks, then they had a very good chance to live to adulthood. After that, we sold about 15-20 of the juveniles to other people also interested in raising a few turkeys for themselves.

We put ads in the *Aegis* newspaper, offering started turkey poults for sale, and sold them without difficulty. Other people were glad not to have to order 25 young turkeys at a time, especially if there was a chance that they could die in the first couple of weeks. The income from these sales paid all of our expenses up to that point, so it worked out for us, too.

Raising young turkeys is not too difficult. They require heat, supplied by a 60-Watt light bulb shining on the cardboard box in which we kept them at this stage, food in the form of turkey and game bird feed that we bought at the Southern States Farm Store, and a shallow container of water. For this, we usually started out with a jar lid full of water in which a colorful marble was placed to draw the attention of the young birds; they would naturally peck at the marble and find out that there was almost-transparent water to drink. If we hadn't used the marble, they might not have recognized the presence of water.

This went on until they started to develop their real feathers to replace the silky fuzz that they were born with. When that happened, they would start to escape the box by flying over the sides. It was time to move them outside.

We raised the turkeys in portable cages that were moved to new grass every day. The cages protected the young turkeys from predators and gave them a chance to eat fresh grass and insects on a daily basis. That made happy, healthy, and good-tasting turkeys. They left behind manure that fertilized the area that they had just left. Our boys had the job of moving the cages, and providing fresh feed and water each day. It wasn't too hard to do this job, but our eldest son, Paul, had a squeamish stomach, perhaps stimulated by the manure, which caused him to throw up almost immediately after moving the cage. Whatever the cause, the routine was to move cage, vomit, move cage, vomit, etc. We could count on it.

The turkeys grew healthy and large. One grew to be a 50-pound monster when dressed. He tasted great, but cooking him took almost all day. After that we tried to harvest them earlier when they weren't so big.

For several years, we killed and dressed the turkeys by ourselves. Art played the role of hatchetman and chief plucker and cleaner. Holding a large turkey while it is being dispatched is not easy; they are very powerful and can easily and often escape the grasp of the person holding them. They have strong wings that can bruise the person holding them when they beat reflexively, even without an attached head. After a while, Art wised up, and cut the corner out of a 100-pound feed bag. The turkey was placed into the bag with the head and neck sticking out of the hole in the bag. It was a lot easier to hold the turkey when the bag limited the movement of the strong flapping wings.

We discovered a business in Galena, in Cecil County, that killed, dressed, and wrapped chickens, ducks, and waterfowl shot by hunters. They had all the equipment and trained personnel to handle birds as large as our turkeys without any problem. We soon decided that bringing our turkeys the 60 miles or so to this place was well worth the fee that they charged. So, we would bring over our turkeys and bring back ready-to-cook birds.

Transporting 5-10 turkeys in a car trunk can also be an adventure. Although we finally found a cage large enough to accommodate several turkeys at a time, convincing the birds to climb into the cage was not easy. The stubborn turkeys had to be convinced to get into the cages, and, as we said, they were large and strong, and resisted as best as they could.

This continued for years until we had no more time to spend with them and no more sons to move the cages, whatever the process entailed. We sometimes miss those turkeys; they tasted better than the ones we have bought from the store since then, and they were always tender. We reminisce about the days when we used to raise our own. Those were good turkeys, and those were good times.

HAIL, BOYS, HAIL

One summer Saturday when sons Paul and Eric were almost grown, they and Art were all out in the back apple orchard doing some work. The weather was warm and sunny, so they were just humming along, working on the trees. At lunchtime, they came in to eat. When they were finished, they would go back to finish their jobs. As usual, Art was the first back into the orchard. Paul and Eric dilly-dallied for a short while longer before they started out.

While they were eating lunch, the weather began to change. Thunderstorms were predicted for early afternoon as a weather front approached the area. The sky soon looked dark and threatening off in the west, and Art shouted to the boys on his way out, suggesting that they might want to hurry out, finish their jobs, pick up their tools, and bring the tractor and trailer back in before it stormed. But they didn't hurry.

Art walked out to the orchard, finished what he was working on, picked up his tools, and began walking back to the machinery shed. The sky was becoming more and more ominous as big black clouds continued to roll in. The boys were just heading out.

Art reached the machinery shed just as the storm hit. Wind, rain, and hail. The boys were still in the orchard, and he expected them to gather their tools and take shelter beneath the trailer. By now the hail was coming down heavily. Hail hitting the metal roof of the shed where Art had sought shelter raised a deafening din.

Art could not see more than 75 feet away in the hail, so he did not know what was happening to the boys. He was confident that they would be alright as long as they were together; they, in their young lives, certainly had already come through more threatening circumstances than this with nothing more than each other to lean on. But, this might be different. Hail storms are not that usual at SweetAire Farm, and Art had not seen hail falling as heavily as this, ever. Already an inch or two of hailstones had accumulated on the ground.

He faintly heard the tractor before he could see it. The throttle was wide open, but he was sure that it still wasn't going fast enough for the boys. As he stood at the edge of the machinery shed, he stared into the fog-like veil of the hailstorm, wondering why the boys had stayed out in the hail. He still couldn't see them, but the tractor noise was getting louder as it came toward him; it began to be loud enough to compete well with the din of the hail hitting the metal roofing over his head.

It seemed like a long time. All of a sudden, he began to make out the orange color of the Allis-Chalmers tractor as it broke into view. And, as it came closer, he could recognize Paul driving the tractor, steering with one hand and holding his other arm over his head for protection. Eric was standing on the trailer, with both arms over his head.

It was a relief to see them, but it was also an extremely funny sight to see them try to avoid the stinging hail. When they finally got to where Art was standing, Art asked them why they hadn't just crawled beneath the trailer for protection. It was not one of their personal options. As they all stood there in the machinery shed watching another couple of inches of hail accumulation, they all had a good laugh over the incident, and decided that they didn't want that to happen again.

PAUL AND ERIC TEASE THE RAM

Paul and Eric grew into confident teenagers who were not afraid of Rhett Butler, our ram at the time. They took every opportunity to provoke the ram, and he took every opportunity to respond. The boys would purposefully walk or run in the pasture in sight of the ram so that he would try to challenge them. When they were spotted, the ram would run after them and they would run as fast as they could away from him. They saw this as a game to be played to demonstrate their daring. It was fun to watch one or both of them run across the pasture, followed closely by the ram running as fast as he could. The ram never seemed to catch either boy, but it wasn't because he didn't try.

When they were old enough, both played lacrosse. During their leisure times, they would practice for hours throwing and catching the ball with their lacrosse sticks. Sometimes they practiced on the lawn, but they often took their sticks into the pasture. That added an extra bit of excitement to their practice, because Rhett Butler was there.

They would typically each stand near the wooden fences on opposite sides of the pasture and throw the lacrosse ball from one of them to the other. The challenge for them was to run to catch the ball, and run back to the safety of the fence as fast as possible, where they could perch out of harm's way, and then return the ball to the other boy. Rhett Butler would be drawn to the boy who was away from the fence to catch the ball. He would run as fast as he could to try to intercept the boy before he was out of reach. So, what happened was that the boys would fling the ball back and forth, and draw Rhett Butler back and forth to follow the ball.

Back and forth, back and forth, Rhett Butler ran himself silly. The boys loved to tease the ram in this way, and get in some practice time as well. It was never observed whether either boy intentionally sent the ball flying away from where the other boy was safely located just to see the ram chase that boy around the field. But, that would have been tempting for almost anybody.

SOOTY BLOTCH ON APPLES

Art was asked an interesting question by a customer one Saturday. The question was, "Are the apples with the dark green markings on their skins less healthy because of the surface fungus that they have?" We have never seen any research on this particular topic, but we do have an educated guess as to the answer.

The surface markings appearing like dark green patches are called "sooty blotch", and the little green dots are called and "flyspeck". They are fungi that live all summer on the wineberries that grow wild in hedgerows and along the edges of wooded areas. Many people have eaten the tasty, raspberry-like wineberry fruits in mid-summer. In late summer, these fungi jump to the surfaces of apples and, sometimes, pears. This causes unsightly spots on the surfaces of the fruits. Conventional growers must apply a lot of chemicals to avoid having these fungi grow on apple skins, and, even so, an extended wet period may sometimes result in a little sooty blotch or flyspeck even on their apples. Sooty blotch and flyspeck can make conventionally-grown apples cosmetically unsightly and unsellable.

Sooty blotch and flyspeck only grow on the surface of the fruit, and do not affect its flavor. Both can be removed by rubbing the surface, but that is not necessary if the sight of them on the apple skin can be tolerated.

Plants, unlike animals, cannot run away from disease and insect threats, and, so, have developed physical deterrents and natural chemical compounds to protect themselves against these threats. These natural chemicals may interfere with insect life stages (hormonal action), trap insects (that's what latex does), or make the plant less tasty to insect grazers. Plants also have developed natural fungicides to deal with plant diseases. Many of these natural chemicals have beneficial effects for people, and some form the basis for modern plant-based medicines and antioxidants. Some of these volatilize and are sensed by surrounding plants, which are then alerted to nearby threats so that they can muster appropriate responses. Salicylic acid, the precursor for aspirin (acetylsalicytic acid), is one of these natural chemicals.

Apples with sooty blotch and flyspeck are under siege from these diseases. So, in answer to the customer's original question, it is likely that the presence of sooty blotch and flyspeck on the surface of our apples not only does not decrease the healthiness of these apples, but probably enhances their beneficial effects. There have been reports of some organic fruits (notably, strawberries) containing more antioxidants than matched conventionally-grown fruits, with no real explanation about why this should be so. So, we stand by our answer that the two surface fungi on our apples probably enhance the apples' nutritional value and make them better for you.

GREGORY BECOMES VIRGIL

When he was a youngster, our live-in grandson Gregory had always had a keen sense for observation and a talent for imitation. He loved our animals and spent many hours with them in the pasture. They accepted him as one of their own, and he responded by becoming one of them. Gregory stood with them and studied them carefully; then he would transform himself into the animal that was the object of his study by making every move that they would make. It was more than pretending, much more.

Virgil was the name of the ram that we had at the time, and little Gregory identified with this dominant male sheep with the result that he was able to become recognizable as Virgil's double.

Virgil would stand by himself at times, chew his cud, and just stare blankly at nothing in particular; Gregory would stand, stare, and chew his cud in the same way. Virgil would walk slowly and stiffly from place to place; Gregory would walk slowly and stiffly from place to place. Gregory's mannerisms were exactly the same as Virgil's mannerisms.

One of Virgil's faults was that he would butt anyone who turned his or her back on him. We couldn't turn our backs on Gregory, either, because he would butt us from behind. And, if we turned toward him, Gregory would stand and stare away from us and then walk slowly and stiffly away. Gregory was Virgil.

Gregory didn't just assume Virgil's identity on the farm. At any time in public he could switch instantly to being Virgil. We could tell when this happened by the way he walked and stared. One time we had him at the airport waiting for a plane. There were many people looking out the window to watch an airplane arrive. Gregory suddenly switched into Virgil and butted several of them from behind before we could catch him. The people were surprised, and we would have been extremely embarrassed had we not been laughing so hard as we apologized to his victims.

Several times, when Cathy took Gregory to the pediatrician, he would switch to Virgil at some of the most inopportune times. One time, when the pediatrician was evaluating Gregory's level of development, he asked Gregory some simple questions that almost any small child could answer. Gregory, however, switched to his Virgil mode and made the doctor conclude that Gregory was developmentally retarded. Cathy, however, knew differently.

GREGORY LEARNS HIS LESSON

Our grandson Gregory spent many hours with our cows and sheep as they dwelled in their pasture. He developed a habit of chasing the sheep. It seemed that he wanted to be with them, but they didn't always want him there. When he first went into the pasture, he would run towards the sheep, and they, in turn, saw him coming and ran away. Gregory followed.

He identified most closely with our ram, Virgil, and Virgil tolerated Gregory's antics, including his running after the herd.

However, rams do not live forever, and Virgil died. This upset Gregory, and he had his own means to deal with the loss. We replaced Virgil with another ram, Rhett Butler, but Rhett Butler was a ram of a different ilk. Gregory ran after the sheep, as he had many times when Virgil was still alive, but Rhett Butler saw this as a threat by a little boy smaller than he was. Rhett Butler turned on Gregory and butted him, knocking him to the ground. The ram butted Gregory several times while he was lying there.

This cured Gregory of chasing sheep, and it also cured Gregory of transforming himself into a male sheep. He learned that day that he was not a sheep himself.

CATHY'S REFUGE

We have blueberries growing in two places on our farm. There are a few bushes planted in a small area next to the driveway in front of the house. These plants yield berries mostly used by our family, on cereal, in baked goods, and frozen for use in the winter.

There is a larger blueberry patch located far from the house, past the peach orchard, past the apple orchard, past the plums, apricots, and pears, and almost as far away as we could be and still be on our property. There are many bushes in this location.

There is a lyric in the song, "Puff, the Magic Dragon", that goes, "Dragons live forever, but not so little boys". Likewise, dragons may live forever, but not so blueberry bushes. Over the course of years, blueberry bushes decline and eventually die. In their prime, however, these bushes produced an amazing amount of fruit, which we sold at the Farmers' Market.

Cathy is our blueberry picker and she would spend many hours every day, happily picking berries and bringing them back to save until market day on Saturday. She loved to pick blueberries down there. The area was enclosed with nets to exclude the birds that would have loved to help pick ripe berries, and there was a feeling of security that came with spending time inside this enclosed space. Cathy used this time away from household cleaning, cooking, washing dishes, and other chores, as a time of rest. Best of all, she says, she escaped from our teenage boys at that time, and she knew that they would not likely venture that far away from the house. So, the blueberry patch became her place of refuge.

Blueberries grow in clusters, and the berries growing together do not ripen all at once. So, the ripe berries need to be picked deliberately and meticulously a few at a time. Nevertheless, Cathy didn't mind. She spent many hours doing this, and doing it well. There are 32 dry quarts in a bushel, and that translates to 128 half pints, which is the way we normally sell them. There were times in midseason when Cathy would pick more than a bushel of blueberries per week, which is an amazing amount of blueberries, no matter how you look at it.

And, she looked forward to all this picking because she could get away from it all for a few hours every day.

GOTTA KEEP MOVIN'

The sheep that we had often attracted another kind of animal – vultures. Whenever the sheep lay down to rest in the middle of a hot summer's day, vultures would come by to watch. They were looking for any sheep that did not appear to be alive. A dead sheep meant a holiday feast would be had by all. They loved to eat dead sheep.

The vultures would most often perch on the peak of the barn roof overlooking the sheep pasture. There is nothing more eerie to a human observer than to see a group of four to six vultures sitting at the highest point of the roof, and wishing for death to come to any creature in their sight. The sight of these vultures can send shudders down one's spine, and chills even on the hottest of days. Vultures – they evoke thoughts of the Grim Reaper.

We have had sheep die in the pastures at times, and it doesn't take long for the vultures to spot a dead sheep. They descend on the carcass and devour it, sometimes taking a couple of days to clean all the flesh from the bones. What is left after the vultures do their work is a skeleton that attracts other animals looking for something to chew on. In this instance, the vultures are providing a valuable, if not pleasant, service cleaning up a dead animal. Nevertheless, the vultures are not welcome, and the sight of a ring of vultures circling above a spot in a field gives a feeling of foreboding and dread. What terrible thing has happened to draw vultures to that spot? We can hope it is not one or more of our sheep.

Vultures are not in the area at all times of the year. There are two or three extended times during the year when they are in attendance. But, when they do show up, we certainly know about it, because they park themselves on our barn roof and look around for any decaying animal to feast upon.

This has led us to say to each other, especially when we tire after a long day of working in the hot sun: "You had better keep moving. Otherwise the vultures with get you." We say this only half in jest.

COMPLAINING FARMERS

In the spring of 1998, we had 13 days straight of rain. Each day it rained at least an inch and it really was wet. With water like that, the roots of our strawberries and rhubarb waterlogged, and they never looked worse. With rain like that, Art couldn't spray his apples for insects and diseases such as scab. Not long after, it turned dry, and we suffered through another summer drought. Was this all bad? Not on your life! You see, a farmer always has at least one eye on the sky, and weather is one of his favorite topics. But, when farmers discuss the weather, they nearly always complain about it.

It's too wet to cure hay, or it's too dry to grow good soybeans, or the freeze killed the corn seedlings, or it is so muddy that the combine can't get into the field to harvest the beans. Listening to this, you might think a farmer's lot is a mighty unhappy one, but you would be wrong. The natural state of a farmer is when he is complaining.

Farmer etiquette requires the listener to sympathize with the complainer. Even better, if the listener can add to the complaints, then the two have found a common basis for communication and trust. Farmers may complain to non-farmers, but their complaints are restrained, because they usually find out that the complaints are not reciprocated. Without someone else to really understand, there is no sense complaining.

Farmers who complain to other farmers are in their glory. The complaints fly back and forth as quickly as each party can get a word in edgewise, and this adds gusto to conversations among farmers. There is a tendency to try to top the last story with one with worse misfortune or more pervading gloom. The worse the stories get, the better the farmers feel.

Ask a farmer how his machinery is, and he will soon come around to telling you how his tractor needs a clutch, and the last time he tried to fix a clutch, the rest of the tractor fell apart. If you are a farmer, it is your turn to talk about how much it cost to put new tires on your tractor, and it looks like they are almost worn out already. Then, if there is a third farmer in the group, he will tell about the time when all his tractors broke down together, and how his crop was ruined because he couldn't get into the field to harvest it.

About that time, someone will remind everyone that the weather has been so dry that all the corn is withering in the field. And everyone will shake their heads and feel wonderful, because the misery that visits one farmer visits all farmers.

Farmer etiquette also demands that, if you have irrigation, and your corn is not withering in the field, while the corn of all your neighbors has turned to dust, you must not mention that fact. In fact, you must turn the conversation to the field of corn that you have that isn't irrigated, and describe how bad it is doing, and how you will be ruined if it doesn't rain soon. Furthermore, if you are going to put in irrigation and, your neighbors don't have irrigation, you must not irrigate everything. You must have at least one field left unirrigated so that you can show that you are still one of the crowd, and are still taking the same risks that your friends are taking. It doesn't hurt, either, if the unirrigated field is the one in front, where everyone can see it.

Art once made a classic mistake. He and others were in the midst of a midsummer drought, and the farmers with corn, soybeans, and hay were facing ruin because of it (at least they said they faced ruin). Drought, on the other hand is somewhat good for tree fruit. The sun and warm weather produce more sugar, and the fruit is sweeter. Also the lack of moisture helps to protect the fruit against fungal diseases. So, Art was contented with the dry weather; as long as there was moisture in the ground within reach of his tree roots, his crop would be better off than normal.

One farmer he was talking to began to talk about the drought, shaking his head as he spoke about the prospects of doom. Art smiled and told him that the dry weather was actually good for his fruit, and he didn't really care if it stayed dry for a while. All of a sudden, Art realized that he had made a terrible mistake. He had turned the farmer's commiseration into self-pity. Art had isolated the other farmer so that they did not share a common challenge. Quickly, Art had to explain that some rain really soon would probably help his fruit size, and that there was a drought a few years back so bad that some of his trees died. He said that he really didn't want to see that happen again, so he hoped it would rain. At that, the complainer again relaxed, and they were again talking the same common language.

Low prices are also a common topic for complaints. But when farmers complain about low prices, they have to be very careful who they complain to. Low prices are bad for grain farmers, but they are good for livestock farmers. Low poultry prices help chicken farmers sell more of their product, but take market share from cattle farmers. High vegetable prices are good for vegetable farmers, but bad for other farmers who must buy vegetables.

You can imagine that when farmers complain about prices, they only complain about prices to other farmers who have farms like their own. They cannot complain if the other farmers are not in the same boat as they are. That's part of farmer etiquette.

So, if you hear a farmer complain, don't feel too bad for the farmer. A farmer needs to complain about something. Too wet, too dry, prices low, machinery broken, no help, it doesn't matter. The farmer has to complain just to feel good about everything. If everything is going well, the farmer will complain that it won't always stay that way. It makes him feel better just to say it. Farmer complaints? When have you not heard a farmer complain?

GREGORY'S CLOSEST FRIENDS

The girls grew up, and soon we had a grandson named Gregory who lived with us for the first six years of his life. Gregory has always had a keen imagination and a talent for quick learning. He especially liked animals, and spent a lot of time among our cows and sheep, observing them closely and imitating their demeanor.

His closest friends were the cows. He stayed in the pasture with them for many hours and became a cow himself. Gregory could walk like the cows, could chew his cud like the cows, would eat grass with the cows, and would lie down and sleep among the cows when they lay down and slept. He became a cow.

For their parts, the cows came to accept him as their own. They were very gentle with him, and would never harm him. In fact, they would protect him when necessary on occasion. So, we were never afraid of harm to him when he was among his cows. We left him alone to be with his closest friends. Whenever we needed to find Greg for some reason, we first looked for the cows, and he was often likely to be there.

Gregory liked to run off by himself and was given the freedom to do so. There was not a lot of danger or trouble that he could encounter on our farm; the farm was pretty much contained: there was a road at the end of our driveway, and another entrance at the other end of the farm, a long ways away, but the rest of the farm was enclosed in fences or bordered with wooded areas where Greg had no interest in going. He knew well not to run to the road at the end of the driveway.

Greg was a fast runner who could disappear in an instant. He could not be spotted easily as he ran among the trees in the orchard or in the pasture with his cows. But, we did like to know where he was at any particular time.

Our solution was to buy a cow bell and tie it to a harness; we put the harness on him whenever he went outside. That way, even if we could not see him, we could hear him as he ran; that was usually enough for us to know that he was safe.

Because it was a cow bell, Gregory was proud to wear the harness and asked to have it put on even when it was not necessary.

His favorite cow was named Eve. She was a large Hereford and the dominant cow in our herd of five or six. She had brown rings around her eyes, which were very unusual markings for a Hereford cow. She was not always gentle with the other cows, but was always gentle with Gregory. He had complete trust in her, and, because he was as close to a cow as a human could be, his judgment was surely correct.

One day, Eve choked on an apple, and despite a visit by a veterinarian, died soon after. Gregory was devastated. His emotional attachment to Eve was so strong that he had a hard time accepting her death. He didn't cry, but reenacted her death and burial with a toy cow that he owned. He never again attached to another cow the way he had attached to Eve.

MUSCOVY DUCK TALES

Along with many other types of animals, we at one time raised ducks on SweetAire Farm. There are three kinds of ducks that we had at one time or another: Pekin, Mallard, and Muscovy. Pekin ducks are the garden variety always pictured in children's books; they are totally white with an orange bill; Donald Duck is a Pekin. Both male and female ducks are totally white; the only sure way at a glance to tell a male Pekin duck from a female duck is that the male has a curly tail feather sticking up near its backside. Pekin ducks do not fly.

Mallard ducks are small and brown, like the type of duck found in wild marshes and waterways. Male Mallards are more brightly colored, with green heads, grey breasts, and some white bands on their necks and tails. Males also have the curly tail feather. Mallards can, and often do, fly well.

Muscovy ducks are a little harder to describe. Their feathers can be either white, or black, or a mixture of the two. Parts of their faces have globs of bright red skin without feathers. Males are considerably larger than females (about 2 pounds larger when adults). Adult females can "quack" like other ducks, but males can only "hiss". Both have sharp spurs on the backs of their legs near their feet. Muscovy ducks are strong flyers.

Muscovy ducks originated in South America, grow to adult size much more slowly than other barnyard ducks, but are very prolific. Young females can hatch up to four clutches of 20-25 eggs per year. We once had a female account for 60 young in one summer, although the norm is closer to 30.

Once someone begins keeping Muscovy ducks, it is hard to stop, because there is always one more female hiding away somewhere setting on her eggs.

When newly hatched, Muscovy ducklings are very cute. They are covered in bright yellow fuzz with a greenish tinge, and take several weeks to begin growing feathers. Joy always loved small, fuzzy, cuddly animals, and always volunteered to care for the ducklings when they were young.

When they do grow feathers, they pass into a second distinct stage in their development. We called this stage the "teeny-bopper" stage because they became somewhat gangly, and just brash enough to be friendly. When we would walk among them at this stage, they would stand there and talk up to us, all at once, like groupies around their favorite rock star icon. They would come running to us if they were called (or sometimes if they were not), and stand around looking up and expecting food or other gifts. Their voices were still high-pitched peeps, although they were still not as soft sounding as baby ducklings.

When they became "teenagers", the sexes started to become distinguishable. The males began to be larger, with more red on their faces, and the females seemed not to grow at all. At this stage, their voices changed, too. The males lost their voices and could only communicate with a guttural "hiss". The females developed a true "quack", but tended not to use it unless disturbed. They began to develop spurs, which made it somewhat more tricky to handle them without it hurting us. They began to fly.

Their wing feathers developed and they began to flap their wings while running along the ground. It seemed that when one duck finally rose from the ground he greatly encouraged the others, and very soon they all began to fly.

The first few times they fly can be funny or dangerous, depending on whether or not you are in their flight path. They haven't developed their flight skills at this point, and don't quite know how to avoid tree branches or buildings; they certainly don't know how to land without tumbling a bit. However, they soon learn to control their movements. After that, they can be seen perched along the peak of a barn roof, on top of a house, or even on the roofs of cars and trucks. There, they relieve themselves, causing quite a mess that takes a good rain to wash off.

With the ability to fly, Muscovy ducks sometimes exercised a new freedom of movement not limited by the boundaries of our farm. Muscovy ducks have been known to appear at many, locales throughout our neighborhood. Our neighbors sometimes phoned to let us know about the appearance of our ducks in their yard or on their house roofs, but there was not much we could do to recover them.

When fully grown, the males have become too heavy to fly, and females don't fly as much as they did when they were younger. Adult females like to swim and clean themselves in puddles. Males usually won't go near water unless to drink. Adult males fight among themselves during breeding season, which can be very intense with animals of this size and strength.

Muscovy ducks are more comfortable on land than on water, but there was one time when something different was the case. Our buildings at that time had eave troughs and barrels to collect rainwater runoff from our roofs. One day, when we went to the barn, we heard a small peeping sound coming from the vicinity of the barrel. The noise was not so unusual at the time, because it was breeding season for ducks and chickens (which we also had at that time), and new bird nestlings appeared quite often.

We looked around to see where the sound was coming from, but saw nothing until we looked into the barrel. There, swimming for its life, was a fuzzy, little, yellow baby Muscovy duck.

How could it possibly have gotten there? The top of the barrel was 4 to 5 feet above the ground, and ducklings can't jump that high. Could someone have carried it there? The duckling was rescued and put into a box with a lamp to let it dry.

Returning to the barn in a few minutes, there again was a peeping sound coming from the same barrel. This time, there were two frantic ducklings trying to swim. They were also rescued and put into the box with the first rescued duckling.

The rest of the morning, whenever we went back to the barn, there were between one and four ducklings in the barrel. It took a little investigation to determine why they were there.

A mother duck had made her nest in the barn hay mow, just above the barrel. There was a space between the barn roof eave and the wall, and, when the newly hatched ducklings began to move around, they had fallen through the space right into the barrel of water and their first swimming lesson. Case solved.

Another time, when a bunch of ducklings hatched just before we were scheduled to leave on a trip for a few days, we decided to lock the ducklings and their mother in the barn for safe keeping. We provided water and food, and closed the door. Four days later, when we returned, the mother was still locked inside the barn, but the ducklings, all 21 of them, were missing. We looked and looked, into all corners of the barn, but there was no evidence of rats, skunks, or other wildlife likely to have eaten the ducklings.

We heard a "peep" coming from the tractor shed, another "peep", and a "meow". When we got there, we saw all 21 ducklings under the tractor and one of our female cats sitting close by. She had recently lost a litter of kittens and probably thought that these warm, fuzzy, little things would substitute well. She had gone through the open window and carried them out one-by-one, until she had them all. When we discovered her, she looked at us as if to say, "Boy, am I tired trying to keep them all in one place. Please take them back." We brought them back to their mother, and the ducklings soon forgot to be kittens.

With new ducks arriving at a rate of 40-50 per year, we had to cull about that many if we and our neighbors were not to be overrun. We sold a few at auctions, sold some to individual buyers, eaten some, and sold a large number to a man who dreamed of becoming rich raising Muscovy duck eggs for a hatchery. At one time we had over 200 ducks. That's a lot of ducks.

We made a unique deal with one of the local veterinarians to trade live ducks in return for some that he had killed, cleaned, and smoked. Smoked duck is delicious and tastes similar to other types of smoked meats. We found out that farmers, in this case us, can eat like gourmets.

MORNING GLORIES, LIKE DIAMONDS, ARE FOREVER

When grandson Gregory was in second grade in school, he wanted to provide the flowers on the altar at church. It was summer, and he wanted red, white, and blue flowers for an Independence Day theme. So, he convinced his grandfather to take him to the farm store to buy some flower seeds. He picked out several packets of flower seeds that appealed to him and brought them home. He would plant the seeds, grow his own flowers, and pick them at the proper time for church bouquets.

He planted them in pots in front of our house. The flowers grew rapidly that year, and he was able to provide the church with flowers, not only on the Fourth of July, but on many other dates as well. He was pleased.

One type of flower that he planted was Morning Glories. They were an intense blue color, and very pretty. But, the trouble with Morning Glories had not been recognized at that time.

Gregory had grown into a teenager, and then into a young adult, but Morning Glory plants were still sprouting where they had been planted years before. Morning Glory plants produce an abundance of seeds, and they remain viable forever, it seems.

Not wanting to leave a perennial legacy of Morning Glories growing in front of our house for the rest of our lives and for generations to come, Art pulled the seedlings as they emerged each year. He continued to do this for at least ten or twelve years after the year when Gregory first planted them. It has now been several years since new plants have no longer appeared, but Art remains vigilant, lest an errant Morning Glory seed decide to repopulate the Earth with Morning Glories. We may never be fully free of the threat.

A SHEARING TO REMEMBER

Each spring, our sheep needed to be sheared. And, each spring, after shearing had been done, we had more farm stories to tell. One year's shearing was clearly a lot different from the others. This one stunk, literally.

We had decided that year to shear in the barn, where it was dry. It had been very rainy, and the pen where we usually sheared was not suitable for shearing. So, in the barn it was to be.

We had, until a year or two before then, kept geese in the barn at night to protect them from foxes, raccoons, and other potential predators. The geese were gone at this stage, but the nests that they had made in which to lay their eggs and raise their young were still in evidence. Our idea was to use the part of the barn away from those old goose nests to shear the sheep one at a time.

As usual when he was a teenager, Greg helped catch and hold the sheep as Art sheared them with his electric shears. All was going smoothly until one sheep got loose from Greg's grip while Art was shearing it. It began to run around the barn. It could not escape completely because the barn door was closed, but it tried anyway. It did not want to have any part of being sheared.

Once it was loose, Greg chased it and tried to catch it to bring it back to where it would be sheared. On the way, however, the sheep ran to the corner of the barn where the old goose nests were located. Underneath layers of old hay were years-old goose eggs, which had been left behind. Greg accidentally stepped on one of the eggs, and with a muffled pop, it exploded and spewed very stinky hydrogen sulfide gas all over the barn. There had been a slow buildup of gas and pressure in the egg as it sat there for a year or two, and the egg shell had apparently been impermeable to gas escape.

Hydrogen sulfide gas, the smell of rotten eggs, was more than evident as it permeated the atmosphere of the barn for most of the rest of the day, even with the barn windows open. That made shearing a lot less pleasant for all involved, both animals and humans, as if that were possible.

After that episode, Greg was directed to very carefully remove all the old eggs hidden under the hay and deposit them, again very carefully, far away from where we could smell them. He was able to do this without breaking any more rotten eggs, but he was especially cautious when he did so.

RUNNING DOWN THE AISLE

When he was young, Gregory loved to be acolyte at our church. He always volunteered whenever he could, and he was very enthusiastic when he served. There was one time, however, when he panicked.

He had learned the duties of being an acolyte under our pastor at the time, Khrista Ferguson. She had shown him how she expected him to light the altar candles at the start of the service, how to give the collection plates to the ushers to take the offering, and how to extinguish the candles at the end of the service. The last part she wanted done in a particular way.

Symbolic of the Word moving from the church out into the world, she trained the acolytes to light the brass candle lighter before the candles were extinguished, and to walk around the altar railing ahead of her at the end of the service. She would wait until the acolyte was in place before she came down from her position at the pulpit, and then she would follow the acolyte back down the aisle to the back of the church while the postlude was played on the organ. The acolytes could then extinguish the lighter and she would shake people's hands as they exited the church. Gregory knew the routine well, and performed admirably.

Every few years, pastors change. Gregory was not with us for the first couple of weeks when our new pastor, Finley Gray, came to serve at Darlington. As is the usual case with different pastors, he had a different style of service and made changes immediately. One change that he made was that he did not expect the acolyte to lead him down the aisle at the end of the service.

For one thing, Rev. Gray was quicker to descend from the pulpit than was Rev. Ferguson. For another thing, he really did not know that the acolytes had been trained to walk ahead of the pastor to the back of the church when the service had concluded.

So it was that Gregory was the first trained acolyte after Rev. Gray came to our church. Things started well for Gregory that day. The lighting of the candles, the collection plates, Gregory was confident enough to handle it. But then, everything changed. Pastor Gray gave the benediction and descended immediately down the two steps from the pulpit. He was around the railing and started toward the back of the church before Gregory realized it.

Gregory had lit the candle lighter and was extinguishing the candles when Pastor Gray hit the aisle at a brisk pace. Gregory's face turned to panic; he usually had enough time to extinguish the candles, but Mr. Gray was way ahead of him by now. Hurrying as fast as he could, Gregory extinguished the candles and ran as fast as he could around the railing; his face showed determination. He accelerated in front of the railing and ran as fast as he could down the aisle, the flame angling backward as he sped. But he never did catch up.

The look on his face as he ran around the railing will forever be among the most amusing things to remember. The look of panic and determination, his gaze on the pastor disappearing quickly toward the back of the church, and knowing that somehow he had failed to be the one to lead. All of us in the front of the church were rolling with laughter.

It's just a good thing that Gregory did not run over some elderly person moving slowly to the back of the church to shake the pastor's hand.

PUT UP ANOTHER BUILDING

There were several sheds and a small barn on our property when we first bought our original five-acre farm. They had not been maintained well for several years while the previous owner had spent his time and money on rehabilitating the house. So, as soon as we had some time, we had to work on the sheds and barn. We painted them first of all, so they looked better. When we could afford to do so, we hired a cement truck to deliver a load of concrete mix, first to one of the sheds (that we subsequently used for growing pigs, and later for housing our refrigerator coolers in which to keep our picked fruit), and, second, to the Bernie Barn (where we kept sheep and hay). Art moved the concrete mix around and smoothed it to make nice hard floors to replace the soft dirt floors that had been there when we first owned the buildings. These buildings were sufficient to satisfy our needs for several years.

Art has a saying that, when he runs out of space for the things he needs to store in the buildings that he has, he needs to build another building. That happened several times during our time here.

When we bought some tractors and haying equipment that needed to be stored under cover, he decided to build a machinery shed. But he did not build it all at once. What was needed first was a bay big enough for our John Deere "A" tractor. So, Art cleared some trees and some brush at the far end of our sheep pasture and prepared to build a tractor storage shed. The machinery shed was to be built near the upper boundary of our farm at that time.

All of our new buildings are of post and beam construction, which has several advantages for farm buildings; that type of building is relatively fast to construct and can never be considered for tax purposes as anything other than farm buildings. In post and beam construction, large poles are sunk several feet into the ground, and beams are attached, followed on top with smaller beams to which to nail sheet metal roofing. The main beams were of rough-cut oak, bought from a local sawmill and lumber supplier, Amos Stolzfus. The smaller beams were soft poplar wood also from Mr. Stolzfus. The posts were either old creosoted electrical poles that had been replaced by the electric company, or they were large Black Locust trees cut on our property. Finding the used electric poles required scouting the area around Darlington for poles that were lying on the ground, sawing them by hand into useful lengths, and then bringing them home on our truck before other people had spotted them. The Locust poles had to be large enough to consist mainly of mature wood, so that they would not rot when put into the ground.

The posts were about ten feet long and all were at least 10 inches in diameter. This made them extremely heavy to handle. After the hole was dug in which to place a post, Art had to lift one end of the post, slide it to the hole, and then hope that the bottom end would fall into the hole and stay there. Then, with all his strength, he had to lift the end of the post high enough so that it was standing upright. Sometimes this required extra grit as he pushed upwards with all his might and then some. This was no job for someone who was not used to lifting heavy objects.

After the posts were settled into the hole, and dirt tamped around them, they were checked with a level to be sure that they stood perfectly vertical. A surveyor's level borrowed from Art's place of work was used to assure that the roof was not tilted from one bay to the next. The tops of the posts were then notched to accept the beams, and the beams attached with lag screws. All these operations were made with hand tools: bow saws, hammers, chisels, brace and bits, and socket wrenches. Building this shed was not an easy task. Once the small poplar beams were attached, again with lag bolts, nailing the metal roofing was relatively easy.

As we expanded our items of machinery, the number of bays was increased until the machinery shed ultimately spanned the entire back of the sheep pasture with ten bays. Most of these were built by Art alone. A couple of the last bays were added after our sons Paul and Eric had come to join our family, and they helped somewhat. Paul, especially, could be a big help with his upper-body strength.

We also made several additions to our Bernie Barn, one to house and feed our sheep, and another to store our newly-acquired Allis Chalmers "C" tractor. Some dirt excavation was needed and all used post and beam construction.

After purchasing our last parcel of land, we now had another barn, the Aunt Renee barn, on the new piece of property. This was a good barn in which to store our hay, but we needed an extension on the barn under which to park our wagon full of hay so that we did not have to unload the wagon in the middle of the night. Sometimes, it would be raining when we brought the hay back from the field, and an under-cover spot would be particularly helpful.

The Aunt Renee barn has a high roof that we used as the pattern for our new barn extension; we continued the roof line from the barn through the extension. Again, we used post-and-beam construction. The posts, in this case, were very large Black Locust trees from our farm. The posts were still green and particularly heavy. Art, Paul, and Eric had to use all their collective strengths to sink them into the ground and raise them upright. Building the roof was a challenge because it was so high. Fortunately, Eric was not afraid of heights, and so he nailed both wooden frame and metal roofing in place while Art and Paul stayed on the ground supporting the pieces in place while Eric nailed them.

That was not the last building to be added. We needed some place in which to store our sensitive plants, including our collection of citrus trees, over the winter. The Caldwell Conservatory was added first to the front of one of our original sheds. The Knight Nook was built inside another of our original sheds. The Gregory Greenhouse was added on to one of the sheep sheds where hay and straw had previously been stored. Electric service was added to all of our new buildings.

By now, we have not run out of storage space and do not need new buildings to be added to our farm. At least not yet.

SHADOW

This is a story about a dog, not just any dog, but Art's favorite dog. If you are a dog lover, then you will understand.

Shadow was the fourth dog that we had on our farm. The first was named Timin, a rather small dog with a lot of spunk when it came to hunting ground hogs with or without Art. Next came Ouija (pronounced "weejee"), who was a nice enough German Shepherd who was obedient and protective of our children, but who lacked an overriding affection that turned to detachment as she aged. Oliver was the only male of the group; he was fun-loving and full of energy, but he wandered the neighborhood and was not obedient.

Shadow, however, was different. She was a 6-week old puppy when she came to live with us. She was a blend of Black Labrador and German Shepherd, and a fuzzy little ball of fur that you could hold in both hands. To say that she was friendly was an understatement, because she seemed to genuinely like to be with people. She did everything she could to keep up with the human she was with, and her legs bounded a mile-a-minute in the grass and across the field. She was a bundle of energy directed toward her human companions, and she expended all that energy just to be with us. Whenever we stopped walking, and turned to pay her some attention, she rolled immediately on her back to expose her tummy to our petting, scratching, and even a little tickling. We must have hugged her a lot during this phase of her puppyhood, because she grew to crave hugs later in her life.

She had not been separated from her momma until she came to live with us, and she used to whine somewhat mournfully at night. She would stop whining when we paid attention to her. The bond with humans was a substitute for mother.

Ouija was by that time quite old and slow. She didn't really take to this youngster who intruded into her domain. Of course, any playful puppy is going to test the patience of her elders, and she tested Ouija by running around her and nipping at her legs. Ouija growled and snapped back, which stopped the action for only the shortest of times. Then Shadow was back at it, nipping Ouija's legs, or neck, or ears, if she was lying down.

Eventually, Ouija ran out of growls and snaps, and began to tolerate this furry intruder. Sometimes she would even play with Shadow. Ouija began to show more pep and look a little less tired.

Shadow was cute, and she certainly was persistent. She seemed like there wasn't a human she met that she didn't wasn't to be with. Because she always followed us, and was always right under foot, we gave her the name of Shadow. She seemed to like the name just fine.

Now, a good dog is a treasure, but a special dog may be found only once in a lifetime. Building that relationship with a special dog takes time and cannot be hurried. So it was with Shadow.

Art was looking for just such a dog. She had to be unquestionably attached to him, and had to be fun to be with. She had to be full of energy. She had to accompany him wherever he would go on the farm, and not wander off. Very importantly, she had to be intelligent enough to learn that squirrels and rabbits could be chased, but sheep and geese were not for chasing.

Shadow developed into that dog. She would always be there, running alongside Art with her head held high, her tail curled upward, and her tongue hanging from the side of her mouth. She always seemed to be laughing and enjoying life. She radiated joy and enthusiasm. She pranced, and when she did, she made Art smile.

She had an endearing idiosyncrasy in that she would raise her head to the sky and yowl every time a siren was within hearing distance. Fire vehicles, police vehicles, it made no difference, Shadow bayed mournfully.

There were days when Cathy was at work and the boys were not home. On those days it was easy to feel alone without someone to be with and talk to. Shadow somehow made it all better. No matter what mood he started with, Shadow would bring cheer and happiness to Art. She had such enthusiasm and such unreserved love that she could make the grayest day bright and the saddest time happy.

She was not to be denied. Whenever Art would take his work shoes out to the back step and sit down to put them on before going to work, Shadow would run over and bound up the steps, nuzzle next to him, and wiggle her way under his arm. She wasn't satisfied until he gave her a whole series of hugs. She loved hugs, but it also cheered Art to know that she loved them. While he hugged her, she would lick him any and all places that she could, most often his ear when he turned his face. After this ritual was over, she would run around and bound up the hill with him. She had a way of gently nipping at his hands as he walked and she pranced up the hill together. It was if she was saying that she was so glad to be going with him wherever he was going.

Her enthusiasm for people wasn't always appreciated by others. She had a habit of jumping on people, and those wearing good clothes, or small children, didn't care for this behavior. She was not trying to be bad; she just wanted to be close. Art admits to feeling angry with her a time or two when she put her dirty paws on his good clothes, but he couldn't stay angry with her; she was just so enthusiastic.

In her first winter, she developed mange. Her hair fell out, and she began biting and scratching her raw skin when it itched her incessantly. The itching was so intense that her walk lost its sprightliness and her tail lost its upward curl. Because mange was so hard to cure, Cathy suggested that we might have to have her put to sleep to end her suffering. And suffer she did.

Art had heard that smearing used motor oil on a dog's skin could cure mange by suffocating the mites that caused it. So, in the middle of winter, he donned a pair of rubber gloves, and rubbed motor oil into her skin. She liked the rubbing, for it must have helped relieve the itching. The oil, however, decreased the insulation value of her little remaining hair, and she sometimes shivered through cold days and nights tied on a chain. Because she left oil stains wherever she rested, she spent the nights in an outside shed. She soon found a comfortable bag of fertilizer to lie on at night, and accommodated to her new condition.

Itching badly, oiled every few days, and spending her time alone and tied on a chain, her spirit had reached a low point. Through all of this, however, she unquestionably came when we called and cooperated fully. The uncurled tail wagged whenever we paid attention to her, so she still had faith in us.

This was the time of the year when Art was pruning trees on weekends, and he would always try to bring Shadow out to the orchard with him. She remained chained to one tree or another, however, because we did not want her running off and either spreading the mange or becoming reinfected. She whined and was not happy during this time, but she was showing some of the spunk that Art had long admired in her.

Ever so gradually, her condition improved. She still had little of her shiny black coat, but her scaly skin seemed to be healing. A few baths with miticidal soap, which Cathy gave her on days when it was warm enough, and Shadow began to look like her old self. The tail began to curve upward again, and her hair began to reappear. She began to prance again, and we knew she was feeling better when she once again started playing with Ouija (who, through all of this, developed not the slightest symptom of mange).

We continued to keep her chained during the day when we were not home so that we knew she would not be running around the neighborhood. Shadow could be very patient on the chain, except when Art came out of the house, and, especially, when he started walking up the hill. Then she would fuss and bark to beg to go with him. Very often, he let her off the chain so that she could go with him. Then she would jump up a couple of times to let him know that she was extremely happy to be with him. Once again, she would prance and nip gently at his hands as they walked together up the hill. There was no place that she would rather be, and there was no friend he would rather be with. They had been through a lot together, although it had only been a year, and a special bond had formed. She had become that special dog that one can only hope for once in a lifetime.

In mid-June of that year, she was in the orchard with Cathy, who was thinning peaches. Shadow had wandered a little while out there, and came back stumbling a little. Art was busy trying to get hay cut and in the barn, and fighting his time schedule, machinery, and the weather. Nothing new. Alas, there was not time enough to worry about anything else, and that included Shadow.

When he came home, Shadow was on her chain, and as was his custom, Art went over to let her loose. She tried jumping, as she usually did, but fell, due to weakness in her hind legs. When he rested on the outside glider, she came over and stumbled over her rear legs. She had a huge thirst, and that night she howled until Art let her out. She disappeared into the darkness, but in the stillness of the night he could hear her lapping water from the stream. A lot of water.

The next day she was weaker, and Cathy suspected poisoning. However, Ouija had once exhibited some of the same symptoms, and had recovered. Art was still busy with his haying to pay much attention.

Shadow lay on her side, occasionally moving location, and occasionally drinking more water that we brought to her. We patted her head and offered words of encouragement. She responded by wagging her tail. We had saved her before when she had the mange, so she seemed to have confidence that we would make it all better again.

We couldn't make it better. By Sunday morning, she was comatose and breathing shallowly. For the first time, she didn't wag her tail when she was stroked. We moved her into the house, where she died several hours later.

She had been with us for just over a year. She had given unconditional love and showed enthusiasm for life. She had reinvigorated Ouija and had given Art more joy than he could ever have imagined, hoped for, or deserved. She had become a favorite with grandsons Gregory and Clay. Shadow had minded well, and several times tipped us off that strange dogs were in our sheep. She had learned how to play with the cows, sheep, and geese so they didn't feel threatened. She had become that special dog. But the lovable howling at sirens was gone.

She left us too early. She left before her prime and before she could reach her full potential. Who knows how all would turn out if she had lived? Who knows how long one very special dog could have given love and brought smiles to the faces of those she touched?

Perhaps 11-year-old Gregory said it best, for he was visiting us when she became sick and died. He left a note for his grandfather that said:

Dear Poppop,
I have left here because of Shadow's
death. I just wanted to tell you good
luck with the hay, I want to ask
you to barrie here with a gravestone
with the following words:

March 1998 to June 1999
In the memory
of Shadow Johnson
who helped bring good
and break the bad.
She was a good dog
to everyone.

Sincerely,
Gregory Pierson

BUZZING BUMBLEBEES

Others have said that a bumblebee can go faster than a John Deere tractor. Art knows from experience that a bumblebee is also speedier than a Massey Ferguson tractor. He found this out when he used his

Bush Hog mower to cut grass and brush on fields that were otherwise not recently cared for.

Bumblebees nest in the ground, and the only clue to their presence is a small hole in the ground where they come and go. This entrance is easily hidden in the surrounding tall grass, and is hard to spot even when its location is known or suspected.

When a tractor and mower pass overhead, bumblebees get very annoyed at the disturbance. They come out in droves to defend their territory. And they are not easily quieted when alarmed.

The sting of a single bumblebee is painful. Stings of a phalanx of bumblebees, however, are unthinkable, and need to be avoided with every possible effort. A strong sense of urgency motivates the offending person to escape as fast as he or she can. If the interloper is on foot, there is nothing that could make the person run any faster. Waving of the arms is good for seeming to ward off the swarm of bees, but only takes attention away from the job of running away as fast as possible. On a tractor, the offender's escape speed is limited by the speed of the tractor, and waving of both arms can't happen without letting go of the steering wheel.

It was soon after we had purchased a parcel of land when Art looked at the field and knew that the weeds and brush needed to be mowed in order to prepare it to become a decent pasture for our sheep. He brought his used mower to do the job.

With all the tall weeds, small trees, and brush that populated that field, he decided that the best way to mow was in first gear of his Massey Ferguson tractor. The brush was tough, but the mower was tougher, and, as long as he went slowly enough, the mower was doing a satisfactory job; everything was working according to plan. That is, until he disturbed a bumblebee nest.

There was no apparent sign of a bumblebee nest as he mowed along. If there were bees coming and going from the nest, they were so small as to be unnoticeable from the seat of his tractor. The first hint of a problem was when a swarm of bumblebees began to fly around Art and his tractor. They were not happy, to say the least, and they made it known that they were going to do something about being molested. They buzzed around the mower, the tractor, and, most importantly, Art himself.

The bees were drawn first to the hot exhaust pipe of the tractor engine, and some of them were toasted there. But, some of the bees homed in on Art, and he began waving his arms to ward off the bees. Dressed in light summer clothing with bare arms, there were no extra layers of clothes for protection. The only means of escape was to put distance between him and the disturbed bumblebee nest. There was no time to stop and change gears. Desperate, and determined to escape as quickly as he could, he opened the throttle of the tractor all the way up to speed up the tractor. But, even at full throttle, the tractor in first gear still could not outrun the bees. The tractor's engine roared, but escape was not happening. The tractor, mower, and Art were still moving in slow motion, much too slowly for comfort. After what seemed to be forever, he finally put enough distance between himself and the disturbed bumblebee nest that the bees gave up their attack. In the end, he escaped with little harm, but the memory of the trauma remains.

He has since had other close encounters with bumblebee nests while mowing. But, the intense feeling of panic that was evoked in that first encounter was never duplicated. Art always made sure that, when he mowed where bumblebee nests were possibly located, it was always in a higher gear.

CHILD LABOR ON THE FARM

Our children have always been given a job to do every day. We always thought that it was necessary for children to learn responsibility and the rewards of successful work by helping out with the many chores and needs of our farm, and, helping out as they did, to give them a genuine sense of ownership of our family and our farm.

Child labor often has a bad name. When children are required to work to the extent that it interferes with their physical and emotional development, then child labor should not be expected, and should even be prohibited. But, there is a level of work that supports learning, self-reliance, and a sense of reality. Work of this nature relocates some of the children's attention from themselves, and helps them learn to give of themselves to contribute to the common good of the group. This type of work can foster a feeling of generosity and interest in the welfare of others. The work does not need to be physically overwhelming, but it can help to make the worker stronger physically as well as emotionally.

Giving a weekly allowance of cash may sometimes be related to performance of daily chores, but that wasn't our plan. Their work was expected as part of their family obligations, and not as a means to earning a monetary reward. The rewards for their efforts were more valuable and lasting than mere money.

Our children learned how to work, which served them well later in life. They knew from experience that they could handle the challenges of many of the tasks or opportunities presented to them when they were finally on their own. And, they were confident that they could become independent adults when they reached physical adulthood because they had already had practice working at jobs appropriate to their levels of abilities.

The daily jobs that our children were assigned were as wide-ranging as the entire scope of activities on our farm, and they were chosen by us to be able to be handled capably by each individual child. And yet, the jobs that they did helped our family to accomplish the many things that needed to be done. The types of chores included: moving cages for chickens and turkeys to new grass, painting fences, weeding garden rows, putting down papers for mulch, pruning trees, moving prunings from the orchard to the pasture with our tractor, feeding or watering cows or sheep, burying dead animals, helping catch sheep for shearing, cleaning manure out of the barn, painting buildings, loading and unloading hay, greasing equipment, and more.

Each of our children had turns helping Art at the weekly Farmers' Market. It was necessary at times to deal with multiple customers at the same time, and our children would be partners who could help to deal with occasional rushes at our stand. They learned how to talk to customers, help people pick out the products they were seeking, add prices in their heads, and make correct change. And, they were responsible as assistant salespeople.

We did not consider asking our children to work on our farm as exploitation. We did not withhold love, attention, or other needs that they might have had. We did, however, consider our children as fully responsible members of our farm family. If there was a time when a large amount of schoolwork had to be done, it always had priority over daily chores. If a child was ill, that child was not required to work outside that day. There was always an alternative. But, even if a child complained about a particular assigned job, that job may still have had to be assigned, especially if the job had to be done anyway, or if not doing the job affected the welfare of some of our animals.

Our children grew up to be capable and responsible adults who knew the level of real-life challenges that they could meet and be successful. We know this for sure: other children who grow up without these opportunities are the ones who are truly deprived and disadvantaged. We feel sorry for them.

IT CAN BE DARK IN THERE

Our walk-in pantry is located just off the kitchen. It has many shelves for food items and other utensils, and a door that we normally keep closed when no one is using the pantry. There is no window to let in light, so it is normally dark inside unless the electric light is turned on. When someone uses our pantry, they must usually step inside to reach items on the shelves. They normally turn on the light and leave the door ajar. And therein lies the dastardly devilish dark deed.

For years, visitors to the pantry have taken the risk of a prank that consists of another devious family member quietly sneaking around the corner, surreptitiously reaching for the door, quickly shutting the door before the person inside the pantry knows what has happened, and, just as quickly, reaching for the light switch to turn off the light. If the prankster has successfully maneuvered through this ritual, then he or she laughs loudly as a signal of a successful prank accomplished. The victim inside the pantry immediately tries to extricate him- or her-self from the pitch-black darkness by reaching for the doorknob, opening the door, switching the light on, and glaring at the prankster. If the victim had really been disturbed, as if he or she was on an urgent mission or in a hurry, then various epithets may be hurled at the prankster. Such an outburst only makes the prankster more proud of the accomplishment. But, the prank can never be repeated often, especially on the same victim, because retaliation in the form of other penalties is possible for retribution, especially if the victim was the woman of the house and the prankster was the man she lives with.

If the visitor is aware of the possibility of a potential prank, usually by the proximity of the prankster and a recent history of being locked in the dark pantry, then a defensive posture can be assumed while inside the pantry. This consists of assuming a wide stance, with one foot close enough to the shelves to be able to reach the needed item, and the other foot in a position to block the door closure. This posture assures that the prankster will only achieve frustration, and not the air of satisfaction that accompanies a successful prank. He may try the prank anyway, but the conclusion is unsatisfying to him. In that case, the prankster must wait for a certain length of time before the visitor lets down her guard enough for another attempt to be made. The results of all this is a big waste of time and a developing sense of paranoia among the occupants of this particular household.

GREGORY LIES WITH THE LAMBS

Back when he was 3-4 years old and living with us, our grandson Gregory used to spend a lot of his days communing with our animals. He loved them all. He had special friends among the ducks, the cows, and the sheep. He was not too keen on our pigs, turkeys, adult chickens, and, especially, our geese. He particularly loved to spend time with the sheep and cows.

And they accepted him as one of their own. The cows, notably, protected him against harm. We soon grew to realize that Gregory had nothing to fear from the animals that he spent his time with, and we knew he was safe among them. If he was playing outside, and that was almost all of his time awake, we were sure where he was and what he was doing. As long as he was with his animals, we did not have to watch him every minute that he was outside.

He studied the animals closely. He knew all their movements. At times, Gregory would imagine himself as one of them and assume their mannerisms. And he was very good at it. He could walk like a cow or a sheep, he could stare in just that way that a sheep stares, and, at times, he even grazed in the grass as they did. He became a cow or a sheep.

Once, he remembers, he lay down in the pasture to rest. Soon, several half-grown lambs ambled over to where he was lying, and they began to nibble at his ears. It may be that they were being weaned from their mothers, and Gregory's ears reminded them of a milk bar. Then again, maybe they just wanted to find out the taste of a human being. But, whatever the reason, lambs of this age would normally shy away from any other human that they saw. But, Gregory was special. He was, indeed, one of them.

WHAT WE CAN LEARN FROM SHEEP

We had a small flock of sheep on our farm, and we had always thought of them as somewhat stupid: when you wanted them to go one way, they often attempted to go another, and they didn't always choose to do what was obviously (to us) best for themselves. They were small and cute as lambs, but lost that cuteness as adults. However, sheep have some admirable qualities, including some that we can learn from.

1. Communications

Sheep are herding animals; they belong together in a group and become upset when separated from the others. Part of this cohesiveness rests on communications exchanged among themselves. This is illustrated with several examples:

Sheep have leaders and followers. We sometimes saw them reinforcing their hierarchy when some upstart ewe challenged the social order by butting another ewe higher up the social scale. They continued this contest for quite a while, and, in the end, figure out who was to dominate the other. It is mostly the females (ewes) that do this; males (rams, or bucks) only contest each other when there are more than one of them, and only during breeding season. Ewes are always the herd leaders; rams always follow dutifully.

So, when the leader ewe decides that it is time for the herd to change location, to move to a different part of the pasture to seek new grass, or to walk to the stream for a drink, or to lie down and rest, she usually communicates this to the others with some "baahs" and begins to move in the direction she wants everyone to go. The others follow.

If several sheep have dawdled in a shed or barn where they were unaware of the movement of the others, and then suddenly realize that they have been left behind, they make a loud commotion, seemingly in a panic, "baah-ing" as if crying "where are you all?", and running around trying to locate the others.

The second example of communications among our sheep occurred in the winter, when we turned them out to graze in the orchard. They often became separated from each other as they sought succulent grass among the trees. When they realized that they could no longer see each other, they would call to the others with a series of loud "baahs". Soon, other sheep joined in the chorus. They don't come together at this point, but they do know that the others are close by, and that is fine with them.

This type of communication helps to coordinate the actions of the herd to aid their collective survival and well-being.

Sheep also communicate by smell. In the spring time, when the sheep are sheared and lose most of their wool, they also lose most of their unique bodily odors. Their lambs lose their abilities to distinguish their moms from the rest of the ewes. Not yet independent, they cry loudly for their moms. In turn, their moms answer back. But the lambs don't recognize the moms by their sounds, so they continue crying. The moms and their lambs can be standing right next to each other, and still be lost. The days after shearing are certainly noisy ones as moms and lambs adjust to the sudden change.

2. Coordination

The prior paragraphs have already shown that sheep are social creatures. They are not entirely unselfish, but they do look out for each other in sometimes surprising ways.

One time our sheep were in their pasture, far away from the barn, busily grazing on grass. One or two were closer to the barn, and could see that I fresh grain had just been put in their feed trough. The closest ewe came running, because they really like their grain, and they don't get much of it. The first ewe to reach the grain might be expected to furiously gobble as much grain as she could before the others realized that there was grain to be had. The others, by the way, had not yet seen me at the feed trough and continued grazing. Instead of selfishly eating her fill of grain, the ewe that was aware of the grain turned around and called the others, telling them, in their own language, that they should come to feast. They all came and shared, in a competitive fashion, the grain that they had been given.

This was an impressive example of altruism in an animal that is largely regarded as stupid. We all should be as generous.

3. Don't Run From Your Fears

One thing that sheep do not do well is to face danger. They will run from anything that seems to threaten them. Even the ram, as belligerent as he is at times, will not turn to protect the herd. This trait can sometimes lead to disaster.

One real threat to sheep is loose dogs. Normally, mild and well-mannered dogs on the loose will readily kill sheep. What happens is this: sheep are afraid of dogs, and will run from them if they get close. The dogs, seeing running sheep, will chase and catch them. The dogs will nip at the sheep once they catch up to them; all they get is a mouthful of wool. However, the wool tears from the skin of the sheep and causes bleeding. Once the dogs taste blood, they go in for the kill. Many of our sheep have fallen victim over the years to loose dogs, and that was our biggest threat.

Other things, besides dogs, also frighten sheep. There was once a helium-filled mylar balloon that landed in our pasture. The balloon was not inflated enough to rise into the air, but it wasn't deflated enough to fall completely to the ground. Instead, it hovered in one spot, about two feet off the ground, with its trailing string mostly coiled on the grass. There were small breezes that made the hovering balloon slowly sway to and fro, as if in a trance.

The sheep acted somewhat between suspicious and terrified. The balloon was strange, and the sheep stood there at the edge of the pasture, facing it and watching lest it make threatening moves toward them. If it had, they would have run away as fast as they could have. They dared not graze, although they wanted to do so. It was only after the balloon was taken away that they relaxed.

The 23rd Psalm mentions a shepherd leading his sheep beside still waters. This has real meaning. Sheep are so terrified of quick motion that they will not drink from fast-moving streams. They prefer to drink from still or slowly-moving water.

Being so afraid of threats can paralyze. Running from fears can lead to disaster. We need to act more bravely than sheep; we need to face our fears, fight them, and try to conquer them. Only in doing so will we be able to overcome adversity and control our own lives.

4. Take Time for Rest and Relaxation

Ruminants, of which sheep are a part, cannot digest the cellulosic materials they eat until they grind them small, mix with saliva, and allow the bacteria in their stomachs to decompose cellulose into simpler sugars. So, sheep take time out of their days of busy grazing to lie down and chew their cuds. This usually happens at the same time every day, and these sessions may last for an hour or more. As one might expect, the whole herd usually chews their cuds at the same time.

Whereas sheep need to engage in this activity as a requirement of digestion, we need to set aside some rest time to pause, reflect, and rejuvenate ourselves. The human body, although made to be able to adjust to periods of intense activity, is not made to run continuously at full speed. Our nervous system needs time to slow our activity level, to allow healing, and to maintain stability. So, just like the sheep, we need time to return to normal and to recharge our energies for the next bout of stress. In so doing, our coping capabilities will be improved, and our lives will be healthier.

As one can see from this collection of instances, there are lessons to be learned form observations of all kinds. In this case, sheep were the ones being observed. Taking time to observe, and reflecting upon what was seen, can be of great benefit to living the good life.

BEING SELF-SUFFICIENT

It may or may not be a typical farming goal, but there is some fascination with trying to be self-sufficient, and, as operators of a small farm, we may have been in a better position than most to actually achieve such a goal. And we tried.

For years, we raised most of the fruits, vegetables, and meats that we consumed. There were seasonal variations in the availabilities of each of these, but Cathy bridged the times of scarcity by canning or freezing produce during times of abundance. Our pantry was full of jars of applesauce, peach halves, string beans, tomatoes, and pickles of several different varieties. There were jars of grape jelly, currant jelly, elderberry jelly, and more exotic kinds of preserves. Our freezers had packages of berries of all kinds that we grew, including raspberries, strawberries, blackberries, wineberries, and more. There were packages of frozen winter squash, sweet corn, peas, string beans, and so many more. We had beef, pork, lamb, goose, chicken, and turkey among the many kinds of meat that we raised, had processed, and froze. We shredded cabbage and made our own sauerkraut. At one time Cathy made our own bread and baked cookies, cakes, and pies for our family's benefit. Cathy spent nearly the entire summer canning and freezing, when she wasn't spending her time baking, cooking, cleaning, doing laundry, washing dishes, and raising our children.

Cathy owned a portable sewing machine, for a short time, and made some clothes for our girls. After a while, she could not find the time to continue this effort with all the other tasks she had to do. She also knitted comforters for our beds and sweaters for Art. She knitted and crocheted during her resting time when she sat down in the evenings following her busy days.

We had two large gardens in addition to the beds and patches that we used to grow berries. Our children helped to maintain these areas, and we made it more enticing for them by planting fun crops like watermelons and cantaloupes in the garden located far from our house. Our boys would visit that garden daily, just to monitor how these melons were doing. Each little improvement in size or color was noticed. When there were melons that had ripened, the boys eagerly picked them, carried them in slings consisting of the tee shirts that they were wearing, and held on the far side with their teeth, and rode their bicycles back to our house with their valuable pickings.

We raised and harvested all the hay needed for our animals. This required a very large commitment of time and a lot of effort for the whole family. Cutting, baling, and stowing hay needs to be done when the weather is just right, and when everyone can jockey their schedules to make themselves available to help. But there was almost nothing with a higher priority than to help with moving the hay into the barn when it was ready. The most important thing was the weather; it must be sunny and dry for several days to allow the cut hay to cure and be dry enough to bale, and then to stack in the barn. It was usually hot, as well, and made for sweaty days for all of us. We found out after a while that the hay usually had to be harvested at the same time that our fruits needed to be picked. This conflict was one consideration that led to giving up cutting hay. The other important factor was that, given the cost of all the fuel used, machinery parts needed to repair breakdowns in the field, and the amount of time and effort it took to bale our own hay, it was much cheaper and easier to buy the same amount of hay from other farmers.

We still needed electric power delivered to our farm, but we installed solar panels on the roof of our house to generate our own electricity. The amount of electricity generated depends on the sun shining, and there are multiple months out of the year for which our solar generation exceeds the need of electric power from the grid.

Our business card that we had printed labeled our farm as an "Ecologically-friendly Farm". We believed that this slogan was justified because we used very few pesticides on our fruits, fed to our animals whatever wastes we had from our fruit and vegetable endeavors, and used the manure that they produced as fertilizer for our plantings. We had cages for our turkeys and chickens, and moved them every day so that the birds could eat fresh grass and simultaneously fertilize the grass with their droppings. We fed our tree prunings to the cows and sheep and, after they had eaten what they wanted, chipped the remains for mulch. We tried to cycle and recycle as much as we could.

Of course, total independence from outside supplies and services is not possible in the modern world. We still had to fill our vehicles with gasoline, we had to buy grain for our animals, and we needed parts to repair our equipment when repair was needed; we had to buy new trees, seeds, and plants; we needed to buy our clothes and school supplies Although we didn't use much, we still had to purchase a small amount of fertilizer for our gardens and fruit crops. We required electric power to be supplied to us to heat our house, pump our water, and run some of our tools. And, of course, the biggest input that we needed was the energy from the sun to power the growth of all the vegetation that we had around the farm.

We learned how much extra time and effort these activities required. After a while, we could not sustain the necessary energy and still be active in other endeavors. So, we eventually decided to specialize. We would grow fruits, and sell them at the Farmers' Market. While there, we began to buy the vegetables that we needed in our household. Specialization allowed us to be much more efficient by concentrating on what we did best.

The idea of self-sufficiency is good in theory, but impossible to realize. At one time, we probably came as close to being self-sufficient as anybody could reasonably achieve and still be connected to the outside world. There really is no crime to have some dependence on other people and suppliers with more skill or efficiency than we could reasonably aspire. But, self-sufficiency is still a nice ideal, one that carries a sense of pride for each small portion of it that one can successfully accomplish. We still carry that pride.

GREETINGS FROM SWEETAIRE FARM

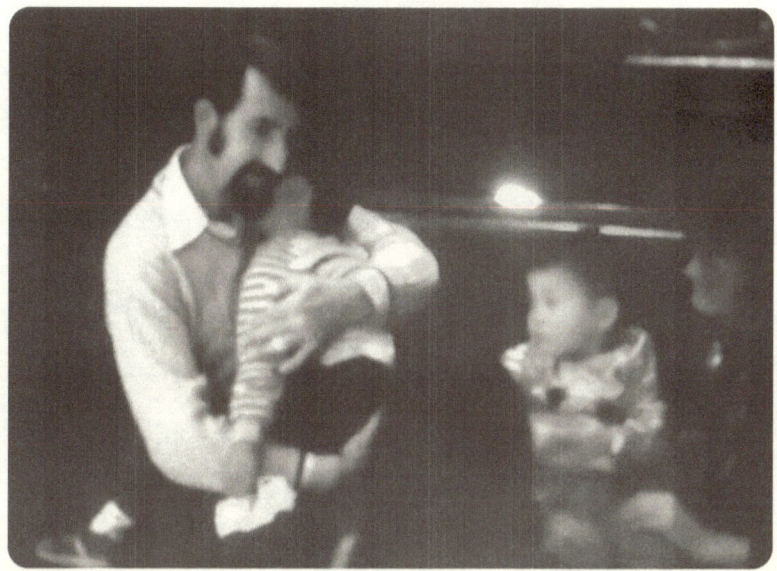

On the evening of 10 November 1984, two small boys came from Korea to join the Johnson family. It was very late at night at BWI airport, and the tired boys had been on the airplane for many hours. The airport was nearly dark and deserted when they all finally united. Here, Art cradles his new 6-year-old son, Paul (Korean name, Hyun), while Cathy holds 3-year-old Eric (Korean name, Hoon).

A year and a half after Paul and Eric had joined our family, they had been completely accustomed to their new life. Paul was doing extremely well in school and Eric would start soon. Jodi was dressed for a special occasion as the boys play in the driveway in front of the house.

Paul accompanied Art at the Bel Air Farmers' Market in 1985, three years after we began selling at the market. There were several venders who brought their young children, and Paul was among them. Joy and Jodi had had their turns at the market, and Eric's turn was yet to come when he became old enough.

Wherever there is a mud puddle, there will be a little child who wants to play in it. This is Gregory at age 4, who got his wish.

GREETINGS FROM SWEETAIRE FARM

When additional property adjacent to our original 5-acre farm was purchased in 1987, it was largely overgrown with trees and brush that had to be removed. Fences also had to be built to enclose new pastures for our cows and sheep. Here, Cathy, and friends Jerry Watson and Jim Caldwell work to help us with putting in fence posts. The posts were cut from locust trees growing on the property. It took many hands and a lot of time to finish the project.

There was need for some place to keep our growing number of citrus trees and other sensitive plants over the winter. So, Art started to build a place with many windows and electric heat. This is Art, with Paul and dog, Ouija, beginning construction of the Caldwell Conservatory (named for good friend, Jim Caldwell). Additional greenhouses were added years later.

We were able to buy a small, used lawn tractor cheaply at a farm sale in 1988. The boys loved to drive it around all over the farm. The original purpose to buy the tractor was forgotten once the boys monopolized it for their recreation. The tractor did not last very long, but the boys soon graduated to real, regular-sized tractors.

Paul, Eric, and grandson Greg watch as a backhoe works on our farm. The boys were fascinated with power equipment and machines, and could watch for a long time.

GREETINGS FROM SWEETAIRE FARM

Paul drives our Allis Chalmers "C" tractor while Art sprays his trees by hand from a spray tank on the trailer. It took several more years before we could afford to buy a better sprayer. Paul and Eric helped around the farm in many ways, including restoring the tractor in this photo with new paint and decals.

1994 was the year of the big ice storm. Two to three inches of ice coated almost everything in the entire state of Maryland, and almost everything was shut down across the state. The thick ice was extremely difficult to melt or to remove, so it took more than a week to return to normal activities. The ice on SweetAire Farm made walking outside treacherous for humans and animals, too. We watched our cows, sheep, and geese try to maneuver without slipping and falling.

We operated a small fruit stand at the end of our driveway for several years. The stand operated on a self-serve, honor system for paying for the fruit. Some local people patronized it, but it never really caught on. We finally decided to close the stand for good when somebody consistently came at night to break into our cash box.

When lambs are abandoned, or their mothers have no milk to feed them, then they have to be fed from a bottle. It is especially important that they get colostrum within a few minutes of birth. Here, Cathy has brought two lambs inside the kitchen and is bottle feeding them. When young, they need to be fed every few hours through the day and night. Cathy is particularly good with young lambs.

We have occasional snow in winter, and this picture, taken in 2014, shows our house taken from the back-sheep pasture. When we have snows like this, we usually get out the shovels and clear the driveway by hand. Art used to take the tractor and plow to clear the driveway, but getting the tractor out, attaching the plow, and putting chains on the wheels was a lot of trouble; it was just easier to shovel snow than to plow it. Besides, shoveling is not as cold as riding on the tractor while plowing.

We had some really big trees that overhung the machinery shed. Storms took down some of these trees before we recognized that they should be cut down before they toppled by themselves. When they fell on the machinery shed, they caused a lot of damage, breaking the roof, overwhelming oak beams, and trapping a tractor. Here, Art stands in 2011 beside fallen branches before cutting them into chunks that he could move.

When he was a teenager, grandson Greg wanted to build himself a house on our farm, so, with money he earned, he bought the materials and constructed a building where he spent a good deal of time when he was with us. He studied techniques for constructing buildings and learned how professionals do things. Every once in a while, but not too often, he consulted his grandfather for advice.

Springtime is the prettiest season on SweetAire Farm, with all the fruit trees in blossom. Here is a closeup of the brilliantly white blossoms of a pear tree with the Bernie Barn in the background. This photo was taken by Ira Silberberg.

The Later Years

INTRODUCTION

The boys had all grown, and the house was empty of children for the first time in about 35 years. Art and Cathy continued to operate their farm, which by now was dedicated to producing fruit with organic methods. The expansion of fruit production was able to supply enough product for the Famers' Market. We added additional fruits to our holdings to offer more exotic choices for our customers. Art retired from his outside job, followed a couple of years later by Cathy's retirement. We gave up raising sheep during this period when it became too much for Cathy to care for the lambs in the winter and for Art to shear them in the spring time.

THUNDERSTORMS: SOME LIKE THEM, SOME DON'T

We once had a dog, Ouija (pronounced "weejee", and named because she was a MEDIUM-sized German Shepherd dog). Ouija used to disappear during thunderstorms, and would turn up later seeking refuge in our neighbors' garage. The neighbor would call us and ask us if we knew where she was (of course not; it was raining too hard outside to go checking on where our dog was). When we said "no", the neighbor would ask us to take Ouija home once the storm was finished. This we did, the many times it happened.

On the other side of the thunderstorm issue, our daughter Joy, who now lives in the San Francisco area, loves thunderstorms. Thunderstorms are reportedly rare where she lives, so she always hopes for a thunder-boomy when she comes east to visit us. A thunderstorm doesn't happen every year when she comes, but she has not always been disappointed. And, our granddaughter, Emma, who was 8 years old at the time, probably heard her first clap of thunder one year when she came to visit with her mom. She was not too impressed.

HORSE COMES TO VISIT

As the farmers who all too often were responsible for sheep running up and down the road, visiting neighbors along the way, and eating whatever green morsels they found to their liking, there was a time or two when the tables were turned. One time, in particular, stands out because we had an unscheduled visit from a horse.

Art must have been doing something outside around the house when he spotted a horse trotting up our driveway. He knew that it didn't belong to us, because, when we had last checked, we had no horses of our own. Someone else was going to miss an animal as big as a horse, so Art planned to call around to locate the owner.

No sooner did he turn to walk to the house to make his calls, when the horse spotted Art, and it must have been love at first sight. The horse began following Art; even as he stepped onto the porch. The horse was right there with him. This wasn't going to work, because the horse might try to follow Art into the house and into the kitchen where the phone was sitting.

So, change in plans: Art needed to go get Cathy, who was working away from the house at the time. Maybe Cathy could call while Art kept company with the horse. Or, maybe they would be able to figure out something else to do; it wasn't clear what was the best course of action: we had no rope that we could use to tie the horse to something that it couldn't move if it had wanted to, we thought about locking the horse in the pasture, but were not sure that our that were fences high enough to contain sheep could also contain an animal as big as a horse, and, we had no idea who we might call to notify that we had their horse.

All the while that Art walked out to get Cathy, the horse followed him. When Art moved, the horse moved, when Art stopped, the horse stopped. And, when Cathy spotted this duo, she became apprehensive; she had no experience with horses, and didn't know if a horse could be trusted not to hurt either of us.

We finally decided that Art would stay with the horse in the pasture while Cathy called someone, anyone, to see if we could locate the owner. She was on her way into the house when a pickup truck came into our driveway. The owners had come to us.

Out of the truck came a woman and an older man. They were, it turns out, a father and daughter. The daughter was glad that she had finally found her lost horse; the old father was just grumpy. The woman explained that her horse had a companion horse that shared a pasture with it, but that had been taken away to be shod. So, the horse that was now with us must have gone looking for its pal.

While this was going on, Art stayed with the horse in the sheep pasture. When the horse looked around and spotted the flock of sheep nearby, it decided that they were at that point more interesting than was Art (the story of his life!). So, the horse trotted over in the direction of the sheep.

The sheep had not seen anything like a horse before. Some of them might have remembered the cows that they once shared their pasture with, but this guy was no cow. So, they panicked, and ran from the horse. Now, you can't really run from a horse and expect to escape from him; horses also know how to run, and run fast. So, at that point, there was pandemonium going on in the pasture, and Art could do nothing about it.

The grumpy old man was still not satisfied about anything, but the woman finally told him that she would walk her horse back home, which she was able to do.

After she left with her horse walking alongside, the sheep settled down, but remained vigilant lest some other monster creep up on them. And Art had lost his new good friend.

CATHY HAS A BAD FALL

In 2009, Cathy suffered a bad fall that threatened her life and had some lasting effects. It was early in the month of September, and Cathy was due back from working as chief librarian at the Darlington Public Library. She worked on Mondays at the library until it closed at 8pm, and usually arrived home a few minutes after. Art waited in the house for her return. The rest of the details of that evening were seared into his memory.

When she had not come back by 8:30, he became concerned. She could have had some extra duties to attend to after the library closed, but she still should have been home by then. Unless something was wrong, she should have returned long ago. He checked out the window to see if she had returned and not come in yet, but saw nothing in the darkness outside. A few minutes later, he was really worrying, and went into the back room to see if she had arrived. It was then that he noticed the dim light of the ceiling light of her van. The vehicle was parked there, but the door had been left ajar. Something was wrong. He put his shoes on and went outside to investigate.

What he found outside sent dread through his being. There was Cathy, lying next to our ramp to the porch. Next to her were things that she had been carrying in her arms: mail, her pocket book, and things from the library that she had apparently been attempting to bring into the house before she fell. She was not moving. He checked for breathing, which she was doing, but, other than that, she was completely unresponsive.

She needed medical care quickly. Art lifted her up, put her into the van, and drove as fast as he could to the Harford Memorial Hospital in Havre de Grace. When he pulled up to the emergency entrance, he quickly rushed inside and called for help. A nurse came out with a wheelchair, and they both moved Cathy's limp body out of the van and into the wheelchair. She was wheeled inside.

At that point, Cathy was wheeled in one direction while Art was asked to provide identity and insurance information. He did so as quickly as he could. The hospital staff paged the attending physician.

Art's confidence was not helped when the doctor appeared; he was dressed in green scrubs and leaning on crutches when he walked in. He had a stethoscope draped loosely around his neck.

It got worse. Cathy had to be intubated so that she could be mechanically ventilated, if need be. Huddled over Cathy at that point were the doctor, an emergency medical technician (EMT), and several nurses. The doctor turned to the EMT and said. "Do you know how to intubate this patient? I forgot how." So, the EMT intubated her successfully. Art was filled with emotions at this point: dread, sorrow, anger, disbelief. How could a hospital staff person be so incompetent?

Hospital staff decided that Cathy's case was serious enough that she would need to be flown by helicopter to the University of Maryland Shock Trauma Center in Baltimore. In the meantime, she was left alone by medical personnel. Only Art continued to watch her vital signs on the monitors that were set up by her bed. At one point, her electrocardiogram flatlined, and Art was panicked. He was about to call for help, but the heartbeat resumed in a few seconds. There was no one except Art paying attention. He was exasperated.

It had now been over an hour since she was admitted to the hospital. Art was assured that the helicopter had been summoned, and was on its way from Baltimore. He was advised to drive to leave the hospital and drive to the Shock Trauma Center; the helicopter would be there before he could arrive. He was not completely convinced about the helicopter, and hung around at the hospital for another half hour or more. Every few minutes, he would inquire about the status of the helicopter. He was assured that it was on its way. But, it was taking much too long for the flight from Baltimore to Havre de Grace. The time was dragging on. Finally, with nothing more to be done at the hospital, and assured by the nurse on duty that the helicopter was, indeed, finally in the air, he left the hospital and drove as fast as he could the 35 miles to Baltimore.

When he arrived at the Shock Trauma Center, the helicopter carrying Cathy had still not arrived. It should have beaten him there by ten to fifteen minutes. His concern grew. Where was she? And was she still alive?

Within another ten minutes, the helicopter landed on the roof of the Center, and Cathy was admitted into the hospital. Once she was in the care of the medical personnel at the

Shock Trauma Center, she would be given the best of care; she would be ok, Art kept telling himself.

He called his church pastor, Gary Sieglein, and Gary came to sit with Art in the waiting room. They both kept a vigil through the night. Upstairs, Cathy underwent several x-ray and MRI tests that showed that she had fractured her skull and there was bleeding into her brain. Tests later that night indicated that the bleeding had stopped and her condition had stabilized. Art was relieved to some extent.

Cathy spent nearly a week in Shock Trauma. Her condition had improved enough by that time that she was out of immediate danger of dying. She was transferred to Kernan Rehabilitation Hospital near Catonsville, in Baltimore County. Art was assured by Shock Trauma personnel that Kernan was the best facility for rehabilitation. We soon found out otherwise.

The first night at Kernan, Cathy was found out of her bed and slumped on the floor. She had gotten up by herself and could not walk. Nurses on duty had not been watching her.

Later during her stay, Cathy had regained consciousness of a sort, and complained of pain. The nurses had promised Tylenol, but had not given it to her. It was not until Art complained to them about her care that she received the medications that she needed. This scene was repeated many times. If Art had not been there to advocate for her, she would have been largely ignored by the nurses. Art made many trips the 60 miles or so to sit with Cathy, and it is good that he did; she would not have had the care she deserved it he had not been there. At one point, Art's sister, Geri, who had worked in hospital settings previously, visited Kernan with Art. They played good cop (Geri), bad cop (Art) with the nursing staff to get them to care for her as she needed.

Cathy made slow, but steady progress. She regained the ability to walk, with some effort, and she even worked on a Baltimore Sun Friday crossword puzzle to relieve some of her boredom.

She was being given 12 medications, some of which were only prescribed to counteract the side effects of some of the other medications that she was taking. Seeing this, Art requested an appointment with her doctor-in-charge. When that took place, several days later, they went over her entire list of medications. Art asked the purpose of each, and the doctor answered. They discussed whether each was really needed. When the session was over, Cathy was down to only 4 medications.

Three weeks after her fall, Cathy came home. She was mentally alert and capable, but still weak physically from lying around for all that time. She needed to walk with a walker and could not walk alone. She was able to solve crossword puzzles and balance the checkbook, but still did not feel as if she was fully connected to herself. Her mental abilities had mostly recovered, but there was still a spacey quality to her responses.

To help her regain her physical strength, Art took control of her exercise regimen. As soon as she could, she and Art walked once to the end of our driveway and back. She walked using her walker. This continued each day for several days. Once she felt comfortable with one trip to the end of the driveway, they increased it to two trips down and back. After a few more days, three trips were required. Within a couple of weeks, Cathy was much stronger, and her mental awareness improved, also.

A month after her accident, Cathy was so much better that she accompanied Art and Greg at the Farmers' Market. She helped a lot and supervised some. After that, she regularly attended the market from then on.

By the end of December, Cathy was taking the opportunity, every chance she had, to prune apple trees. She had come a long way since her fall, and apple tree pruning had been her job for many years now. The only accommodation she made to her accident was that she did not prune the very top branches. But, she was climbing up the ladder, and feeling good that she could be productive again. This was entirely voluntary on her part.

Our farm is really a two-person operation, so her help (as well as her person) was very much missed. With the time it took Art to travel to and back from Kernan Hospital, Art had little time to do a lot of the things that should have been getting done at the farm. It was good that there was a natural slowing that time of the year of things that had to be done immediately. It's in the fall that we have time (usually) to perform maintenance chores, such as painting, fixing roofs and fences, and laying out new plantings. There is a natural cycle of major tasks that must be done, with winter being pruning time and lambing time, spring being planting and spraying time, summer being harvest time, and fall being building and maintenance time.

Cathy described her first few weeks out of the hospital as chaotic; she was unable to process the many sensory inputs that she experienced, and had trouble separating a few important inputs from environmental noise. She had trouble adapting to her environment outside of the recovery center. Her first trip home as a passenger in our vehicle was overwhelming to her. Her first visit to the supermarket, with its many selections of shelved foods packaged in brightly colored boxes and containers, flooded her brain with so many visual images that she could not cope. She can, fortunately, now visit the supermarket and focus her vision on only those groceries for which she seeks. She has regained the ability to properly focus her attention on something manageable.

She has permanently lost her sense of smell, which is a common lasting aftereffect of head injuries. Her sense of taste is also impaired. Art has to describe to her the wonderful odors emanating from the Thanksgiving turkey baking in the oven and the pleasant smells from the other foods that she cooks. She remembers what they smelled like; otherwise, to her, everything smells like air.

MOTHER AND LAMB RODEO

A lamb born on a winter Friday morning in 2018 was different from the others in a number of ways. First off, it was our first male lamb of the season. Males are usually not quite as hardy as female lambs, we have found, so it was good that the weather was milder than it had been in the weeks before. Another difference was that it was born out in the peach orchard, where we pasture the sheep during the wintertime, rather than in the pastures behind the house, as the others had been. But the third difference was the real kicker.

The other lambs were born to docile mothers. They were easy to get into the barn and they were easy to handle once they were inside. But this mother was wild, and caused the rest of the sheep to be frenzied as well.

It all started when Cathy was returning from her pruning in the apple orchard. She spied the new lamb with its mother, and, having to move them into the Bernie Barn so that they would be isolated together for a few days, picked up the new lamb and cradled it into her arms. It snuggled right in. She then began walking back to the sheep pasture behind the house, frequently showing the lamb to its mother so that the ewe would follow. The problem came when Cathy attempted to get the mom into the barn; she wouldn't go. Cathy tried several times, but the mom would not leave the rest of the flock, which, by now, was all in the same pasture. So, becoming increasingly frustrated, Cathy closed the gates between the pasture and the pathway to the peach orchard. This limited the distance that the flock could run when chased. Meanwhile, Cathy had put the lamb down near the barn, and it was bleating loudly for its mom. The mother answered back, but would not leave the flock.

At this point, Art walked back from his pruning activities, found the gates closed, and, closing them behind himself, entered the upper pasture. The sheep, by now all upset, ran through different open gates into the lower pasture. Cathy told Art what had happened, and they both decided to let things stand while they went to eat lunch. Cathy and Art soon changed their minds, however, realizing that it might not be any easier to get the mom into the barn after lunch. So, they chased the flock into the upper pasture and closed the gates to the lower pasture behind them. The sheep ran for the upper gates closed so that they blocked the pathway to the peach orchard. Seeing the gates still closed, they waited there. Art walked up to chase them back down towards the barn. He realized again that he is not very good at running anymore (he used to run all the time).

The sheep, including all the ewes and their small lambs, ran back down, but would not run into the corral near the barn. If they could be chased into the corral, then it would be relatively easy to divert the new mother and her lamb into the door to the Bernie Barn. Art and Cathy tried chasing the sheep into the corral, but all that accomplished was for the sheep to run back to the upper gates several times, and then try to run to the lower pasture.

Greg had been replacing the fence separating the upper from the lower pastures over several weeks, and it is a good thing that he had completed his fencing project, because the frantic sheep would have jumped through holes in the fence and escaped. One tactic that the sheep attempt is to split up. Once they do that, humans can only chase one part of the flock. The rest of the flock finds a means to escape, and then the remainder of the flock runs as fast as possible past the humans to catch up with the escaped sheep. This happened multiple times, adding to Cathy and Art's frustrations.

All this while, the lamb was lying near the barn, bleating loudly, and the mom was loudly answering.

Finally, Art and Cathy were able to position themselves so that the sheep had no choice but to run into the corral. Cathy shut the gates to the corral. It did not take too much effort to get the sheep to move into the shed adjacent to the corral where we usually give them their daily grain. The door was closed to lock them into the shed. At this point, there were two lambs left outside the shed: the new lamb, and one of the others born earlier in the week. Both lambs were bleating, and two moms inside the shed were loudly answering back. Art went into the shed to catch the new mom and bring her out and into the barn. He asked Cathy, who was outside the shed controlling the doors, to catch the older lamb and place her inside the shed. This would, at least, quiet one frantic mother.

The new mom was still not cooperating. When sheep are chased inside the shed, they tend to group together, with the target of the chase trying to hide among the others. Art grabbed the new mom, but she was strong and not cooperating. She escaped several times, and hid among the others.

Finally, Art grabbed the new mom by her front legs, and was able, with much difficulty, to drag her out of the shed and near the entrance to the barn. Cathy reclosed the shed door and moved the new lamb into one of the pens inside the barn. Once released, the mom ran to her lamb inside the barn, and was locked inside the pen. At last glance, the lamb appeared to be eating fine and standing, none the worse for wear. The mom was still nervous, but taking care of her lamb.

The lamb and his mom were released back outside after several days in the barn together to get acquainted. They both did fine. The ewe was happier being with the flock, but the lamb was not so sure that the cold and wet outside was any better than the dry and comfortable inside. He was also being run ragged by his mother as she and the rest of the sheep ran back and forth from barn area to the peach orchard several times a day. He would be fine as long as he was still being fed by his mother.

WEEDING STRAWBERRIES

Art has spent a lot of time over the years weeding the strawberries. Despite his utmost diligence in past years removing weeds by hand, there are sometimes many, many weeds germinating for some reason in the strawberry rows in the springtime. He expected that, if he kept removing weeds as they appeared, there would eventually be few, if any, weeds growing there. Perhaps the cool spring weather is just right for sprouting residual weed seeds in the soil. Whatever the reason, the concentration of weed seedlings can be a surprise some years. If there ever was a temptation to use chemical herbicides, this would have been the reason. Of course, we don't use such things, but we have noticed that many farmers and gardeners try growing strawberries for a year or two and then become discouraged because the weed problem gets out of hand unless chemical herbicides are sprayed on the plants.

SMALL HOUSES

We view houses with a simplistic perspective. Small houses are honest; extremely large houses are ostentatious. Small houses take up little precious land; large houses are unnecessary. Small houses require just a little energy to maintain; large houses require a lot more energy. People who live in small houses are in cozy constant contact with each other and learn to live with other people; people who live in large houses can escape too easily. We live in a house that is comfortable. It was small when there were five humans living here, but is a nice size for two. With two, there is still the opportunity of escape and isolation, but not so much that a determined search can be quickly successful.

There is something desirable about a simple life, and small houses exemplify the essence of simplicity. Life can sometimes be very complicated, and a lot less enjoyable than it could be. We have plenty of material things, and they are supposed to make living easier and fuller. But, material things can also take time and attention from other things that matter more. Activities can help to fulfill our needs to some extent, but activities can also keep us so busy that we forget to smell the roses of life.

There is nothing more fulfilling than hard work to accomplish a meaningful task. Work hard during the day, accomplish some task as a result, and sleep well at night. That is as simple as it gets.

The simple life can sometimes be boring. But, boredom is a gift during which dreams are formed. Boredom has the potential to open the mind for wonderful thoughts, if we just let them wander in. It is when the mind is free of constraints that memories are recovered, plans are made, or creativity asserts itself. Simple life can be focused or unfocussed, but it is not tightly packed with complications that steal our attention from more expansive considerations.

It seems that during trying times that societal values drift toward more simplicity. During these times, people are more empathetic and caring for each other than they are during times with many more distractions. We have seen this tendency through several economic cycles. During high-flying times of economic abundance, there develops a competitive sense of hedonistic accumulation of material goods; people judge their sense of worth on the material things that they have compared to the things other people have. That includes owning large, majestic houses that impress family, friends, and neighbors.

So, small houses can be homes; large houses are too often pieces of property. And, as Robin Hobb observed, "Home is people. Not a place. If you go back there after the people are gone, then all you can see is what is not there anymore." Small houses enhance our sense of oneness.

WHERE HAVE ALL THE WILD ANIMALS GONE?

Looking out over the yard at SweetAire Farm, we are pleased that we have so many beautiful butterflies flitting about. They are sure pretty and interesting to watch as they fly from one flower to another, especially among the flowers of the Anise Hyssop and other perennials. We are reminded of other wildlife that we have seen over the years. We used to have quails that ran in front of our vehicles on the farm lane. They would rather try to run as fast as the vehicle than to turn off into the tall weeds on either side. There are no more quails. It was also not unusual to hear the crow of a cock pheasant in the morning and evening of every day; now we haven't heard one of these in decades. There used to be Box Turtles all over the place. Now we don't see any. And bluebirds, where have they disappeared to? Spotting foxes used to be easy; there were times when we would catch sight of whole families, mother and frolicking kits in our fields eating dropped peaches. Now to see a fox is a rarity.

Reptiles and amphibians are a lot more rare than before. For a while, toads were seen everywhere and at all hours of the day. Then they disappeared. We now have a few toads that can be heard trilling to each other on warm days at various places on our farm. Salamanders could be seen in our driveway many years ago. Then they disappeared. Coming across a snake or two warming in the midday sunshine in our lane used to be a common occurrence. We don't see any snakes anymore.

Where have all these gone? There is no shortage of deer, rabbits, squirrels, and ground hogs at this time. At least we haven't lost the beautiful butterflies.

BEWARE OF FLYING OBJECTS

On Saturday afternoon, Art was trying to hand weed the elderberry row before it started raining again. He had a window of maybe 3-4 hours without rain. He was crawling on his hands and knees in order to reach into the row to pull weeds between the plants. Over the years, with persistent efforts to remove the weeds that grew in among the elderberries, there are many fewer weeds than in the past. Nevertheless, if only one weed is missed and goes to seed, then years of efforts can easily be nullified. So, he was intent to find and remove every weed possible.

Grandson Greg had used the rainless period to mow our grass. He was trimming some grass just outside of the area where Art was weeding, but could not see past the thickly-populated row of black raspberry canes to where Art was moving about. Greg knew that Art was outside doing something, but he had thought that he had heard Art take his Gator and go back on the property somewhere. So, when he heard some noises near the elderberries, he assumed that there was a big animal over there. He couldn't see Art, who was crawling low about the elderberry row, so he had no idea that it was his grandfather. Greg said later that he seriously considered throwing an available rock or stick to where the noise was coming from in order to chase the animal away. If he had thrown a projectile, then Art would probably have found out that more than rain was falling from the sky that day. He may have been tempted to say a few words, if he were still able. His weeding activities could have been seriously interrupted, and he would likely have been found by the next day, at least. And Greg would have had to hide for weeks.

A DOG INCIDENT WITH THE SHEEP

We had an incident with the sheep in January 2013. Art was luckily out in back of the house pruning a grape vine when he heard dogs yelping and barking. He looked up and saw three dogs chasing our sheep all around the pasture. If dogs chase sheep, the sheep run, and if the dogs manage to grab some of their wool, they can tear it out and make the sheep bleed. Once they taste blood, then dogs mutilate the sheep and often kill them. The result is gruesome. Art quickly ran to the animals, and was able to grab one and then two of the dogs. They were half-grown lab types, and together they were terrorizing the sheep. With one heavy, squirming dog under each arm, he managed (with a lot of heavy breathing) to carry them down to our cat shed, which has been sealed so that hungry wild animals can't get in to eat cat food when it is locked.

Once the two dogs were locked in, he was able to catch the third and also lock it in. We called Animal Control, and they came to take the dogs away. Almost end of story. Sheep when terrorized by dogs scatter and stand in a stupor for a long time afterwards. Our sheep flock had broken into two bunches, one headed out to the peach orchard and one stayed near the barn in the pasture. The nearby ones stood motionless for a long time until the Animal Control person led the dogs on leashes out of the shed. When the dogs started barking again so that they could be heard loudly, the sheep in the pasture took off running for parts unknown. All the sheep eventually came back together and lay down as of the next morning. We hoped that this experience did not adversely affect their lambing, as it sometimes had in the past.

ALMOST INTO THE HORNETS' NEST

Art was picking under the lower branches of a Fuji apple tree, and was making great progress. When he turned to pick the other side of the tree, he saw that he was almost face-to-face with a HUGE white-faced hornets' nest. The nest is made of something like gray paper and shaped as a holiday globe. It was more than nine inches in diameter and just as long. Before he had a chance to panic, he noticed that the nest appeared to be abandoned; there were no hornets flying in and out of the nest.

Whew! If it had been populated and he had not known it was there, he would have had a hard time escaping from under the lower branches of the tree. There was no direct way out. He probably would have plowed a new path out of the tree, but he would have been stung many times for sure. Talk about being lucky!

A NEW LAMB FOR CHRISTMAS

On Christmas morning 2013, the temperature was finally sufficiently cold to freeze the ground solidly enough to be able to drive the truck up the hill and through the pasture to its parking place in our machinery shed. So, at 7 am that morning we went outside to put the truck away before the ground thawed. Art drove the truck while Cathy closed the pasture gates behind him and the truck.

Up on the hill, a ewe stood by herself, and tiny bleats could be heard from her vicinity – newborn twin lambs.

So, Art went over to the three of them and picked up the lambs. He coaxed the ewe to follow him into the barn where they would be kept for a few days until they were mature enough to be with the rest of the flock. One of the lambs, both females, was dried and strong. The other, slightly smaller, was still wet and covered in her membrane. And she was cold.

It was now Cathy's turn. She has such patience with newborn lambs. First, as was her routine, she checked the ewe for milk. No milk. For some reason that year, our ewes seemed to be dry immediately after lambing, although they would produce milk later on. So, Cathy returned to the house to mix up some powdered colostrum, warmed it in a bottle, and brought it back to the barn to feed to the lambs. The little one wouldn't drink. Cathy stuck her finger in the lamb's mouth to gauge its temperature. It was getting colder. Back to the house Cathy went for her hair drier. Directing the warm air from the drier over the lamb, she slowly warmed it. We have found that the fastest way to warm a lamb is to put it in a pot of warm water, but this washes off all the identifying smell of the lamb, and the mother often will reject the lamb after that, so the hair drier is the next best alternative.

Cathy must have spent at least an hour on that lamb. Finally, the lamb warmed and drank several ounces of colostrum. The lamb crisis was averted, at least for that time. The lambs turned out fine, drinking from their mom with gusto, and the mother soon had more than enough milk for both of them. The little one was not as frisky as the other one, but both survived and were fine.

The lamb crisis was over, but the dinner crisis was developing, because all this time in the barn had delayed cooking of the meal scheduled for noon. So, there was a little delay for dinner. Son Paul and grandson Greg come over to share in the meal. After they had been fed, they were frisky, too.

BANANA NUT BREAD

Art's grandmother used to make a dark banana bread that he liked very much. That recipe has been lost since then, and Cathy has been trying to reproduce it ever since. This recipe is a good substitute. This is a delicious dark banana bread that we have enjoyed many times.

Ingredients:

2 cups flour
⅔ cup brown sugar
1 teaspoon baking powder
½ teaspoon baking soda
1/8 teaspoon salt
2 eggs
1 cup mashed ripe bananas (2 medium bananas)
3 tablespoons milk
⅓ cup melted butter
1-¼ cup golden raisins
⅔ cup chopped black walnuts

In a large bowl, combine flour, sugar, baking powder, baking soda, and salt. In a small bowl, beat eggs, bananas, milk, and butter. Stir into dry ingredients until moistened. Fold in raisins and walnuts. Transfer to a greased 9×5×3-inch loaf pan. Bake at 350°F for 60 minutes, or until toothpick inserted near center comes out clean. Cool for 10 minutes before removing from pan to wire rack. Makes 1 loaf.

CRICKET WARS IV

With August, one or more interloper crickets usually come into our kitchen. It is not easy for a cricket to get there; the visitor has to jump onto the porch, go through a door and into the back room, and then under the door into the kitchen. Once there, a cricket almost always goes no further. It's almost as if our kitchen is a cricket's Valhalla. In the still of the dark night, the cricket chirps its song, hoping to find another cricket to share its good fortune. Sometimes there are more than one, but, so far this one August, we only had one. There have been years when Art has laid in wait for the cricket to crawl out from under its hiding place, so that he can capture the cricket and send it flying outside again. Catching a cricket is not so easy, because crickets are quick on the jump, and Art is not quite as quick with his cupped hand. This year, the cricket that had taken up residence in our kitchen had not yet aroused Art's hunting tendency, much less his prowess, so the cricket was safe for now where it was. European folk wisdom allows that a house without a cricket is a poor house indeed. If that is true, then our cricket proves how rich we are.

Cathy and Art had just retired on Monday evening, had turned out the kitchen lights, and had settled down in front of the living room television, when a loud cricket chirping sound began to come from the kitchen. Cathy and Art don't often watch TV in the evening, but when they do, they like to hear the dialog. The noisy cricket in the kitchen was interfering with their hearing. That was the last straw that led Art to leap literally into action. Both Art and Cathy quietly got up from their comfy seats on the couch and snuck to the edge of the kitchen. Cathy suddenly turned on the kitchen lights, and, lo and behold, there were two crickets- not one, but two- in the middle of the kitchen floor. Art quickly dropped on all fours, cupped his right hand so as not to harm the crickets, raised his hand above the first cricket, and then down. The first cricket had no chance. Mighty hunter Art was too quick, and the first cricket was captured. The second cricket had not moved, so Art repeated his demonstrated prowess and captured the second cricket in his cupped left hand. Two tries, two crickets; what a feat! Cathy opened the doors, and Art released the crickets outside, where they belonged. Art and Cathy then turned out the kitchen lights and returned to the living room. It may have taken five seconds for the chirping to begin anew, but no longer. So, they again crept to the kitchen and turned on the lights. Yes, another cricket was in view, this time near the wall. This one would be a little harder to catch, because it could escape beneath any appliance or under the desk. Art, on all fours again, tracked the cricket, cut off its obvious avenues of escape, and, after several tries, caught that cricket, which was subsequently released to its natural habitat outside. But, the adventure was not to be ended there. Another cricket came into view, sneaking along the wall. This one was wily. It hugged the wall and jumped away every time Art came nearer. It hid inside the electrical wallboard heater, and was not able to be seen. Art asked Cathy to turn on the heat, which she did, hoping that the cricket would feel the heat and vacate the heater. While we waited for the inevitable, another cricket was spotted, and, after several impressive, Olympic-quality leaps and turns with many near misses, Art was able to capture that one, too. Four down, one to go. The last cricket came out of the heater, much energized, and jumped and avoided Art's clutches for several minutes. That cricket hugged the wall, and leaped out of Art's range time and again. Once it leapt toward Art, so that Art lost its location, but, without the aid of a GPS, Art again homed in on that cricket. Art had almost met his match. But his cat-like sleuth and parry-and-thrust skills eventually caught up with that talented cricket. Out it went. When Art and Cathy returned to the living room, all was quiet in the kitchen. No more chirping. They could finally clearly hear the dialog on the TV. They had missed some of the show that they had been watching, but returned to the TV just in time for a commercial, and, this is true, would you believe the commercial was to advertise an internet service from Cricket Wireless!

MUDDY FEET

The corral area near the Bernie Barn gets very muddy in late winter and early spring when the sheep repeatedly walk over the ground in the area. When muddy conditions prevail, the sheep, who hate to walk through mud if they can help it, sometime take to staying overnight either in the hay-feeding pen or the shed where they are fed grain. It is dry and comfortable in both of these places.

When Cathy went out to feed the sheep one day, she tried to get the sheep to vacate where they had been staying and slog through the mud to the other side of the corral gates where they could be locked out while she poured grain into their feeding trough. They were used to the procedure, and knew what they were supposed to do, but, on this day they wouldn't go. She tried to chase them, and she tried to reason with them. She reminded them, first nicely and then a lot more adamantly, about what they were supposed to do, all to no avail. They had turned obstinate.

She kept at it. They simply moved from one pen to the other without getting their feet wet and muddy. She tried again and again. The sheep said, "nuh-uh, nope we won't go there. It's too muddy for us."

Finally, tired of all of the running from one place to the other, one large and probably very hungry ewe tired of the chase and decided that it was time to go; she led the others out of their nice comfortable refuge, through the mud, and to the other side of the gates. Cathy closed the gates, and they waited patiently outside the corral for Cathy to let them back in.

When she did, they were eager to trade wet feet for a chance for a few mouthfuls of grain, so eager, in fact, that they did not even notice the mud in their mad rush to get to their feed.

GREGORY RIDES A SHEEP INTO THE FENCE

Shearing was always so much fun (that was said sarcastically). Art had always sheared our sheep in the late spring so that they were cooler in the summer than they would have been with that thick coat of wool grown since the springtime before. As it was, even when sheared, they still suffered during some of the hottest days of midsummer, lying in the shade and not eating most of the time. If we were to lose any adult sheep during the year, it would almost always be in the summertime when they were weaker and more malnourished than at any other time of the year. So, shearing was important for the health of the animals.

When he grew big enough to help, Gregory was recruited as a sheep catcher and holder. Sometimes he was able to do these things, and sometimes the sheep would do them to him. This is the story of one such time when Gregory had an exciting and memorable adventure while helping his grandfather shear sheep.

Before they were to be sheared, the sheep were herded into their shed, usually given an incentive by a little grain poured into their feeding trough. They were locked in the shed and caught one at a time to be brought out to the pen where shearing took place. It was Gregory's job to catch the sheep one at a time when Art was ready to shear it, bring it out of the sheep shed and into the pen for shearing, and help hold the animal while Art used his electric clippers to cut the wool. There were only three major obstacles that Greg had to overcome; first, sheep do not like to be caught, and they tend to crowd together when cornered. This makes difficult separating one sheep from the rest. If one sheep senses that the catcher is after it, it will try to lose itself in the mix of sheep all packed tightly together. Catching a sheep like this is usually accomplished by grabbing a handful of wool and holding on while the sheep frantically tries to get loose of the catcher's grip.

The second step is to separate the sheep from the rest. That can be accomplished with a little muscle and a lot of determination; a lot more determination is needed by the human catcher than is demonstrated by the sheep once caught. The sheep then would typically run around the shed, as fast as it can, to try to escape and rejoin its other herdmates. The catcher must, at this point, hold on as hard as he can to demonstrate to the sheep that there is no recourse; there is no rejoining the group. Desperate sheep can be very determined, and this stage in catching can be very intense.

Art would have been watching all this happening, and enjoying the fact that it was not he who had to catch the next sheep victim. He may also be rolling with laughter, especially if the sheep had wrestled Greg to the ground and was walking all over him, or if the sheep defecated or urinated on him, or if Greg was tossed into fresh manure on the floor of the shed. But, Art had a job to do. It was his responsibility to open the door to the shed when Greg seemed to have a sheep under enough control that one and only one sheep would be brought out of the shed and into the shearing pen. If any of the others were to escape, there would be no catching them for the rest of the day.

This brings us to the third obstacle: the shed door was narrow and only wide enough for either the sheep or Greg to pass through – only one at a time. The sheep had to go first, because dragging a sheep is nearly impossible if the sheep is bracing and putting on the brakes. On the other hand, the sheep, in desperation to escape the grip of the catcher will accelerate out the opening once it sees that the door is open. Greg has to follow as best and as fast as he can through the doorway, holding on tightly so that the sheep doesn't escape entirely. Recapturing an escaped sheep is almost impossible during the same shearing session.

As soon as the sheep and Greg have cleared the doorway, Art's job was to close the door as quickly as he could so that the rest of the sheep, seeing a way out of their predicament, were prevented from rushing en masse out the door. This prevented Art from assisting Greg with controlling the sheep and to help steer it into the shearing pen. This was a very exciting stage in the process, because Greg had to try to maneuver from behind the sheep to its side where he could turn the sheep into another pen where it really did not want to go.

There was one time when Greg could not perform all these many moves as he should have. Instead, when the sheep that he was desperately holding from behind by a handful or two of wool bolted through the doorway, he landed on top of the sheep and went for a ride. The sheep, loose except for the heavy weight on its back, headed for open space. But, instead of getting entirely free, it saw that there was a relatively low spot in the fence that stood between it and total escape. It frantically ran toward its potential liberation.

The fence was constructed of boards and barbed wire. The sheep jumped. The sheep escaped scot free out of the corral area and out of the pasture into the lawn around the house. Gregory ended up stuck in the barbed wire, unhurt in all but his pride.

Art ended up laughing as hard as he ever has.

IT WAS THE BEST OF TIMES; IT WAS THE WORST OF TIMES

"So Satan went forth from the presence of the Lord, and afflicted Job with loathsome sores from the sole of his foot to the crown of his head." (Job 2:7).

Whereas the afflictions that we endured during the first week of July, 2015, were not nearly as extreme as those inflicted upon Job, we were wondering just what was going on and how to respond. Many large trees surrounding our orchard were blown down by the strong wind on the previous Tuesday; Cathy discovered that another large tree had split and fallen, blocking our direct access to the bottom of the orchard and to the blueberries. Another large tree fell on the last row of peaches.

Then, we had a torrential rain on Saturday, the Farmers' Market day. That cut into the number of people who came to our stand. We had struggled all week to pick the fruit that had ripened that week, and then had to bring home a large portion of it. A total of 3 ¼ inches of rain fell that day. The ground is still squishy.

Luckily, we then had a couple of better days to work on the tasks that needed to be accomplished. During that time, we set insect traps, sprayed, weeded, and mowed. Then, during the night the following Tuesday, we had a strong thunderstorm with wind and 1 ½ inches more of rain.

Thursday morning was, would you believe it, rainy. All this rain and wetness washes our weak organic protective sprays from the trees and promotes diseases in our fruits. Even the berries are crying "uncle", we've had enough.

So, these are the best of times and these are the worst of times. We just have to decide which of those two is the truer characterization. Our optimism has been sorely tested.

AN ARTHUR JOHNSON INSTEAD OF AN ARNOLD PALMER

Many of you have probably heard of an Arnold Palmer, the drink named after the famous golfer. An Arnold Palmer is half lemonade and half iced tea. Art has a favorite drink that he invented, and he eponymously calls it an Arthur Johnson. This drink consists of one half unsweetened iced tea and one half Ocean Spray Ruby Red grapefruit juice. Art drinks a lot of these during the summer on days that he works hard outside on the farm. He usually fills a large plastic Slurpee glass with the Arthur Johnson concoction and downs it in a few gulps. The drink tastes so good. Anyway, Cathy had the quip of the week; when Art told her that he had five or six Arthur Johnsons one hot and humid day, she retorted, "In other words, you're full of yourself."

Case closed.

A WEEK'S WORTH OF SHEEP TALES

We let the sheep into the peach orchard in the wintertime so that they can graze on the extra grass growing there. We don't however, let them into the apple orchard because the apple orchard fences are not good enough to contain the sheep.

Cathy was going back to the apple orchard one day to prune trees when she came to the closed gate between the peach orchard and the apple orchard. The sheep were there, but waiting on the wrong side of the gate for someone to let them back into the peach orchard and the way back to their home base. The sheep had been getting out of the peach orchard the previous year, and their escape route yet to be found. They had visited several of the neighbors last spring, eating the grass that looked so much greener on the other side of the fence. And that's how things stood until, in desperation, we locked the sheep into their summer pasture later that spring. It looked like it was happening again this year.

Art was scheduled to leave for a couple of days for a meeting in Pittsburgh on Wednesday of that week, and Cathy had no stomach for chasing sheep while he was gone, so she closed the gate that lets them into the peach orchard, trapping them near the house until he came home.

She walked the fences, and found no place where the sheep could have escaped, but she did find some places in the apple orchard where the fence was down due to large trees having fallen across it. These places could not explain how the sheep kept escaping from the peach orchard, but, if they did manage to get into the apple orchard, they could then escape from SweetAire Farm property over those downed fences.

In the meantime, it snowed three inches on Tuesday. Cathy is always anxious to clear the driveway after snow, so she went outside as soon as the snow stopped in early afternoon. She spotted a ewe that was about to give birth, so she called Art to help move the ewe into the barn. Cathy and Art separated the ewe from the rest of the flock, and got her into the barn. Then they shoveled the driveway. After that, Cathy checked the ewe, and it had given birth in the barn to twin female lambs. The lambs appeared to be healthy, but Cathy takes no chances; she mixed up some artificial colostrum, put it in a bottle, warmed it, and brought it to the lambs. They drank a little, but not much, so they must have been drinking enough from their mom. They would be fine, but they did keep bleating for some unknown reason.

Soon after Art left on Wednesday, another set of twin females was born, but this time outside in the cold wind. Cathy found them and moved them into the barn. They were both cold, so Cathy dried them and heated them with her hair dryer. Once warm, they had a chance to live. Again, following her standard operating procedure, she mixed some artificial colostrum and brought it to the new lambs. One drank some, but the other did not. Over the course of the next few days, one of the lambs appeared to be doing well, but the other did not. When she went out to check on them on Friday morning, the weak lamb had died.

Art returned. Wanting to find out where the sheep were escaping from the peach orchard, he opened the gate to the peach orchard. Perhaps following sheep tracks in the snow would lead to their escape route.

Saturday morning came. Despite the cold, Art bundled up and went to fix the apple orchard fence where Cathy had found it flattened. He cut the offending trees with his chain saw and removed them. He pounded metal posts into the ground and hung the fence wire high enough to keep the sheep inside. But, he couldn't find the sheep. They were nowhere around. Lunch time.

After lunch, Art went to the barn and gave the lambs their shots, docked their tails, and put identification tags on their ears. Once they recover a short time after that, the lambs are usually let out of the barn for the first time. While waiting for this time to elapse, it was time to find the rest of the sheep.

Cathy had walked out to the peach orchard, following the sheep tracks in the snow. She found the hole in the fence! This was the way the sheep were getting out last year and this year as well. Without the snow, we would never have found it, because it was low, so the sheep could crawl under rather than jump over, and it was beside a tree where it was hard to spot. The hole was located in a place where the sheep could escape from the farm without going through the apple orchard first.

They had probably been going through the hole every day and coming back every afternoon.

So, where were the sheep? Cathy got down on her hands and knees and slithered through the hole to follow the sheep tracks. Art went back to the house to get Cathy's van to cruise the road to try to spot the sheep. Driving down Smith Road, he spotted the sheep in a neighbor's yard. He opened our gate to the road side of the apple orchard, so that the sheep could be chased back into the apple orchard. According to the mass of tracks near the gate, the sheep had been looking to return to the apple orchard either through or around the gate, but Art had fixed that part of the fence. The sheep could not get back with the route they had been in the habit of using.

The sheep had disappeared from view without going through the gate into the apple orchard. Where had they gone now? Art returned the van to the house and walked back to the peach orchard. Cathy had come back to our side of the fence without spotting the sheep. The sheep finally figured that the way back was to return through the hole where they had escaped in the first place. As Cathy and Art watched, the sheep slipped under the fence and walked back to the barn.

Art prepared to fix the hole. Before he did, however, he let the mom and her two lambs out of the barn. Cathy made sure that the sheep did not go back to the peach orchard and escape again through the hole in the fence.

Art spotted a ewe lying on her side, told Cathy about it before he walked out to fix the hole. It took several trips, but he had it fixed within a half hour or so. As he came back, Cathy informed him that the ewe that had been on her side had had a lamb. Cathy had gotten her and the lamb into the barn, just where the previous ewe and her lambs had been released an hour before. Because the ewe with the new lamb was one of the sheep that had been in the neighbor's yard, we almost had a lamb born while they were off the farm.

And it doesn't end there. On Sunday, Art and Greg went to get a truck load of hay for the sheep. While they were gone, Cathy spotted a ewe trying to give birth. The lamb was huge, its head and one leg were showing out the back of the ewe, but lambs, especially large ones, need to be born with their heads between their two front legs. Without the two legs, the lamb's shoulders are too wide to pass naturally through the birth canal. The way to solve this problem is to pass one's hand inside the ewe and past the lamb's shoulder to locate the other leg, pull the other leg forward so that it is on the side of the head, and pull the lamb gently from its mom. Cathy tried this, but couldn't locate the other leg. At this point, Art and Greg returned, and Cathy had Art come over to the shed where the ewe was located. Art rolled up his sleeves, thrust his hand into the ewe, and attempted to locate the other leg. No success.

What could we do? If we did nothing, the lamb would die and the ewe would die. At the very least, we had to sacrifice the lamb to save the mom. So, while Cathy held the ewe, Art pulled as gently but firmly as he could on the lamb while trying to avoid hurting the lamb too badly. All of a sudden, the lamb came out, and the mom was relieved. Cathy placed the lamb in front of the ewe, and she began to lick it and make gentle noises to it. This was the largest lamb we have had in many years. After bringing both mom and lamb into the barn, Cathy helped the lamb stand on its legs and drink artificial colostrum from a bottle and suck from its mom. She observed that this was the hungriest lamb that she had ever seen. The lamb seemed to be fine, and none the worse for the difficult birth experience.

ART AND THE RAM 1

Art had a rough few days. It started on a fall Sunday afternoon when he went into the sheep pasture to switch the sheep to a new pasture section. Along with the ewes; the ram was there.

All of our rams were mild-mannered when young, but, as they aged, they developed a hostile attitude toward humans, especially during breeding season in autumn. This ram, Jack, remained in a more docile state longer than the rest because we tried hard not to antagonize him for the first several years of his life. If, at times, he attempted to hit into Art, Art would stop and confront him with a loud threatening sound and a wag of the finger; that was enough to stop him in mid-charge before contact was made.

He was feeling belligerent that Sunday afternoon, but Art didn't feel the need to carry a stick with him when he went in to change the sheep pasture section. This time, however, the ram didn't stop, and it took Art by surprise. The ram knocked Art to the ground.

Art has not been knocked to the ground very many times, but, at no other time did a ram come back for a second time; but this ram did, and hit Art hard while he was on the ground. Art got up as fast as he could, and went after the ram for retribution, but left the pasture as quickly as he could after that.

It felt to Art like he had a cracked rib just under his left arm. It hurt really badly for a few days. Whenever he had to sneeze or cough, the pain was murder. He also had a hard time sleeping. Art has had cracked ribs before, and knew that it would heal sooner or later, so resisted taking any pain medicine. The rib had begun to feel better after a few days; it still hurt at times, but the pain was tolerable.

For a long while, he still tried to avoid coughing or sneezing, but, when he was forced by nature to engage in either of those two involuntary activities, at least it didn't feel as if he was being stabbed. He recovered his health, but his distrust of the ram remained. Ever after, he would not enter the pasture without a stick in his hand when the ram was there

ART FALLS IN THE MUD, AGAIN

It had been a very wet year, in 2018. There were places where the mud was so slippery and deep that vehicles could get stuck if we were not careful. So, Art decided to dig a ditch to divert water from a particularly mucky place in our lane. He was doing fine, although he lifted a ton of mud that stuck to his shoes with every step he took. At one point, as he was attempting to drive his shovel into the ground one more time, he began to lose his balance, Normally, that would have been just a minor detail, but this time his feet stuck in the mud; he could not step backward, forward, or anywhere, to regain his balance. Over he went, splat, right in the mud! Now that is how his status was confirmed as a dirty old man. After getting up again, with a yuck score of 8 out of 10, he continued to dig, but being a lot more careful this time.

BLENDER OATMEAL PANCAKES

Regular pancakes are not nearly as filling as are these oatmeal pancakes. When you sink your teeth into these, you know that you are eating something. And, they stick to your ribs through a whole morning's worth of farm work.

Ingredients:

1 cup quick oatmeal
1-½ cups buttermilk (or 1-½ cup of milk with 1-½ tablespoons vinegar)
¾ cup all purpose flour
1 tablespoon sugar
¾ teaspoon baking soda
¾ teaspoon salt
2 eggs

Put all ingredients in a blender until everything is mixed (about 30 seconds).

Pour small circles onto a well-greased and moderately hot skillet (a droplet of water dropped onto the skillet should "dance").

Cook the first side until the edges are done and have little bubbles; turn and cook on the other side for an equal amount of time, or until cooked through (about 2 minutes per side).

Serve hot with your favorite topping. Pancakes can be kept in the refrigerator to eat later either hot or cold.

BIRDS IN OUR FRUIT

We usually need to pick our berries quickly before birds devour them. Birds must think that SweetAire Farm is their meal ticket, because they sometimes eat more than their share. We don't mind if the birds have a few; that is just the price we pay for ecological tranquility, but, when they eat a large portion of the ripe berries, then we have no benefit for growing them. Birds start early with the Goumi berries, eating most of them, and move on to the tart cherries. One year, Art had picked about 2/3 of the cherries, and had to wait a day or two before he could pick the rest. In that time, the birds had cleaned them up. Then they moved to our black raspberries. Next, they try to finish off our elderberries. After that, they eat some of our apples. They are worse during some years than others for some reason. We could put nets over some of our fruits to protect them from the birds, we suppose. We have nets over most of our blueberries. If we didn't, we would have none of those for ourselves. But putting nets over all our fruits is impractical. The elderberries, for instance, are 10-12 feet tall. So, we are in a race to see who can get to the fruit first.

We have a particular problem with crows in our pears and Asian pears. Perhaps because of the location of these trees toward the back of the orchard where we do not often go, crows are free to eat all they can. If these fruits are not picked before they are fully ripe, then we may not get a single fruit. This is discouraging after having cared for the fruit all season up to the point of ripening, seeing the trees respond each with a full crop, and then getting nothing. We do not know how to stop the crows. We had a few years reprieve when West Nile virus decimated the crow population in our area, but the crows eventually repopulated and again began eating more than their share.

Some people use explosive noise-makers to scare off the birds. These shoot off a loud "bang" after some time interval. There are also audio speakers that emit the sounds of birds in trouble. These are supposed to work particularly well with crows. Both of these methods not only scare the birds, but they disturb the neighbors, as well, so we don't use them. Other growers have different means to cope with birds in their fruit. Some are more successful than others, we suppose, but we have not yet found the ideal solution for our operation, so, for us, it's still a race of us against them.

CAROLING WITH PATIENTS

A small group of us from our church went one Saturday before the holiday to sing some Christmas carols at a local nursing home. We walked through the halls, stopping at each occupied room to ask if they would like us to sing a carol for them. What could they do but say "yes"? They were there in their rooms, some confined to their beds, and we had the door blocked. So, we had no one turn us down. We sang one carol per room, and moved on.

We each had sheets of paper in our hands with the words to the carols so that we would seem to be coordinated enough that we were all singing the same words. This worked pretty well, and there were no complaints from any of our captive audience listeners.

We soon reached a point where we could see several patients sitting together in wheel chairs watching a television program. "Look", cried one of our singers, "a bevy of beauties lies ahead." And, indeed, if that is what a bevy is, then we saw them, too. They were engrossed in the program, but, when we asked about singing a song for them, one or two, at least, said "sure", and we sang. Some of the beauties continued to watch the TV, but the ones closest to us had no choice but to turn and listen. When we were finished, and left, the ones who had had to listen jockeyed their positions so that, if we should turn around and ask if they again wanted us to sing, there would be others who would have to be courteous and pay us attention. It was like watching a Black Friday sale stampede in slow motion.

When we reached the end of the hall, we turned around to exit that particular ward, but when we reached the set of closed doors near the end of the hall, we found that we could not get out. The doors were locked, probably to keep patients from running off by themselves and enjoying some freedom. There were numerical touch pads by the doors, and we tried all of the codes that had been given to us. Nothing worked. It was starting to look like we might have to spend Christmas in the nursing home with the same people that we had subjected to our

Christmas carol singing. What irony! There were some panicked looks on the faces of some of the patients: they were probably thinking that they might have to hear a second carol from us, or worse, three.

Fortunately, we found an attendant working on our side of the closed doors who was only too happy to let us out. We are not sure, but she may have been one of the ones with the panicked facial expression. In any case, we left, and decided that we had sung enough for that evening. We all went home with warm, joyful hearts for having been so good as to sing mostly on key and for being able to walk out under our own power.

CATHY'S LAMB EUPHORIA

"I am completely besotted", said Cathy to Art the one morning. She had just come in from outside where she had fed the sheep their grain for the day. She had never before said these words to Art, at least as far as he could remember, and he wasn't quite sure of what she meant. He didn't know whether to hug her, to hide from her, or to get her a large swallow of high-test coffee. Instead, he just listened to her talk.

She had fallen in love with this new lamb. When it was in its pen in the barn, it would hop around its mom, and act just act as happy as could be. It even would come up to Cathy so that she could pet it. No other lamb in recent years has been as friendly.

So, Cathy calls her "Sunshine".

On the day when she told Art about her besotted condition, she had been out feeding the sheep, and this was the first morning outside for Sunshine. Consequently, Sunshine did not know the drill: how Cathy would put the grain in the trough, open the gates so that the sheep could enter, and watch as the sheep made a mad dash for their shed where the grain was waiting. Sunshine just stood there as her mom, along with the rest of the sheep, disappeared inside the shed.

Very soon, she realized that her mom was not coming right back, so she started bawling in her little lamb voice. Cathy saw this happening, and thought that she could perhaps get behind Sunshine and push her into the shed to be with her mom. Instead, Sunshine came up to Cathy, who then was able to lead her into the shed. Sunshine followed Cathy all the way.

Once inside the shed, Sunshine's mom was still not paying any attention to her; there is only a limited opportunity to eat as much grain as she could while competing with all the other sheep for the contents of the trough. Sunshine began bawling again. At this point, the largest of our lambs turned to Sunshine, as if to say "What is your problem?". Soon, the grain was all devoured, and things returned to normal. That is, normal for the sheep. Cathy was still besotted.

UNSCHEDULED DELIVERY

As if things weren't busy and exciting enough ... a furniture delivery box truck made an unscheduled, unauthorized, and unwanted incursion into SweetAire Farm on a mid-August afternoon in 2015. By way of explanation, the driver said that a county dump truck had been coming down our road in the opposite direction and he moved to the right to avoid a collision. His right front wheel went off the road and he headed straight for our "SweetAire Farm" sign at the end of our driveway. He plowed through the sign and into a cedar tree near the driveway entrance, taking half of the tree with him and the truck as he rode out of control. The tree and our electric service wire stopped the truck. Neither the driver nor the passenger in the truck was injured. Art and Cathy were not home at the time, but Art arrived shortly thereafter. Soon, a sheriff's deputy came. After a while a Delmarva Power guy came to cut the tree from the electric wire. Then another furniture delivery truck came to transfer the remaining furniture from the errant truck into the one that had just arrived. In the middle of all that, we had a brief thunderstorm. After what seemed like a long time, a large tow truck came to pull the box truck out of our yard. The tow truck operator had to be very careful because the fuel tank of the box truck was in contact with the tree root ball and he wanted to avoid a rupture. He was eventually successful, and the truck was towed away. Next, a Delmarva Power crew came to straighten the electric pole which had been tilted when the box truck stretched the electric service wire to our house. That's when Cathy arrived, and several trucks had to do-see-do to let her enter our driveway. We spent the rest of the evening cutting and removing the tree and trying as best we could to repair the deep ruts made in our grass and flower bed. The "SweetAire Farm" sign remained a casualty for weeks.

CRAISINS OATMEAL CHOCOLATE CHUNK COOKIES

This recipe was found on the back of a Craisins package, and makes really good cookies that satisfy after working hard pruning trees or picking from a ladder. We enjoy them when really hungry after a morning or afternoon of hard work.

Ingredients:

2/3 cup butter, softened
2/3 brown sugar
2 large eggs
1-1/2 cups old-fashioned rolled oats
1-1/2 cup flour
1 teaspoon baking soda
½ teaspoon salt
1-1/4 cups dried cranberries
2/3 cup white chocolate chunks

Preheat oven to 375°F. With electric mixer, beat butter and sugar in a medium bowl until light and fluffy. Add eggs, mix well. Combine oats, flour, baking soda, and salt in a separate bowl. Add to butter mixture slowly, mixing well often. Stir in cranberries and white chocolate chunks. Drop by rounded teaspoonfuls onto ungreased cookie sheets. Bake 10-12 minutes, or until golden brown. Cool on a wire rack.

CATHY'S SHUDDERING ADVENTURE

On a Thursday night some time ago, Cathy had what can euphemistically called an adventure. The episode began in the evening, when a rustling sound was heard near a window facing the deck of our house. Art thought that there might be an animal that had climbed on to the deck, so he went to investigate (we have had, on rare occasions, small wild animals getting on the deck). Even shining a flashlight out the window disclosed nothing – no animal, nothing else that could make the noise. It happened again, and he investigated a second time; still nothing.

Later that night, Cathy was in bed, sleeping, when she felt something move in her hair. It felt larger than a spider or even a stink bug that sometime crawl around where they are not wanted. She sat up, shuddered, and turned on the light. She looked around, put her fingers through her hair, but felt or saw nothing. So, she crawled back underneath the covers, turned out the light, and tried to return to sleep. It happened again. There was definitely something crawling through her hair. This time, she shuddered even more, sat straight upright, and turned on the light. There was nothing to be seen for a minute or two, and then she spotted a movement over by the closet - a mouse. As she watched, the mouse climbed up some blankets that were touching the floor and reached the top of the other bed. She saw how the mouse was running back and forth in front of the closet, so she tried to arrange a handy plastic bag so that the mouse would run into and she could catch it. No such luck! Realizing that she could not catch the mouse that night, she rearranged the blankets on her bed so that they were not dragging on the floor, and moved her bed out from the wall. Reasonably sure that the mouse could not return to crawl through her hair, she warily tried to go to sleep again.

The next day, she scoured through the house for her mouse traps. It took some searching, but she found them and baited them both, one with peanut butter, and the other with cheese. She placed them in front of the closet where she had seen the mouse the night before. Art was upstairs brushing his teeth that evening when he heard "Snap, Snap". The mouse had paid the ultimate price for upsetting Cathy the previous night. Let that be a lesson to all outside mice that are tempted to come inside our house. Don't mess with Cathy, or she will get more than even. This lesson was not lost on Art, either.

CONFUSED CONVERSATION AT THE APPLE FESTIVAL

The Darlington Apple Festival is held annually in our small town on the first Saturday in October. Art takes a wagon load of apples to the Festival to sell to the roughly 65,000 visitors who roam the street partaking of the many booths and events on that day.

This conversation between Art and a customer happened for real at the Darlington Apple Festival in October 2016. Nothing in this conversation has been changed. It went like this:

Customer: "Hi."
Art (as he often responds to a customer saying "Hi"): "Not now, but maybe later."
Customer: "Huh?'
Art (repeating himself): "Not now, but maybe later."
Customer stares blankly.
Art (starting to explain): I meant that I am not high now, but maybe I could be later."
Customer: "I don't understand."
Art: "I think we have a communications problem here."
Customer: "Maybe. It could be because I had a little cannabis this morning ... for my migraines."
Art: "Oh."

And that's the way it was. Art and the customer eventually settled on a sale of some apples, and they separated, one confused and the other amused. It really happened.

CRICKET WARS V

Art and the Cricket: We returned that Saturday evening from a restaurant dinner and opened the door to our kitchen. Right near the table was a cricket that had somehow crawled into the house. We often have crickets come in at this time of the year, an old saying is that it is a very poor house that doesn't have a cricket, but Art was not about to concede house privileges to this particular upstart. So, he quickly dropped to his knees, cupped his hand and covered the cricket. Oops! It escaped out of the side of his hand. Quickly recovering, Art scrambled as close as he could to the cricket, which by now was in panic mode, jumping for all it was worth ahead, sideways, and even more sideways still. Art lunged and lurched after that little guy. Several times Art had that cricket in his grasp, and just as many times the cricket found a way to escape. But Art is stubborn, if not half-fast, so, he scrambled after that cricket and eventually corralled it in his cupped hand. Out the door with that interloper!

But that is not the end to the story. Sunday morning, returning from church, what did Cathy and Art spy when they opened the kitchen door, but a cricket in the middle of the kitchen floor. Was it the same one? We don't know, but for sure, the action drama of the night before repeated itself. Art quickly dropped to the floor, church clothes and all, and cupped his hand over the cricket. The cricket escaped his grasp. Again and again Art scrambled and tried to capture his prey. The cricket almost made it under the dishwasher, but with one last lunge, Art had captured that critter and, quick as a bunny, threw it out on the lawn.

But that is still not the end of the story. Art got up in the middle of Sunday night and went downstairs to the kitchen. He heard a cricket cheerfully chirping away. It seems that he had won the battles but lost the war. Was it the same cricket? We don't know, but the next morning, Cathy spied the little critter as it crept out from under the dishwasher. Art sprang into action. He played the same cat-and-mouse routine, slapping his cupped hand over the cricket, cricket escaping, Art trying again and again. After many tries, he finally captured that cricket once again, and out the door it flew.

But that, again, still isn't the end of the story. We could still hear a cricket chirping from somewhere in the kitchen. We still had more crickets to catch. Art had caught two and so had Cathy, one in the kitchen sink, of all places. Last week, when Cathy was putting on her shoes to go outside, she felt a small lump inside. She knew it wasn't one of her toes (she is smart that way). Taking the shoe off and shaking it revealed a cricket that had wanted to hitch a ride in the worst way possible (can you imagine being inside a shoe next to a foot?). So, these crickets are really fanatic about coming inside to be with us.

CONVERSATION WITH A PARK ATTENDANT

Immediately after the Farmers' Market one August Saturday, Cathy and Art drove to upstate New York to attend a reunion of Art's family (and a couple of friends). The reunion was held on Sunday in a small park in the hills of New York's Chemung County. There is a fee for entering the park, and it is $1 cheaper for Chemung County residents than for others. The following is a conversation that occurred between Art and the entrance attendant as he pulled up to the guard house and rolled down his window:

> Attendant: "Do you live in Chemung County?"
> Art: "No. Why would anyone want to live in Chemung County?"
> Attendant: "Then that would be $8."
> Art (handing over the money): "I'd even pay another dollar extra so that I wouldn't have to live in Chemung County."
> Attendant (giving change): "I live in Chemung County."
> Art (feigning amazement): "And you are wearing shoes!"
> Attendant: "Some of us know how."

Anyway, she let us enter.

CRICKET WARS VI

Crickets! We had more cricket incidents with the removal of four from our kitchen. There were two episodes involving the sport of capturing the little critters, each time ending with the removal of two crickets. The first event occurred in the middle of the night, when Art turned on a kitchen light and saw, first, one cricket in the middle of the floor, and, then, another not too far away. They had come out of hiding under the cover of darkness, not expecting anybody to ruin their face-to-face conversations. The second time was right after we returned from church on Sunday morning when the two crickets must have been lounging around, taking it easy, and meeting and greeting each other, as they probably do on a typical quiet Sunday morning.

As with his method of dealing with unwanted crickets, he quickly dropped to his knees, raised his cupped right hand, and brought it down over the interloper, trying to capture it without harming it. After all, a cricket saved is a cricket earned.

It takes a special manual and digital technique to close the natural gap between thumb and forefinger so that a cricket cannot escape through the tiny opening, but Art has practiced enough that he has nearly perfected this part of his technique. Anyway, the cricket was captured.

Now came the hard part: capturing the next little trespasser. Art does not have the same skill with his left hand as he does his right hand, so, before the second cricket could be dealt with, he had to transfer the cricket in his right hand to his left hand, all without allowing the squirming hostage to escape his grasp. With some care, this maneuver was accomplished.

On to the next cricket, and that one was relatively easy to capture. In the shadows of the partially-lit nighttime kitchen, it was not so easy for the little monster to see where Art was, so the cricket didn't move much. Art moved faster, even on his hands and knees.

Getting up from a hands-and-knees position with a cricket in each closed hand was not an easy maneuver for Art to accomplish. But, with some difficulty, he rose to his feet, then walked out the back door, and sent those guys flying onto the lawn. Case closed.

The Sunday morning episode was similar, except that the second cricket was much more aware of Art's presence, and kept hopping out of range of the big guy trying his best on his hands and knees to keep up, and to block the cricket's path to cover. Cathy helped by pointing out where the cricket was each time it moved, although Art could very well see that for himself. However, he appreciates directions from Cathy whenever she offers them to him.

DARK ACRES

There must be a logical reason why it takes us so long to complete the many chores that we are tasked with on SweetAire Farm. The pruning in winter, the fertilizing and spraying in the spring, the picking, mowing, and weeding in the summer, and the building and repairing in the autumn; these should not take nearly as long to accomplish as they do. There must be a good reason.

That reason, we have decided, must be Dark Acres. If physicists can invoke the existence of dark matter to explain the mysteries of the universe, then it stands to reason that we can use the concept of Dark Acres to explain the unknowns here at SweetAire Farm. Dark Acres certainly is a better explanation than the excuses that we get tired, or are getting older, or that we have taken on more than we can easily handle. No, Dark Acres must be the answer.

SweetAire Farm was actually formed from three different parcels of land. The original house, sheds, and Bernie Barn were located on nearly 5 acres (more or less, as the deed said) purchased in 1972. To that was added a parcel of land of 15 acres (more or less) purchased in 1979. Finally, another 22 acres (more or less) were added in 1987. Adding those numbers results in a total of 42 acres. However, back in 2004, when we wanted to sell to Harford County the development rights to our land, we were required to have the property surveyed. When that was done, we ended up with 49 acres (someone quipped that we should have it surveyed again, and then maybe we would end up with an even 50 acres). Anyway, somehow we ended up with 7 extra acres. This is a good practical example of Dark Acres finally made visible.

Without all the SweetAire Farm Dark Acres, we would be able to complete all our daily work at a leisurely pace, and have time at the end of our days for fun and frolic. We could read, watch television, go to good restaurants, enjoy musical theater productions, take up exotic hobbies, and probably be as lively as people who do not have to contend with work that seems to have no end. We would not moan and groan at the end of each day like old folks do. We would be exciting people leading exciting lives. We are not all these things because of the effect of Dark Acres on our farm. It's the only possible explanation.

DEAF CHEF

One Saturday at the Farmers' Market, a man came up to our market stand while eating a banana. Art asked him why he was eating a banana when there was all this good, fresh, locally-grown fruit in front of him on our tables. He said that he was eating the banana because he suffered from bad leg cramps, and the banana added potassium to his system. We know about leg cramps; Cathy, especially, suffers from leg cramps quite often, and the quick cure that she uses is a teaspoon of yellow mustard taken orally when she first feels the cramp. This really works, and works almost instantly. Art has tried it, too, and it works the same for him. So, Art explained to the man eating the banana that taking a spoonful of yellow mustard when he got the cramp would solve his problem. He said that he was a chef, and called it salad mustard rather than yellow mustard, but that he would try it and let us know the next week.

So, he did show up the next week. We asked him if he had used the mustard cure, and he said that he had, but only for one day. He had taken the mustard prophylactically, not when he got the cramps. He expected that the mustard would prevent cramps before they occurred. Art then started to tell him that he had not listened to what we had been telling him; the mustard was only supposed to be eaten after the leg cramps first appeared. Art no more than said to him that he had not understood what we had told him, that he hadn't listened correctly, when a female (presumably his wife) came over to him, talking to him as she approached, and completely ignoring that Art was in the middle of a conversation with the man. The man, oblivious to what Art was saying, turned toward the woman and then left without listening to another word from Art. He still hadn't listened! He is destined to have leg cramps forever. But, at least, he listens when a female says something to him. He is destined to live a long, if painful, life.

FOOD RULES

From his book entitled "Food Rules", Michael Pollan writes these things:

1. Don't eat anything your great-grandmother wouldn't recognize as food.
2. Avoid food products containing ingredients that a third-grader cannot pronounce.

3. Eat only foods that will eventually rot.
4. Buy your snacks at the farmers' market.
5. Don't ingest foods made in places where everyone is required to wear a surgical cap.
6. It's not food if it arrived through the window of your car.
7. Don't eat breakfast cereals that change the color of the milk.
8. Be the kind of person who takes supplements – then skip the supplements.
9. Pay more, eat less.
10. Don't get your fuel from the same place your car does.

He writes lot of other things, too, but these give the idea.

MORNING GLORY MUFFINS

These muffins are filling and very good. They are moist with all the crushed fruit in them. Cathy made them once with her cranberry relish instead of pineapple, and they tasted wonderful. Eat them for breakfast or for a snack in the middle of the day when you need energy and something that sticks with you for a while.

Ingredients:

1-¼ cups sugar
2-¼ cups flour
1 tablespoon cinnamon
2 teaspoons baking soda
½ teaspoon salt
½ cup coconut
¾ cup raisins
1 apple, grated
1 cup crushed pineapple (almost any crushed fruit will work)
2 cups grated carrots
½ cup nuts
3 eggs
1 cup oil
1 teaspoon vanilla

Combine all but last 3 ingredients. Whisk together last 3 ingredients and add to the mixture. Spoon into muffin tins. Bake at 350°F until a toothpick comes out clean. Makes 2 dozen muffins.

GOOD PEOPLE ARE EVERYWHERE

News media bring you awareness of terrible events everywhere, even in living color right into the sanctity of your own homes. It is extremely difficult to avoid bad news nowadays. It is tempting to start believing that the world is a dangerous and nasty place where no one is to be trusted. One cannot tell the good guys from the bad guys, because they all look alike. So, we are tempted to look over our shoulders at all the strangers around us and to be afraid. We want to withdraw and exclude everyone else not close to us as we lose trust in every outsider we see.

But, look around. If you want to see good people, just realize that they are all right here. We see some of them every week, and we can attest to the goodness of the people, both buyers and sellers, at the Farmers' Market and elsewhere. We know, because we have learned enough about each of you that we consider you to be among our friends. You are good people. You care and you try to do your best. Because of you, the world is a better place. Each of you has your own way to do this, but you do it, and make it better for all of us. Do not stop.

And the vendors: each of them is a hard working, honest individual, the salt of the Earth. We do not know all of them personally, but we would attest, even without knowing their names, to their essential goodness. They have big hearts in their chests and calluses on their hands. If they had no optimism, they wouldn't be here.

So, do not change your outlook on life and your faith in the quintessential goodness of the vast majority of the people, not only those whom you know, but also those who you may have the good fortune to meet eventually. It takes a million people working hard together to build the world into a better place; it only takes a couple of deranged people to upset what the million have built. It takes courage to rise above the fear that the latter two can evoke from the good works of the million, but we have that courage; we only have to realize it. Do not lose the trust we have in others. Now, more than ever, we need to cultivate trust and connectedness. That is the wish we have for all.

GROUNDHOGS GO FOR A RIDE

We had a surplus of groundhogs on the lawn around our house. A surplus means anything more than none. These pests get into some of our plants growing in the flower beds, eat fallen fruits, and sometimes even climb on to our porch. So, it was time to get the Have-A-Heart trap and capture them one at a time. It is said that some people who catch groundhogs then bring them across the Conowingo Dam and release them on the other side in Cecil County. It is also said that groundhogs are a dietary staple for some over there and a delicacy enjoyed by other Cecil county inhabitants. In addition, they say that groundhog is best served warm after having been tenderized by the tire of a three-quarter ton pick-up truck with a gun rack in the back window. We have no means to verify these things that people say, except to note that there is a long line of groundhogs signing up for swimming lessons so that they can cross the river and return to Harford County where they would be safe from human consumption.

INDEPENDENCE DAY TRADITION

Our tradition for the Fourth of July is rather simple. Usually with our grandson Greg, we drive up to the small town of Strasburg, Pennsylvania and visit one of our favorite stores, Tractor Supply Company (TSC). Before other TSC stores were built closer to us, this visit was unique, but, even now, it is still a welcome part of our tradition. There is always something to look at and usually something for us to buy at TSC, and we leave the store with a few things we had no intention of buying before we went in.

There is an antique store across the road, which Greg likes to visit and browse, and we spend some time there.

Then, after all that excitement, we drive to the ice cream store on the corner of Rtes 896 and 741, order strawberry sundaes, sit on the benches in front of the store, and watch the cars and Amish buggies go by. There is a traffic light at the corner in front of us as we sit and eat our sundaes, and, one year, we were especially noticing the number of cars that drove through the intersection when the light was red in their directions. About one out of every eight or ten cars or trucks transgressed in this way. Nevertheless, no Amish buggy was ever driven through a red light.

Our routine has been going on for many years, and, although not filled with the thrills of a parade or fireworks, is still the kind of simple pleasure that makes Independence Day special for us.

INSECT MATING DISRUPTION

A big job that Cathy has to do each spring is to hang pheromone ties from the limbs of our fruit trees. These emit female mating chemicals that confuse the male codling moths, oriental fruit moths, and peach tree borers. The males look for love in all the wrong places, and never can find any females of the same species that might be flying around. No mating, no worms in the fruit (at least that's the theory). It works pretty well, and enables us to avoid harsh insecticide chemicals. We've been using these ties for many years, and are happy with it. We suspect that there will come a day when the ties will no longer be effective, but, until then, we have a winner.

CRICKET WARS VII

It turns out that crickets cannot jump very well from carpeted surfaces. This puts them at a severe disadvantage when Art goes cricket hunting whenever there are carpets on the floor. There are no carpets or rugs in our kitchen, so catching crickets in that room provides more sport than if the floors were carpeted. There is a carpet in our living room and rugs in our downstairs bathroom. If crickets ever dare to show their faces (do crickets have faces?) in those rooms, they don't stay there long. They can be easily captured with little skill. Besides, the carpeted floor surfaces are easier on Art's knees when he drops down to catch them.

That's why we don't see many crickets in those places. Crickets there are supplied with little white flags to designate that they are giving up their resistance.

INTRODUCING UNFAMILIAR FRUITS

We have noticed a clear pattern that repeats with the introduction of new and unfamiliar fruits to our Farmers' Market customers. There have been a number of them: Aronia berries, che fruits, currants, gooseberries, goumi berries, jostaberries, Oriental persimmons (for some), pawpaws, and shisandra berries, among others. The number of new and unfamiliar fruits that we grow to bring to the market is unusual for a Farmers' Market of its size.

When we first bring a new type of fruit, most people who frequent our stand are usually reluctant to try it. There are a few brave souls who want to try something new and different, and do try it by tasting a sample, which we freely offer to anyone willing to test something unfamiliar. But, they may or may not like it, and tend not to purchase any. At this point, we wonder if we have made a big mistake growing and bringing this type of fruit. After all, the pictures of the fruit in the catalogs from which it has come do not adequately describe the fruit, its taste, its texture, or its growth habits.

After several weeks of exposing the fruit to our friends and customers, and assuring them that trying the fruit will not kill them, more people are willing to try it. Some do not think highly of it, but enough people like the new taste that they purchase some. Over the course of several weeks, more people take some home with them. Eventually, and this may take several years to develop, people begin to ask for the fruit. "Will you have (fill in the blank) this year? When will it be ready?"

This trend continues until some people like the new fruit well enough that they buy large enough quantities of it so that it sells out. Others ask for some, but are disappointed when there is none left. At that point, we realize that we have not grown enough of the product to satisfy everyone's requests. And, then, when we have another new fruit to introduce to our customers, the pattern repeats.

PERSIMMON PIE

We started making this pie when we had significant amounts of Oriental persimmons. Grandson Greg requests this pie for each Thanksgiving. The pie is custardy, similar to pumpkin pie.

Ingredients:

1 single 9-inch pie crust
3 eggs
½ tsp. cinnamon
½ cup sugar
¼ tsp. salt
1 cup half-and-half cream
1 – 1 ½ cup persimmon pulp pureed
2 tbsp. melted butter
1 tsp. lemon juice

Preheat oven to 400°F. Combine eggs, half-and-half, cinnamon, sugar, and salt. Mix in persimmon pulp, melted butter, and lemon juice. Pour into unbaked pie shell and bake for 10 minutes. Reduce oven temperature to 350°F and bake for 30 minutes more.

JUST US

A couple of Farmers' Market customers came to us late in the morning a couple of weeks ago and speculated that we had a farm with 5-6 workers to produce all the fruit that we do. Wrong! We have a Cathy and we have an Art, and we once occasionally had a Bernie, and now a Greg for a few hours, but that is all. The two of us have a lot to do, and we work very hard doing it.

WATCH OUT, LITTLE LAMBS

The winter day with a big snow storm, Cathy went out to feed the sheep as she normally did the first thing in the morning. Because of the snow and sleet, she had to put the hood up on her dark winter coat. Seeing her dressed this way, the sheep thought that she was some terrible monster. They were not used to her in her storm outfit. They huddled inside their shed while she tried to get them to come out before she could distribute their feed in their trough. Normally, they know what they were supposed to do: vacate the area while she closed the gate, put the grain in the trough, and reopened the gate. That morning they had to be chased out. That does demonstrate how observant they were and how they got used to certain appearances of things in their environment.

The small lambs had to get used to the rush when all the rest of the sheep, including their mothers, ran through the opened gates to get their grain. Normally, they stood back and let the adults run into the shed. It's only after the adults passed that they ran behind the sheep into the shed. They didn't eat grain themselves, but, if the rest of the sheep were running toward something, then they thought they should, too. One day, one of the gates was pushed the wrong way by the ram, and it swung back after he went through. It hit one of the lambs on the back swing, and sent her flying. Somewhat dazed, she managed to get up, and run as well as she could to catch up to the others. She seemed to have no lasting effects from the incident, but she was a little wary of the gates after that.

At times, lambs have been in the wrong place while the sheep ate their grain. If they somehow got in front of the adults, between the adults and the feed trough, then watch out! Anything or anybody that got between the adults and their grain was pushed and tossed aside. There was no sympathy extended to them by the adult sheep, and it's a wonder that they didn't get mauled. But, they survived, perhaps a little wiser, if such a thing can be said about a sheep. Our lambs had to be tough.

LOST IN THOUGHT WHILE PRUNING

Pruning the extra branches off apple trees and pear trees can be a daunting task. Both of these types of trees grow what are called "water sprouts", branches that grow straight up from where they originate; some are long and thick, and some are shorter and thinner. Most grow from the ends of other branches, but some grow inside the tree canopy. None of these are fruitful, and all they tend to do is to shade the rest of the tree from the bright sunshine needed to produce bountiful blossoms in the spring and plump, sweet fruit in the fall. They all must be removed during winter pruning.

It is easy to look at a tree and see all the hundreds of water sprouts that must be cut off. From this perspective, just the very thought of all the work that must be accomplished can be exhausting. Each and every one of these shoots must be removed by a separate cut of the shears. There is no shortcut to this process. Each one must be removed as an individual, one at a time. Sometimes, for the thickest of the water sprouts, several cuts and extra effort must be expended just to get each one off the tree and falling to the ground. This is especially true for the shoots at the top of the tree, which are usually the most robust. It is also at the top of the tree that the shoots are the hardest to reach. The view of the whole tree before it is pruned certainly can be disheartening.

The cure for this malaise is to climb the ladder into the tree and look at one shoot at a time. Once that shoot is removed, it can no longer be of concern. It is gone for the year, not to return during this pruning season. Then, on to the next branch; remove that one, and move on to the next. Taken one shoot at a time, the huge, daunting task becomes manageable.

It is easy for one's mind to wander while pruning a tree, and Art has, on occasion, begun to philosophize about other things while working to remove each one of those shoots. He has likened the job of pruning to multitasking. There are people who laud multitasking and claim to be able to multitask effectively. "But", muses Art, "trying to pay attention to all those things that one has to do is just like looking at the whole tree, and being overwhelmed. It is better to look at one shoot, or one job, at a time to be effective at completing the whole multitude of requirements well. Sure, paying attention to one thing at a time in serial fashion is not as glamorous as pretending to deal with a whole bunch of things in parallel, but, to do the best job that one can do with each thing requires enough attention to finish the task so that it does not return to bother the doer, at least until the next tasking cycle. Sometimes, as in pruning, several attempts must be made before the task is completed, but some other tasks may be able to be discharged with ease."

Giving over his consciousness to such thoughts as this, the job of pruning an apple or pear tree is soon completed, rather mindlessly to be sure. And, then on to the next tree and more grand thoughts. But, try not to look at the next tree the whole thing at a time.

MANEUVERS FOR FEEDING THE SHEEP THEIR MORNING GRAIN

There is a much-rehearsed choreography that goes on between Cathy and the sheep every morning when she feeds them their grain. First, Cathy closes the gates to the corral with the sheep outside of the corral. If the sheep had been inside the corral or sheds, then she has to wave her arms and chase them out first before closing the gates. Once they are on the other side of the closed gates, they wait patiently while Cathy doles out their grain into their feeding trough. The sheep are used to this routine, and know what they are expected to do. The flock usually waits back a ways from the gates so that they don't have to stand in the mud. They hate the mud as much or more than we do. When she is ready, Cathy opens the gates and the sheep rush in. The first sheep to reach the grain can choose the best spot to eat. This sheep stampede through the gates slows considerably when they reach the narrow doorway to the shed. The doorway is just about wide enough to allow a fat ewe to pass comfortably, but the sheep don't count very well. Nor are they patient. So, at least two sheep at a time try to squeeze through the doorway. They push and strain, and manage to squeeze through with difficulty. Once those two make it, other sheep try to get through. Eventually, they all get to fight for a place at the grain trough, and eat as much and as fast as they can.

MATH IN THE BERRY PATCH

Mathematical Mental Musings from the Berry Patch:

1. Picking yellow raspberries is akin to integral calculus: an infinite number of infinitesimally small pieces really does total to something real.

2. It takes about 60 hours to pick what we sell in 4 hours; thus, the ratio of picking time to selling time is about 15:1. And that doesn't count time caring for the plants.
3. "I ate some pie!!" expressed mathematically is: " $\sqrt{-1}\ 2^3 \Sigma\ \pi!!$ "

MAYHAW MAGIC

Cathy ran into a friend of hers while visiting the library. The friend had seen our notes on mayhaws explaining that they grow in swampy areas of the south, may have a slightly tart taste, and have the look and feel of small crabapples. Mayhaws are often made into a delicious jelly. We grow a few ourselves for the Farmers' Market.

The friend related about a trip that she had made to the south a while ago. She stopped at a little store in Alabama and noticed some mayhaw jelly on the shelves and asked the lady behind the counter about it.

"What are mayhaws?", asked the friend. "I've never heard of them before."

In her unmistakably thick Alabaman accent, the lady proprietor launched into a long discourse about mayhaws, what they were, where they came from, and their importance to the people of the south and to Alabama in particular. "They are so important; my kids were raised on mayhaws."

So, what could the friend do but buy a jar of mayhaw jelly? She reported that it was delicious.

MOCKINGBIRD NEST IN THE RASPBERRIES

There is a rogue raspberry bush growing among the blackberries, and it had such luscious-looking berries on it that Cathy just had to pick them. As she stood next to the bush, she noticed a bird's nest situated in its interior. A mocking bird had taken possession of the plant and treated Cathy as the intruder that she was. The bird was only a foot in front of her face and threatening further assault if she did not leave. Thoughts of Alfred Hitchcock's movie *The Birds* flooded her mind. At that point, she decided that she had picked enough of those raspberries for the week, and she left. Mother bird remained there, tending to her nest.

MUDDY 2018

What is a farm without mud? The year 2018 had been the wettest on record in the Baltimore area and the whole state of Maryland, and not just by a whisker. Total precipitation that year exceeded that of the previous record holder by the equivalent of a whole ocean. We had gotten more than `175% of our normal annual rainfall, that's nearly six feet of fallen water rather than a normal three and a half feet, and the rain still kept coming down.

When it did rain, there was no place for it to go except to run off into streams and rivers and lakes. Even there, it overflowed. Any depression in the ground, whether large or small, had become a permanent wetland that year. Nothing dried up because there was not enough time between storms. Puddles became permanent ponds, and soil became mire.

That was the year that we could not put our truck away after returning on Saturday afternoon from the Farmers' Market. Even when in four-wheel drive, the truck would slip and slide. There is an upward slope toward the machinery shed where the truck is normally parked, and every time we returned it was problematic about whether the truck would make it home. It did make ruts, however, that would soon fill with more rain water.

We had seen other farms, both near and not so near, as we drove along the highways. Pastures all had ponds in the middle. Cropland had ruts. There were some stands of corn in the middle of fields that could not be harvested because of the mud. Deep ruts told the story. We could imagine that harvesting that year had tested the patience as well as the vocabularies of machine operators trying to get their work done. Sometimes farming operations can become exasperating; the euphoria of a good harvest turned into the disappointment of a harvest partially completed.

A farm is a large expanse of land with few, if any, buildings. For the year 2018, around here at least, a farm was a large expanse of mud.

Could there be any large expanses of land without mud that year? We have seen them - they are asphalt-covered mall parking lots.

RACCOON WARS I

We battled at least one raccoon for several years. The battleground was a shed behind the house in which we fed our cat. We closed the shed at night to keep wildlife from accessing the cat food and making a mess. That didn't work, the raccoon found other ways to get in, so Cathy bought a plastic tool box in which to store the cat food. The raccoon soon figured out, not only how to get into the shed, but also how to open the unlocked, but closed, tool box. So, Cathy bought a lock. The raccoon couldn't open the lock, but chewed on the box until it could be opened without unfastening the lock and the treasure inside could be consumed at will. The raccoon would move the tool box all over the place, making a mess in the process. Art tried to keep the raccoon out of the shed by shoring up the foundation, putting new cement blocks in place and nailing more boards just above them. That worked for a couple of days, and then the raccoon found a way in by lifting the metal roofing ever so slightly to slip inside. Art fixed that with more lumber and many more nails. That worked for a while, and then the raccoon found a way in through a small gap over a back door. It was hard to figure out how he was getting in, so Art locked the cat into the shed and watched as she escaped. He then nailed the door shut and added more boards to fill the gap. The raccoon started tearing boards off the front of the shed. Art nailed more boards behind them. The raccoon continued to get in and eating the cat food, but it wasn't apparent how he or she was still gaining access. Finally, Art found that the raccoon had torn pieces of paneling covering a former window to an adjoining shed, and that was the way in. He fixed that. The next move was up to the raccoon. The cat food in the shed now became more secure than if it were sequestered in Fort Knox. We fully expected the raccoon to bring a wrecking ball one of the next nights, or perhaps calling in all of his friends as a wrecking crew. We kept listening at night to hear the raccoon cussing, swearing special raccoon words, or grunting as it tried to break into the shed that, by then, closely resembled a Brinks armored car. This raccoon did not give up easily.

NAMING OF OUR BUILDINGS

We have a unique means at SweetAire Farm to remember close friends and family: we name buildings after them. We have the Caldwell Conservatory, a part of a shed with many windows, in which to overwinter some of our citrus trees and other tender plants. The Caldwell Conservatory is named for Jim Caldwell, a good friend from our past. Jim used to come over and help Art whenever another strong helper was needed. He was also quite often asked to bring his chain saw to cut trees before Art had developed enough confidence in his own ability to safely handle a chain saw. Jim and family often shared holidays with our family, and we grew quite close.

We also have the Knight Nook, another windowed room in a different shed wherein we keep some other plants from freezing temperatures. That one is named for Bob Knight, who used to put up hay with Art, and with whom we used to play cards every Friday evening. Bob was a telephone company employee who also liked to do farm and mowing work with his old Ford 9N tractor. He was known throughout our little town of Darlington as a generous man who helped a lot of people.

We have the Aunt Renee Barn to remember a very nice sister-in-law. Renee was unusual in that she constantly volunteered to help, not only us, but also many others. She was strong and not afraid to work hard, but often tried to exceed her physical limitations, with sometimes painful consequences. She used to come to our farm with her husband, and Art's brother, Don, from their home in upstate New York. There were years when she came alone or with a granddaughter of hers to help us with the Darlington Apple Festival. She was always pleasant to everyone who knew her.

We needed to figure out an appropriate monument to Bernie Mullen (no, we don't have an outhouse), so we named our lower barn after him. The Bernie Barn was named to remember Bernie, who for years helped us at the Bel Air Farmers' Market, was a stalwart volunteer for us at the Darlington Apple Festival each fall, and would often come to our farm to help pick apples or prune trees. Bernie had a high baritone or mid-tenor voice and he often broke into song while helping at the Farmers' Market. He and Art could sometimes blend their voices on a song or two, but each of them was most comfortable in a different key than was the other, so, depending on who started first singing a melody, that was the key the other had to sing to join in. When they did manage to get going this way, customers would often join in for a melodic good time.

Our Gregory Greenhouse was named for our oldest grandson, Gregory Pierson, who often helped with our farm. He has sacrificed his dignity when catching sheep to be sheared. He has installed beautiful new fences to replace old, broken down fences. He has mown a lot of our lawn, pastures, and orchards, and made our farm look like a really good estate. He has plans for even more projects in the future. He helped to build the greenhouse that bears his name, and is available almost any time we ask him to help.

Each of these named buildings has a wooden plaque bearing its official title and is located in a prominent position. These are reminders of the wonderful people who have been important in our lives on SweetAire Farm.

OUR MARYLAND STATE FAIR SHOW RAM

It was late summer of 2008, and our old ram was definitely headed toward the great green pasture in the sky. He had been getting weaker and weaker, and not moving throughout most of the day. He was not going to live much longer. We had to find another ram to breed our ewes for the next lambing season. Without a new ram, we would have no lambs in the spring.

Finding affordable quality rams to purchase is not easy. We needed a suitable ram for our ewes that were mostly of the Suffolk breed mixed with a little Hampshire in their lineage. There are few local sheep breeders with animals of these types. A breeder about 50 miles away with whom we had previously done business had quit raising sheep, and therefore had no rams to sell. And, going further afar, rams can get to be quite expensive. Purebred rams of most breeds could cost upwards of $1000 or much more. To avoid this expense, we sometimes raised our own rams for breeding, but too much in-breeding is not good for the health of any sheep herd.

After looking around and inquiring a bit, we located a man who was exhibiting some sheep at the Maryland State Fair, and was willing to sell a ram to us for the (to him) cheap price of $500. To us, this was expensive, but we had to have a new ram.

The ram in question was a yearling, raised for exhibition at the state fair. It had been coddled and spoiled. It had been raised on the best grain and high-quality hay that could be had. It had been kept inside for most of its life, and had grown quite large for a lamb less than a year old. Nevertheless, this ram did not place very high in the sheep competition that year, and that may have been one reason that the owner had decided to sell it to us at a bargain (to him) price.

We made the exchange of money for animal on the last day of the State Fair. We loaded the ram on the back of our pickup truck, and drove the hour back to our farm, but not before the owner had given us many instructions about what to feed the young ram and how to care for him. The owner also made a few telephone calls to us over the next few days reiterating what he had told us as we had left the fair.

It was not as if we were new to the sheep business, but what he told us was not how we raised our sheep. Instead of nutritious grains and dietary supplements, our sheep had grass to eat. Instead of the best quality alfalfa hay, our sheep had grass to eat. Oh, they would get a little grain on a daily basis, but they had to compete with each other for a few mouthfuls. We only fed them grain in the summertime to incentivize them to get up and move around rather than lie all day in the shade to avoid the heat.

So, when we brought the new ram back to our farm, we let him out in the pasture with the rest of the sheep.

He had apparently not been with ewes for most, if not all, of his life to that point, but, being a young male, he was interested. He began to chase the ewes one at a time. But they were not ready to have relations with him, so they ran away. They did not have to run far, because he then turned his attention to the next nearest ewe; she ran away, as well.

This did not continue for long, because his luxurious upbringing to that point caught up with him. He was out of shape, and he was out of breath. He could not run with the ewes. He stood there, panting hard, tired to the core, and looking quite pathetic. He was not going to be good for breeding until he toughened up a bit.

Over the next few weeks, he found out that, if he wanted to avoid hunger, he had to eat the stuff that he was standing on. He also learned that he had to walk by himself to the water when he was thirsty; no one brought him water as they had in his previous life. He began to develop some muscles that were not just for showing off at the state fair.

He eventually adjusted, and sired 12 lambs born the next spring. But, for a while there, we wondered if he could survive the excitement and exertion of breeding season.

MACARONI AND CHEESE

When Cathy injured her head in a bad fall in 2009, she spent several months in the hospital. A neighbor brought to Art some macaroni and cheese quite unlike any that he had ever had before. It was so cheesy and yummy that we had to have the recipe to make it ourselves. This is the only mac and cheese that we eat anymore.

Ingredients:

1 pound cut ziti
1 stick butter
3 tablespoons flour
1-½ pound sharp Chedder cheese, shredded
1 cup water
1 large (12 ounce) can evaporated milk
Paprika for topping

Cook macaroni as directed. Drain well and set aside. In a large pot, melt the butter. Add 3 tablespoons flour. Cook until bubbly, but not brown. Add all at one time, the evaporated milk diluted with one cup of water. Stir until the mixture comes to a boil and starts to thicken. Turn off the flame. Add the shredded cheese and mix until well blended. Add the macaroni and mix together. If the mixture becomes too thick, add some regular milk. Pour the mixture into a large oblong baking dish which has been greased. Sprinkle with paprika. Bake at 400°F until bubbly and brown (about 20-25 minutes).

PAPAYAS FOR THE SHEEP

We had two papaya trees planted in 5-gallon buckets that we moved indoors into the house for the winter. The trees had set about 10-12 fruits in the summer, and they were still attached when the trees were moved inside in October

The trees seemed to be doing quite well for a couple of months, and the green papaya fruits grew larger and larger, but still not ripe. In mid December the trees started to lose their leaves despite being located directly in front of a large window and the room temperature being in a tolerable range for this variety of papaya. All the leaves dropped off eventually, and all that were left were two tree trunks and about a dozen green papaya fruits of various sizes hanging from each trunk.

In late January, the fruits started to soften and turn a yellowish green: they were ripening. They also started to drop off the trees, one or two at a time, making a loud thud when they landed on the floor, sometimes making a racket in the middle of the night. By this time, the largest of the fruits were about 3-4 pounds each.

They looked good, so Art cut several open to taste them. They were nice and soft inside, as they should have been, but they tasted sour, not like he remembered papayas were supposed to taste. So, Art was not eager to eat any more of them.

As happens with a lot of the excess fruit that we have at SweetAire Farm, the papayas were thrown over the fence to the sheep. And, that's how the sheep got to taste homegrown papayas. They had not tasted papayas before, so they had no taste memory to compare. So, they ate them hungrily. We suppose that the papayas tasted better than dried old hay. And that's the way that our sheep became connoisseurs of papayas in the winter of 2018.

PESTICIDE-FREE FRUIT

If a fruit is labeled "Pesticide Free", is that the same as "No Chemicals"? The answer is "no". The reason is this: when citing the word pesticides, the writer is often referring to insecticides and fungicides. Some fruits can be grown adequately without these two pesticides, and this is good for you. But often not included in the term "pesticides" are herbicides and fertilizers. Both of these can contain synthetic or unnatural chemicals. Our fruit labeled "No Chemicals" refers to the fact we have not used synthetic insecticides, fungicides, herbicides, or fertilizers on the fruit.

POLICE BLOTTER

Living in a rural area like Darlington is mostly peaceful and quiet. Sometimes, however, some unusual things happen. Take the Police Blotter entry for Darlington appearing one week in the *Aegis,* the local newspaper. Unlike the items for other areas of Harford County, there were no burglaries, stabbings, or shootings in Darlington. Instead, the *Aegis* reported that "A donkey was running in the roads and yards at Castleton and Berkley roads Oct 20." That animal was right in our neighborhood, but we had not seen it. Cathy thought that Art might have been the animal reported, but it couldn't have been him because he wasn't on the loose that day.

SHEEP OUT AGAIN

It happens every year in the early spring; the sheep will test all of our fences, looking for a way to get to new grass. It's not that they don't have enough to eat on our side; it's just that the grass on the far side looks so much better.

So it was that, when Art went outside one Monday afternoon, our ram (Jack) was bleating away in his gruff deep male voice, all alone and looking for his sheep family. His bleats were so plaintive that Art eventually took pity on him and decided to help him find the rest of the sheep. They both went all around the pasture behind the house. Nothing. They looked in the sheds. Not a soul. They walked back to the peach orchard. No one was out there. They looked everywhere. Finally, looking from the vantage of a hill top, the other sheep were spotted on the other side of the woods, in the neighbor's back yard. Art went to the house to change his shoes, because chasing them back would require walking through wooded paths and through wet spots.

Before he could change, though, the sheep, evidently feeling guilty, but not too guilty, for leaving the farm where they belonged, filed back through the hole in the fence where the original transgression had occurred. Their tummies full for now, they walked into the shade of their favorite cedar tree to lie down and ruminate. Jack, happy to have them back, began to eat the grass that the rest of the sheep had eschewed for the better grass that the neighbor had grown especially for them.

Art found the hole in the fence, nicely just the right size for lambs and ewes, but not big enough for rams. By design, we keep a small supply of metal fence posts and wire on hand for just such occasions. Imagine the dreadful fence fixes that would be necessitated if we did not keep these emergency supplies around!

Many times on a farm, extra supplies and parts have to be kept because events such as escaping sheep, clogged sprayers, or broken tractor generators happen at the most inopportune times when it isn't easy to go buy the necessary items. In years past, Art used to use every occasion to fix something as an opportunity to buy a new tool or two. We now have all the tools we need, but still have to stockpile supplies.

Driving a few posts, putting up some new wire, and making sure that the bottom of the wire was firmly enough attached to the posts low enough that the lambs could not sneak underneath, the hole was fixed. Just as Art was putting his tools away, the sheep came down from their resting spot and walked to where they had escaped before. Art watched as they went to where the hole had been, stopped, and tried to fathom what had changed. They stayed there for a few minutes until it became clear to them that their vacation days were over. One-by-one, they turned and began to graze the grass that they were supposed to eat on our side of the fence. Art smiled to himself.

This wasn't the last time that the sheep attempted to steal away through that particular trail. Evidently, they had been going back and forth for some time, because they went many times to where that hole had been, only to be disappointed. Eternally hopeful, they visited that spot on many more occasions. Art smiled to himself again. Art 1, sheep 0 for now, at least.

PRICES OF OUR FRUITS

Art has developed his motto for our fruit growing and selling that he states as:"Grow fruits that require no care and sell fruits that have no competition." Of course, there are no such things, especially the part about care. There are, however, some of the fruits that we grow that only require minimal care: maybe a little fertilizer every now and again, maybe a little weeding, or maybe some slight pruning year in and year out. There are fruits that do not need to be sprayed constantly, or that need a lot of attention during the growing season. Using organic sprays that are much less effective than chemical sprays means that spraying can sometimes be a never-ending job.

We do, however, grow some fruits that have no competition at the Farmers' Market. These are usually unconventional fruits that have not yet come to the attention of other growers, or that are not potential big sellers at the market. We can sometimes be the only seller of these particular fruits as long as we develop the market for them by introducing them to our customers and waiting for them to be accepted enough to make them worthwhile to bring.

Just because we have no competition does not mean that we have *carte blanche* to charge an outlandish price for any of these fruits. There is only so much that customers are willing to pay, especially if the fruits they are purchasing are an alternative to others that they are more familiar with. There are always the prices on similar products sold in grocery stores to put a cap on the prices that we can charge. And, there are instances where the prices charged in grocery stores are so low, because of overproduction elsewhere and because of the benefits of modern transportation from faraway places, that it would not be worthwhile for us to sell them at that price. So, pricing becomes an issue for consideration.

It is rare to hear our customers comment about the prices we charge at the Farmers' Market. One customer noted that our prices for our fruit grown with organic methods (which we call "sweetaireganic") are much cheaper than those in stores for organic produce. On the other side of the issue, two people one Saturday a while back complained that our price for rhubarb was much too high.

We learned many years ago that some people expect their food to be dirt cheap. Back in the first years that we participated in the Bel Air Farmers' Market (since 1982), there were customers who would agonize over the price of our apples, and compare prices up and down the row of venders, but who had no problem with the substantial prices on bunches of dried flowers sold at the stand next to ours. We, in this country of ours, have all been very spoiled by the relatively low prices of our food. How sad that we devalue the nutrition and the essentialness of the food that nourishes our bodies, and of the pleasure that good food can bring to us when we eat it. And, this extends to a farmer we knew who expected high prices when he sold his crops, but, when he took trips to Florida, always looked for the cheapest prices for the grapefruits he would bring back home. You would have thought that he would appreciate the efforts of the grower enough to pay more than the minimum.

We are not out to gouge anyone, but we do try to charge a fair price. We don't want to make our fruit so expensive that young parents cannot afford to feed their children the wholesome food that we grow. On the other hand, we know very well how much of our time and effort, even under the hot summer sun, in the freezing cold winter, in the wind, and in the rain or snow, that goes into bringing our fruit to our customers. We spend a lot of time and effort hidden from the unaware general public. This means that we cannot give it away. So, we try to find a happy medium that is still affordable for you and adequately compensates us.

RACCOON WARS II

We started having trouble from a raccoon coming on our porch and upsetting plants and making a general mess of things. So, the Have-a-Heart trap was baited with cat food and set on the porch where the raccoon was expected to visit. It didn't take long. The trap was set at about 8 pm and, when Cathy checked at 9 pm, there was a raccoon stuck inside the trap. Art thought about taking the raccoon away and releasing it elsewhere at that time, but figured that early the next morning would be good enough. He arose at 5:30, dressed, and went to the porch to pick up the trap with raccoon inside to take it away. When he looked at the trap, he did a double-take; there was no raccoon inside. The trap had been sprung, and the cat food bait had disappeared, but there was no raccoon inside. How that raccoon freed itself, neither Art nor Cathy could figure. It had been there, and now it wasn't. Was the raccoon able to use its tiny hands to pull back the spring holding the door shut or did it call on its friends to help it escape? We may never know. What we have learned from this, however, is that a raccoon is to be moved as soon as possible after it is trapped.

And that is not the end of the story. The next night, we set the trap again, complete with a pan of highly-delicious cat food all the way in the back, where the raccoon would certainly have to trip the trap in order to reach it. Cathy and Art had just settled down to watch a DVD for an hour or so before turning in, when a loud racket was heard downstairs on the porch.

Investigating, Art turned on the porch light and looked for the trap. It wasn't where he had put it. He looked all over the porch, but it took a little while before he found it all the way on the other end of the porch; the trap door had been sprung, and the trap on its side. Some of the cat food had been spilled out of the pan and eaten. The raccoon was nowhere in sight. So, Art replaced the trap to its original location, set it again, turned off the porch light, and went back upstairs. It wasn't more than a couple of minutes before there was another loud commotion coming from the porch. Art and Cathy both went downstairs to see what had happened. This time, the trap was nowhere on the porch. It took a lot of searching before the trap was finally found far away on the other side of the lawn. The cat food was gone, and so was the raccoon. So, the score was raccoon 2, Art and Cathy 0. At this point, the raccoon had clearly outsmarted us, and had had his (or her) fill of cat food, to boot.

We never knowingly did get that raccoon, but we kept trying. It's hard on our human self respect to concede a skirmish to a raccoon.

REAL APPLES

A mother and her little daughter came up to our Farmers' Market table one Saturday. The mother said to her girl, "Look at these apples. What do you notice about them?" The daughter replied, "They are small." "Yes, and what else do you notice about them?" mom questioned. "They have spots on them", said the daughter. "Yes, and that's because they don't use pesticides on their fruit," instructed the mother. And then she turned to Cathy and said, "You have to teach them young. We'll be back next week to get some." And she left.

Another customer came to our table and was given an Elstar apple to taste. The sample she was given looked somewhat worse than the apples in the baskets for sale. She tasted the apple and liked it, enough so that she bought some. "They don't look so good on the outside", she said, "but there's nothing wrong with the inside".

These people have discovered that an apple (or any other fruit, for that matter) doesn't have to look perfect to taste good. And our apples that taste good are better for you because they don't have residual artificial chemical pesticides on them and in them (many modern pesticides are systemic and penetrate all the tissues of the plant, including the fruit. They depend on dilution in all the tissues to bring them below tolerance levels, although eating the entire fruit means consuming the whole pesticide dose.). Apples have been one of the USDA dirty dozen fruits and vegetables found to contain relatively high residual levels of pesticides. That's one reason why we have the slogan: "We sell taste, not looks". And we invite anyone who wants to add that awful chemical taste to their fruit to shop elsewhere.

RETURN OF THE FIREFLIES

The lightning bugs return to June and July evenings at SweetAire Farm. These are fun to watch once darkness begins to fall and they slowly rise from the grass to fly higher and higher. Their little lamps blink on and off as they soar higher and higher, searching for some damsel on the ground who will be enticed to answer their calls. If we watch really close, we may also see faint glimmers from glowworms on the ground responding to the passionate prompts from the many airborne potential beaus.

We were told by an IPM (integrated pest management) scout some years ago that lightning bugs are good predator insects to have around because they prey on harmful pests in our organic orchard. So, their presences are not only beautiful to watch in the warm summer evenings, but we also know that they are our partners during the daytime hours, too. That makes them doubly welcome.

Nighttime darkness comes so late during those early summer evenings that we are often ready to turn in before the lightning bugs are fully active (early to bed and early to rise, etc.). One night, when we were ready to turn in, we looked out the window to watch the fireflies as they rose slowly from the lawn and pasture grass with their little lamps a-burnin'. In the distance were lightning flashes from an impending thunderstorm. The lightning flashes were, of course, much brighter than those little firefly taillights. We could imagine an ethereal voice urgently speaking to the fireflies, "Watch out, little fireflies, there's a big monster brighter than all of you put together, and it can hurt you. Be careful".

Of course, that was all in our imagination. But, then again, that's one thing that lightning bugs are good for.

REVERENCE FOR SWEETAIRE FARM

To us at SweetAire Farm, there is something awe-some about the land that we call our farm and our home. We have a reverence for this place, our home, our sanctuary, and the center of interest for our present lives. For us, it is a magical place, a place where we can feel completely safe and isolated from the troubles of the world. Everyone needs a place like this, and we are fortunate to have this one.

This land is ours for only as long as we live, and then it becomes someone else's to treasure. Because we have it on loan, we need to care for it and not let it become despoiled. For that reason, we transferred the development rights to our farm years ago; we could not bear the thought of houses populating the place where we had spent so much time and effort to bring about harvest abundance. After us, the land will go on, probably not in the same way as it has while we have been in charge, but it will go on nonetheless.

Land is a gift. It is a resource that can be used to produce a bounty of goodness, or, if left to revert to nature, be like cash deposited in a bank savings account, able to be used for productive purposes at some time in the future. We have chosen to do both with parts of our land. With only two of us, we cannot even imagine planting the entire farm to crops. We can hardly keep up with what we have now, as it is. So, we have some orchard, some pasture, and some forested areas, all looking lovely at all times of the year.

SHEEP VISIT NEIGHBOR'S YARD AND ARE REPELLED

The sheep finally had reached the limit of our patience. One Saturday we had gone out to dinner, but hadn't seen the sheep when we left. When we returned, the sheep still weren't in the pasture where they were supposed to be, so we went out in the darkness to try to find them. They were again on the other side of the gates in the apple orchard where they were not supposed to be. We chased them home and locked them in the lower pasture.

The next day, Cathy went looking for a hole in the fence through which they could escape from the peach orchard where they were allowed to graze in the winter. She found a place, and we spent an hour cutting back brambles and installing new wire to fill the hole. Confident that we had finally defeated the wandering sheep, Art let them into the peach orchard and went about doing some things that he needed to do. It wasn't more than twenty minutes later that a neighbor drove in the driveway with the message that our sheep were grazing on Smith Road, outside of our farm. We chased them back, and locked them into their summer pasture, a couple of weeks ahead of when we would have liked. We wanted to let the summer pasture grass grow a little more before we allowed the sheep to graze on it, but the sheep had given us no choice. We still didn't know how they were able to escape the peach orchard so rapidly, but they were at least secure until the next winter.

On another occasion, Cathy went out to feed the sheep that morning. Once they had eaten their grain, the sheep decided to bail out. They began to jump over the fence and through the minihedgerow between us and the neighbors. With some effort, and moving as fast as she could, Cathy was able to keep the rest of the sheep from escaping. Then she went over to the neighbor's yard to retrieve the escaped sheep. She didn't have to worry. The sheep came running back, chased by a small dog and a man running after the dog and yelling at it to stop chasing the sheep. Cathy was never so glad to see a dog chasing our sheep as she was that morning. Anyway, she managed to get the sheep back into their pasture and then came in the house. She had intended to stay inside for the day because of the nasty cold, windy weather we were having that day.

After breakfast, Art put on an extra layer of clothes and walked out to the orchard to do some pruning. The rest of the day was uneventful until it wasn't. Art went out to prune in the afternoon, and Cathy settled down in the house to work on her current cross-stitch project. It was then that she noticed the sheep walking by the kitchen window. They shouldn't have been there. So, she went back outside and chased them back from the road. She got so mad at them that she chased them into their summer pasture, despite the fact that there wasn't all that much grass for them yet, and locked them inside. Then, afraid that Art would come back from pruning and not understand the why the sheep were in their summer pasture, she took a long, cold walk down to where he was pruning to explain what had happened. They both walked back together, both feeling very blue and ready to give up everything.

SHEEPFUL REMINISCENCES

Someone at the Farmers' Market asked us how it felt to be sheep-less after we had sold all of our sheep. Cathy immediately piped up, and said, "Great!" Art was a little more circumspect in his answer, but upon reflection, there were some mental images that came to our minds:

1. Shearing sheep each spring. Readying the shears, and hoping that the shears would work for one more year. And hoping that Art's back would survive another year of shearing.

2. The wonderful taste of a large glass of iced tea drunk in the middle of shearing.
3. Dreading Memorial Day weekend, when we usually sheared the sheep.
4. The year we sheared the sheep on a hot spring day, and the stress was so much for one sheep that it died in the back of our pick-up truck as we transported it to another pasture.
5. The ram that was found floating, having drowned, in our friends' swimming pool near where they were pastured for the summer.
6. Greg lying on the ground under a sheep after he had tried to catch a sheep for shearing, and the sheep won the wrestling match, pinning Greg in record time.
7. Greg, having stepped on a rotten goose egg in the Bernie Barn when we sheared in there one year. The egg popped loudly and released a cloud of very smelly gas that took several days to dissipate completely.
8. The sheep that were mesmerized by a helium-filled party balloon that landed in the pasture and waved on its attached ribbon with each little breeze. The sheep just stood there, not moving a muscle in the face of that strange thing.
9. The many sheep that were killed by dogs over the years, including one episode with 23 sheep killed in one night.
10. The many times Art arose from his bed at night when strange dog barking awakened him from his sleep. He would dress and go to check that the sheep were ok.
11. The times when sons Paul and Eric put young Greg on the back of the ram and made him ride around the pasture like that.
12. The many times the boys had to outrun the ram as he tried to overtake and butt them.
13. The time when the sheep overturned several bee hives located in the pasture. Boy, were the bees mad.
14. The lamb named Wonder, who required bottle feeding, was given to a shelter, and eventually died.
15. The sheep lined up outside the gate awaiting feeding, and rushing to the shed once the gate was opened. Our efforts to

thwart the ram as he tried to be first and beat the others to the grain. The young lambs that had to learn quickly to get out of the way lest they be run over in the mad rush.

16. The many times, especially early in the spring when the grass in neighbors' lawns was more tempting than the grass in the pasture, that the sheep would find holes in the fence and graze the greener grass that the neighbors grew. We knew, when the phone rang early in the morning, what the call was about.
17. The time when the sheep were escaping our winter pasture and we could not find from where they were escaping, until it snowed one morning and we could follow their tracks. The tracks led to a secluded spot where they were able to slip under the fence. Cathy crawled under the fence to find the sheep, and she chased them back.
18. The time when the sheep jumped over the fence into the neighbor's yard right after they were fed and while Cathy watched. She uttered some words to herself, not knowing exactly how she was going to get them back. And then, as if by a miracle, they came running back home quickly, chased by the neighbor's small dog. Cathy was never so glad to see a dog chasing our sheep as she was that day.
19. The time when we had the sheep in a pasture one half a mile down the road and there was a crew installing a gas pipeline through the field. They forgot to close the temporary fence that they had installed, and the sheep got out that night. Art heard on his police monitor that there was a sheep in the middle of the road. He knew immediately what it was and what he needed to do. He hopped into his truck, and removed the ram from the road, avoiding what may have been a very bad situation.
20. How the sheep always came back at night whether we knew where they had been or not. Sometimes, we had not even missed them.
21. The lambs born during big snow storms or very cold nights and that required at least one of us to go to the barn at all hours.
22. The many times we postponed trips because it was lambing season.
23. The newborn lambs brought into the house to be warmed.

24. Preparing for lambing season by inventory of needles, syringes, vaccines, ear tags, rubbing alcohol, cotton balls, banding rubbers, lamb milk replacer, and various medicines.
25. The many new sheep stories that we told to each other every day because of what they were up to that day.

All these memories, and more, went through our minds. Yes, we agree, it feels great to be sheep-less after 46 years of sheep-fulness.

SHOVELING SNOW

Art used to use the tractor and plow to deal with snow in the driveway, but he also used to get very cold just sitting there while doing so, no matter how much he bundled up. Then again, there was always the task of putting the chains on the tractor tires and hitching up the plow. Long story short, he doesn't do that anymore. Instead, Art and Cathy shovel the 150-foot long driveway by hand. Instead of getting cold, they warm up while working, and they usually finish in just a few hours.

SMALL BERRIES

Our everbearing strawberries often show the effects of hot summer days. Mid-summer berries are not as large as they were a few weeks ago, when it was cooler. People used to seeing the large but tasteless strawberries in supermarkets will not see them from us. However, our berries still taste very good. The size of our berries suggests a hypothetical conversation between Art and a customer:

> Customer: "Why are these berries so small?"
> Art: "They just take up the spaces between the big berries."
> Customer: "But there are no big berries."
> Art: "Then it's good that you have all those small berries."

You may find larger strawberries in the food store, but you won't find any that taste any better than ours. As we have said many times before, "we sell flavor, not looks".

SPIDER WEB SEASON

Early fall is the heart of spider-web season, when, no matter where one goes, invisible sticky gossamer strands are everywhere. They are difficult to see, except in the early morning when they serve as the underpinning structures for condensed drops of morning dew. There is nothing more beautiful than the early morning sunlight beaming through the dewdrop prisms hugging intricate web shapes and radiating a spectrum of shining colors. But, after the dew has all disappeared into the atmosphere, spider webs are nearly impossible to see and to avoid. After a web encounter, the sticky strands must to be pulled with difficulty from our faces and arms.

Those spiders sure know how to build imposing structural frameworks. While picking apples in the back orchard, we have been amazed by feats engineered by those little arachnids. Most of their webs were anchored between branches on the same tree. One enterprising spider, however, decided that more prey could be had with a web between the rows of trees where insects usually fly free. This web was strung between branches of trees more than 20 feet apart. Appreciating this splendid effort on the part of the spider, Art ducked each time he had to cross the web location. It remained there for the entire season.

Riding or walking along our farm lane, between rows of trees, or into a shed is just as likely as not to result in an encounter with a spider web strung across the span of the passageway. The result is that we spend the next few minutes trying to remove these invisible strands from our faces, our ears, and our necks. They don't hurt, and they don't quite tickle, but they feel unpleasant enough before removal that we must stop what we had intended to do and try to take those sticky little things off before continuing. Even on our skin, they are not so easy to locate. It's just a good thing that we are not insects; we would be caught for sure.

We only wish that they would try not to catch us in their webs.

SWEETAIRE FARM SOUNDS

What sounds are heard at SweetAire Farm in the summer? The ambience of our farm depends not just on what one can see, but also on what one hears. SweetAire Farm can be a sanctuary afforded by silence. So, what sounds are heard at SweetAire Farm? That depends on the time of day and the day of the week. We start out at midnight, and there is nary a vehicle on the road in front of the house. The only sounds to be heard in the summer are a steady high-pitched background chorus of thousands of chirping crickets accented with sounds from katydids or other types of insects. Very infrequently, the whine of a truck may be heard from miles away on Rte 1. Sometimes a freight train rolls along the tracks on the Cecil County side of the Conowingo Dam, and its rumbling sound can be heard at the farm in the pre-dawn hours of the early morning. Otherwise, the nights at SweetAire farm are very quiet, allowing sleep undisturbed by loud noises

This condition changes at about four in the morning, when dozens of cars travel on our road on the way to and from work at the Peach Bottom nuclear power plant. Such a rush occurs three times a day, reflecting the work shifts at the plant. During weekdays, there is a fair amount of commuter traffic on the road in front of the farm, and we hear cars as they whoosh by the house, accompanied by a quiet hum of the engine when they pass directly in front of our driveway. There are not enough cars to make a steady noise, but instead they can each be individually identified as they go by. Later in the day, the road noise abates, punctuated at times by a truck or school bus, but the noise is not steady. Evenings are usually very quiet; there may be a toad or two chirping, depending on the time of year and the weather.

[How do you describe the sound of a car on the road? The sound is not usually a roar, but more like the sound of a rushing stream. "Rush" is not the best descriptor, however, because many of us do not know what a "rush" really sounds like. So, we call it a "whoosh", and hope that the tintinnabulation of the word brings to mind what sound we hear as the tires roll along the road.

Around dawn, there are birds that begin to sing as soon as there is a faint hint of light. Bird songs are much more plentiful in the spring and early summer than later in the summer or early fall, and they can be loud enough to wake us. Opening the windows let inside the springtime sounds all around. Birds sing to us, a chorus of many different melodies all of which we cannot identify for sure. In the distance can be heard the harsh, raspy voices of crows engaging in a conference call, punctuated every now and again by the shrill shriek of a hawk or two as they fly from tree to tree. Later in the fall, dawn silence is broken by the faint sounds of geese awakening on a pond nearby, and the rat-tat-tat of a woodpecker working on extracting breakfast from the bark of an old tree.

We can often hear toads trilling to each other, especially in wet weather. Trilling toads can be identified individually in different locations on our farm, from near the house to our back orchards. On early spring evenings, there are so many noisy toads that they form a chorus of high-pitched sounds. We like to hear toads, because they eat a lot of insects that could otherwise be bothersome for us and our fruit. There was a time when nary a toad could be found on our farm, but they seem to have returned in large numbers in recent years.

Starting in July and continuing through August, cicadas buzz throughout the day. Sometimes they can be very loud.

Sunday afternoons are some of the noisiest periods during the week. It is at those times when motorcyclists roar along our road going for joy rides starting at the Harley-Davidson dealer just down the road at the corner of Rte 1.

If the flood gates on the Conowingo Dam are open, then we hear a siren on and off throughout the daytime hours. This siren is meant to warn boaters and others above and below the dam that the waters are turbulent and dangerous. This dam siren makes an otherwise quiet day turn noisy, and we try to ignore it as much as we can.

There is an Amish family located up the road a ways, and sometimes we hear the clip-clop of horse's hooves as they pull a buggy along in front of our house with a destination somewhere on the other side of the dam. We hear the sound accelerate as the horse runs and the buggy rolls down the hill in front of our house, and we hear them slow if they are going uphill in the opposite direction. The buggy may be on the road anytime, including in the middle of the night. When it is very quiet out, we can even hear the horse at least a half mile away. The family avoids the Peach Bottom traffic rush and the possible danger with all that many cars, usually going faster than the posted speed limit, represent to a slow-moving buggy.

Vehicles with sirens are easy to hear miles away, and, if there is no local traffic and the wind is in the right direction, we can hear the carillon bells as they ring at noon and 6pm on the United Methodist Church about five miles away in the midst of Darlington.

There are occasional airplanes and helicopters that fly over the farm and make various levels of noise. We are probably on the glide paths for planes landing in Baltimore and Philadelphia. About once a week, Air Force Reserve or National Guard A10 jets flying out of Martin Airport in Baltimore pass just north of us following the Susquehanna River as the pilots log their required flying times. Military helicopters from Aberdeen Proving Ground and commercial helicopters from Exelon Energy fly above us at times.

Away from the house and back in our orchard, the road sounds are greatly attenuated, and, in winter, especially during a snowfall, there is hardly a sound to be heard except for our own breathing. Cathy often wears a set of ear buds and listens to books on tape; Art has a portable radio that he tunes to a station in Philadelphia.

So, there you have it, our acoustic ambience.

THE MOST BEAUTIFUL TIME OF THE YEAR

Springtime is the most beautiful time of the year on SweetAire Farm. First come the light pink apricot blossoms, followed soon by white flowers on the Japanese plums. Then the peach trees are in full pink blossom. The white pear blossoms start opening soon after, and the apple buds show themselves to be pink. The ultimate showy display comes when the apple blossoms open fully and saturate the eye with a gorgeous white profusion. In addition, the currant bushes blossom early; they have much less noticeable greenish blossoms. Blueberries flower at this time of the year with small white bell-shaped blooms tinged with purple. The Goumi bushes are covered with small yellow flowers, and the strawberries also start to blossom. The showy display continues with white blackberry blossoms and, much later, dense, intensely white umbels many inches across adorning the elderberry bushes. Add to the mix: cherry blossoms, redbud tree blossoms, and many varieties of flowers in our flowerbeds.

With all the blossoming, there are usually many bees of all sizes and shapes, from tiny little bees to large carpenter bees, buzzing among the trees. A beautiful butterfly or two can be seen among the later blossoms, also helping to pollinate them. We depend very heavily on these insects to pollinate our fruit. The year that had so much rain and cold temperatures that many of these natural pollinators were killed, we had almost no fruit on our trees. It was horrible.

Springtime is also the season of hope. The trees are beautiful, all the leaves are turning green, the lambs are growing, and the sun shines brightly. Damaging insects haven't yet become a problem with the fruit, diseases have not yet started, there is enough rain and sun, and we haven't had a chance to see if the machinery still works right or needs repair. It's a good time; reality and disappointment may come later. But, for now, all we have to do is concentrate on getting the pruning done before it is too late. And, that's enough.

Cathy counts on strawberries one month after the blossoms first appear, so we mark our calendars for our likely first appearance of the season at the Farmers' Market, about the first of June. Bringing good, healthy food to our friends and customers at the Farmers'' Market is another good motivator to keep moving during the springtime, our busiest, but most beautiful, season of the year.

RACCOON WARS III

When we had sheep, a lot of our food scraps, mostly fruits and vegetables, could be thrown over the fence into the pasture, where the sheep could pick through what they liked and eat it. This was especially true with left-over fruit from the Farmers' Market. Sometimes we had bushels of apples or other fruits well beyond their prime and good only for sheep food. When we no longer had sheep, we needed some other means to deal with food scraps. We first thought about dumping them in the now unused pasture just to rid ourselves of them, but that would attract wild animals that we might not like to have come around, so we soon decided to turn the scraps into compost; we purchased a new plastic compost bin in which to dump our food scraps, and with some leaves, so as not to waste their nutrients and to make good compost for our plants in the spring time. When our first compost bin was full, we were not yet ready to empty it. So, we bought a second bin.

We have a lot of leftover citrus rinds, both from our own fruits and from others that we purchase in the winter when our fruits have not yet begun to be ready. Other food wastes have also been added into the compost bin.

There is a local raccoon that saw this compost bin as a source of a free lunch. There were sliding doors on two sides of the bin, and the raccoon soon learned how to raise them and reach inside for something to eat. He or she pulled out rinds and other food scraps and left them all around the area, making a mess for us to clean up. After picking up after this raccoon's untidy gastronomic indulgences, Art started dumping the food into a corner of the bin farthest away from the sliding doors. This, apparently, made it too hard for the raccoon to reach inside for its tasty morsels. So, for a few days, life was good for Art, but not for the raccoon. Then, the raccoon must have invited a few friends over for dinner, because we found the entire bin dumped over and the contents completely exposed. The raccoon crowd must have enjoyed a grand banquet that night.

In response, Art returned the bin to its upright position, cleaned up the surrounding mess, pounded one metal stake outside each corner of the bin, and tied the bin to the stakes with bungee cords. This secured the bin in place. We suppose the raccoon did not have enough friends to invite to dinner and to prevail over this arrangement, because the bin still stood. Art has taken pride that he is apparently smarter than this raccoon, this time at least.

THE SLEEPY POSSUM

We had been receiving bags of fallen and raked leaves to be used as mulch, and Art unloaded some of these from the truck and put them into a pile for temporary storage. There had already been some bags of leaves in the pile, and the pile was covered with a tarp. When Art pulled the tarp back to add the new bags, he uncovered a very sleepy-looking opossum that had found a nice warm and dry place to rest (hibernate?). It was easy to tell that his possum didn't really want to be awakened.

So, after tentatively opening its sleepy eyes, and trying to figure out what had just happened, it burrowed under some other bags and went back to sleep. Art piled more bags on and replaced the tarp. The pile is located not too far from our sheep pasture where we feed the sheep the apple pomace left from cider making. What a wonderful place for a wild animal to be: warm, dry, comfortably soft, and close to a food source. We should charge rent.

THE THREAT OF HAY

Making hay was one of the hardest jobs for us at SweetAire Farm. Art would mow the hay, ted (turn) it sometimes to help it dry, bale it, help to pick up the bales as they lay on the ground, bring it home, and stack it in the barn. Cathy and the kids would help to load bales on the wagon and remove them from the wagon to place them in the barn. When it came time to make hay, there was no other higher priority activity for any family member than to help with getting that hay safely into the barn.

One episode we remember well involved daughter Joy and her boyfriend, Mike. Now, Mike was a young man with impressive chest and arm muscles, and he and Joy had made plans for a date the evening that the hay was to be ready to be picked up and loaded on the wagon. We needed Joy's help, and told her so. She was not given a choice. Either or both of them decided that they could go on their date a lot sooner that evening if Mike helped Joy pick up bales.

So, late in the hot summer afternoon, we all went to the hayfield to pick up bales. Mike worked very well at first. He did not just pick up the bales; he threw them on the wagon while Joy stacked them. And, sometimes he threw them from a distance. He was out to impress Joy and, we suppose, her parents as well.

Mike did not last more than 15 minutes. He was not able to pace his work to last as long as needed. He had to quit and go home.

Thereafter, Joy was not happy about anything having to do with hay. When she finally left home for college, she would occasionally visit us, but certainly not if there was hay to be done. One of the first questions she would ask before she would commit to coming home in the summertime was, "Are you doing hay today, tomorrow, or the next day?" If the answer was an affirmative, then she would change her mind about coming home to visit. We soon came to say that "the threat of hay keeps Joy away."

THE TRAPPED OWL

We certainly have our wildlife stories to tell. This tale involves an owl trapped in canopy frames covered with netting over our grape vines, which we erected as a barrier against birds that eat all our grapes as they ripen. The netting has mesh openings no larger than one inch, so that keeps most birds at bay (except for a whole family of cardinals that managed somehow to find their way in one year). Anyway, Cathy spotted an owl inside the nets one Monday, and it couldn't get out. We propped up some of the netting and tried to chase it out, but it would have none of it. The owl just would not go out the openings we made for it. So, after many repetitions of flying back and forth past the opening, we left the owl alone. That didn't help; when we came back later, the owl was still trapped. So, Cathy made another opening in the net, this time at the end of the row. After a little reasoning with it, the owl finally flew out to a nearby tree branch.

We still are perplexed about how the owl got inside the net. We did discover a small hole at the bottom in one place, and that was the only hole that was large enough for the owl to get in. Why a self-respecting owl would be walking on the ground looking for a way to get into the net is beyond us. There was no other logical explanation (metaphysics aside). Incidentally, it is said that owls fly without making a sound in order to sneak up on their prey. We have verified that as true: when the owl flew out, there was nary a sound.

ART'S FIRST RULE

Art expects to win the games in which he participates. So, he broadcasts to anyone who will listen that the first rule of the game, no matter which one it is, is that Art is supposed to win. Second, third, and all other places can be up for grabs; he doesn't mind at all the order of placement at the end of the game. As a matter of fact, he will adopt a tone of superiority and congratulate the next person or persons in line at the end. But, first place should be reserved for him.

Needless to say, hardly anyone hears what Art has to say in this regard. At least, it doesn't seem so. And so, competition reigns, and others try to win as much as Art tries to win.

Art is, nonetheless, often the winner, no matter if low score wins or high score wins that particular game. He plays well enough that his competitors try hard to keep him from being the person in first place at the end of the game. It gives them great pleasure when he loses.

We have played board games, such as Checkers, Chess, Parcheesi, Stratego, or Monopoly; we have played placement games, such as Connect Four, Five-pegs-in-a-row, or Dead Pan, and we have played card games, such as Hearts, Canasta, Rook, Uno, or Euchre. Our favorite lately is a card game called Oh Hell, and we play it almost all the time when the occasion warrants breaking out a game to play.

Oh Hell is a game that Art learned while riding a bus on his high school senior trip from Newfield, New York, to Washington, D.C. It has since become Cathy's favorite card game, and we play it with any number of players, from two to five, especially when grandson Greg or son Paul come to visit.

Thanksgiving is a holiday when those two usually visit and stuff themselves with excellent food cooked to perfection by Cathy. But, due to caution in the year 2020 exercised to keep the Corona virus from spreading to other family members, those two did not visit that year. There were no other family members to play cards with us after the meal. That means that they didn't have a chance to abide by Art's first rule of card games in our house.

So, without anybody else to victimize at cards, Art played a card game of Oh Hell with Cathy. Realizing that he expected to win, she dutifully headed the score columns for the two of them as "winner" (Art) and "loser" (Cathy). For a while it looked like the headings would be prophetic. Art had some lucky hands (he maintained that it was his skill), and he took an early lead. But, at the end of the game, when the final scores were tallied, Art had disappointed his biggest fan (himself), and lost the game. He reverted to his habit of complaining about the cards,

Cathy's luck, and the fact that the cards weren't shuffled well enough. He also does this sometimes even during the game, before the outcome is known. It was then that Cathy felt compelled and justified to modify the spelling of the heading of his score column from "winner" to "whiner".

THIEVING SQUIRREL

While sitting on our porch at the end of our early fall workday, we spotted a squirrel running along the top of the wooden wall on the far side of our flower garden. It then jumped to the wooden fence and ran along the fence to the Seckel pear tree, and jumped into its branches. As we watched, the squirrel knocked to the ground one or several Seckel pears, jumped out of the tree, and then retraced its path along the fence and wall, but this time carrying a Seckel pear in its mouth. The squirrel must have either been extremely busy or had a bunch of friends, because the Seckel pear tree that was full of pears on Thursday was almost devoid of pears on Monday. And, the other two pear trees next to the Seckel tree, once also loaded with fruit, were showing less than a handful of pears between them. The wildlife around here must think we grow our fruit solely for their benefit. Actually, as it turns out, sometimes we do.

WE PREFER YELLOW SWEET CORN

We used to grow a big garden with almost all the vegetables that we needed in the summer and, after Cathy canned or froze our surplus, much of what we ate during the winter. We had two gardens, actually, one behind the house and another a ways away where the peach orchard is now. Our boys wanted to grow watermelons, so they were allowed to plant them in the far garden where the vines could take up as much room as they needed. When the melons ripened to their glorious summertime best, the boys would hop on their bikes and pedal themselves back to the far garden, pick a melon or two, and cradle the melons in their shirts. Holding the shirt hems in their teeth, they pedaled back to the house, holding tightly to the handlebars with both hands as they sped over bumps and roots, trying to reach the house as quickly as possible to cut and enjoy the delectable fruit.

We no longer have what might be called a vegetable garden. It is all we can do, and sometimes more than that, to care for and harvest our many types of fruits. Of course, there is always room in our flower beds for a few cherry tomato and zucchini plants, but all of the other fresh vegetables that we consume in the summer are purchased from other venders at the Farmers' Market. One of our weekly purchases in the summertime is sweet corn.

Cathy and Art both grew up in rural upstate New York, she near Binghamton and he near Ithaca. Up there, all the consumed sweet corn is yellow. Neither of us had heard of white sweet corn until we moved to Maryland and had to be satisfied with Silver Queen corn if we wanted sweet corn at all. We still prefer the extra buttery taste of yellow sweet corn, but must settle for bicolor, because growers around here do not grow yellow sweet corn. So, bicolor corn it is, when available.

We have heard some people complain about worms (caterpillars) in the ends of the shucked corn ears. We, on the other hand, would prefer to see worms. The presence of worms means that either: 1) the corn has not been sprayed with insecticides, or 2) the sprays were washed off by rain before they could have an effect. In either case, we feel better eating corn with worms, as long, of course, that we cut them out. We suppose that the worms could be fitted with little collars and leashes and brought to the market as pets, but we won't go that far.

WE SELL TASTE, NOT LOOKS

Some Farmers' Market customers have asked us about fruit seconds. Our sweetairganic fruit first quality has the appearance of conventional orchards' seconds or thirds. We have only two levels of quality: 1) marketable or 2) sheep food.

There was a published article on "clean eating", which was defined as consuming food in as close to its natural state as possible. This includes choosing organic whenever possible, avoiding processed and refined foods, and shopping with a conscience. It is certainly easier to eat cleanly in the summer, when all the local produce comes in. And we don't know if making pies, preserves, or smoothies from our fruit disqualifies it from clean eating, but they sure taste good. People will have to judge for themselves about their shopping consciences. In this regard, we feel good that we can supply people and their families with fruit in as natural a state as possible. We are "clean suppliers".

If customers can tolerate the chemicals that other orchardists spray on their fruits to protect them from insects and diseases, then they will find conventionally-grown fruit to be of much better appearance than ours. But, remember, that systemic fungicides infuse the tissues of the fruit, and cannot be washed off or peeled off with the skin.

A mother and her little daughter came up to our Farmers' Market table one Saturday. She said to her girl, "Look at these apples. What do you notice about them?" The daughter replied, "They are small." "Yes, and what else do you notice about them?" mom questioned. "They have spots on them", said the daughter. "Yes, and that's because they don't use pesticides on their fruit," instructed the mother. And then she turned to Cathy and said, "You have to teach them young. We'll be back next week to get some." And she left.

Another customer came to our table and was given an Elstar apple to taste. The sample she was given looked somewhat worse than the apples in the baskets for sale. She tasted the apple and liked it, enough so that she bought some. "They don't look so good on the outside", she said, "but there's nothing wrong with the inside".

These people have discovered that an apple (or any other fruit, for that matter) doesn't have to look perfect to taste good. And our apples that taste good are better for you because they don't have residual artificial pesticides on them and in them. Apples are one of the USDA dirty dozen fruits and vegetables found to contain relatively high residual levels of pesticides. That's one reason why we have the slogan: "We sell taste, not looks". And we invite anyone who wants that awful chemical taste in their fruit to add it themselves.

WHAT GLOBAL WARMING MEANS TO US

Global warming may or may not mean much to you, but, to us, it means that major adjustments are on the horizon. These adjustments include pruning methods, spray schedules (still organic), and apple varieties. When we first started planting apple trees, forty or more years ago, Maryland was a nice mix of warm and cold climates. We could plant the apple varieties from the north that we were familiar with, and still expect that more southern varieties would do well. Apple varieties, such as Macintosh, Macoun, Cortland, Snow, Empire, and Northern Spy did well. So did Gala, York, Smokehouse, Spitzenburg, Jonathan, and a host of others. For the last few years, we have had almost no apples from the northern varieties named above, nor from Golden Delicious, York, Smokehouse, Lodi, Spitzenburg, Golden Russet, Baldwin, Westfield Seek-No-Further, Summer Rambo, and many others. Part of this may be due to the shift in harvest times. Many apples are definitely ripening earlier, becoming summer apples instead of fall apples. We can tell you that it is a lot easier to pick apples in cool autumn weather compared to hot, sticky summer weather. Then, too, customers have told us that they are not ready for apples in the middle of summer. So, what to do? It is clear that we will have to make some kind of adjustment. Perhaps instead of the 75-80 different varieties of apples, we will have to concentrate on 10-15. In the past, there have been weeks when we have brought more than thirty different apple varieties to the Bel Air Farmers' Market. Those days are probably gone. We will still have enough different flavors and textures to satisfy your needs, but the choices are going to be much more limited.

WHEN THE BIG MAPLE TOPPLED OVER

It was during a very heavy rain storm late one dark evening of March of 2011 when we heard a loud boom, almost like thunder, but not quite. That boom was soon followed by another almost as loud, and extremely close. The large maple tree in front of our house had toppled over, taking the electric feeder wires to the house with it, and blocking our driveway. The second noise was made when a part of the side of our house was torn out when the electric wires pulled on the eye bolt that went through the outside wall. Miraculously, we did not lose electricity to the house. If we had, we probably it would not have been restored quickly, because, when we called Delmarva Power the next day, they sent someone out to look at the damage. We were told that, because the wires were pulled down between the pole in our driveway and the house, it was our responsibility to fix them. And we couldn't do that until the house was repaired.

So, at eleven o'clock that dark night, and in the wind and rain, Art climbed 20 feet up the extension ladder to nail a tarp over the hole in the wall. Cathy was at the base of the ladder, trying to shine her weak flashlight on the nail that Art was trying to hammer. Most of the time he couldn't see the nail, so how he missed hitting his thumb and hand is still a mystery. Maybe he couldn't see them, either. Anyway, rain was blocked from coming in the attic, and we retired for the night.

The next day, Art started his chain saw and began cutting the many branches of the tree lying across the driveway. Cathy helped to clean up brush and pieces of wood. She had called a tree removal guy, but he couldn't come until a lot later. When he finally did come, he had a much larger bar on his chain saw, so he could easily saw the larger branches and the trunk. He was even more at ease than was Art about sawing around the electric wires trapped under the tree branches. It didn't take long after that.

A neighbor was attracted by the noise and came over to ask if he could have the wood. We have tried to give away wood before, without much success, so we were very happy to have him help clean up the bigger lengths of wood.

Judging by the size f the tree, it had stood in that location for many years before Art and Cathy had purchased the farm. The funny thing is that the tree was solid all the way through, and gave no indication that it was about to fall. The only rotten part of the tree was at the roots, and they had withstood very heavy gusts of 50-70 mph wind that we had had a couple of times a few weeks before. This tree came down when it was ready, not a moment before.

The electric wires were propped up enough for us to get in and out of the driveway. We put some temporary barricades in the drive to warn the UPS and FedEx drivers not to bring their trucks in too far when they delivered the many boxes of trees and plants that we expected at any time.

We were able to have the house and the electric service fixed in the next week, and things began to look a lot better. We made it through that one. It was an exciting week.

WILD ANIMALS AND WHAT TO DO ABOUT THEM

We have other animals besides the domesticated kinds. Crows are a big nuisance. They will clean an orchard of fruit before the fruit is ripe and before anyone is aware. They particularly prefer our Asian pears. Whether it is the location of the Asian pear trees at the far end of the orchard, or whether the fruits are particularly delectable for crows is not certain, but crows have been known to rob an Asian pear tree of bushels of fruit in a matter of days.

The ecologically-friendly way to control the threat of crows is to use nets on the trees. This we did for a while, before we ran out of time for such things.

Fortunately, the entire tree does not have to be covered. Crows are large birds and they are smart enough to recognize that they could become tangled in nets. When they fly off from a tree, they fly horizontally or, perhaps, even a little downward. So, a net that covers a good part of the side of a tree, even with gaps big enough that a crow can easily go through, would be effective to deter crows from eating the fruit. Other birds are different; small birds that especially love sweet cherries or grapes can only be stopped by completely covering the plant.

We have stopped using these nets because they are not easy to manage. They can be installed on large trees using pong poles, and that usually takes two people. Removing them from the trees is harder, because the trees tend to grow through the nets while they are in place.

Deer can also be a problem, especially for young trees. Deer like to eat the tender young shoots all season, and, as if that isn't enough, the bucks like to rut on tree trunks in the fall and skin the bark off as they rub the velvet off their new antlers. These things can kill young trees.

Deer are not always easy to control. They visit when people are not usually around. If our habits are to work in the orchard in the evening, then they will be there in the morning. If we usually work in the morning, the deer will appear in the evening. There will be occasions when deer are seen in the orchard during spraying. Art can be spraying one row, and they might watch from the next row. When he moves to spray the row where they had been standing, they move over a row and continue to watch.

Mesh bags with particularly aromatic soap hung from young trees have been known to deter them from eating, and sometimes rutting, those trees. Cheap, smelly soap works best. Trees with soap are not touched when other food is available for the deer to eat. The soap must be replaced when it dissolves in the rain or when birds peck and eat it, as they do sometimes.

It has become standard practice to put a four-foot-high cylinder of welded wire around each new tree as it is planted. Art figures that the wire would keep deer from touching the trees until they grow to at least four feet tall, and that should protect them from being killed. This has worked well for most trees, but has not for young mulberry trees. Deer apparently love mulberry shoots and leaves, and will eat them even as the trees grow above four feet high. Art has installed six-foot-high wire cylinders around mulberry trees, and deer have been known to reach up and nip off leaves as high as they could reach.

Squirrels will eat peaches hanging on trees. If there are only few ripe peaches, squirrels can easily eat them all. Raccoons also love peaches, and will climb into a tree and break branches doing so. Our only recourse at present is to pick the peaches before they are fully ripened, before these thieves do their dirty work.

Groundhogs also love peaches. Cathy has seen groundhogs that have climbed into the trees and are eating the fruit. We have a campaign against groundhogs, and try to keep up with them as quickly as they reproduce. We used to have a dog that would chase them, but don't have one anymore. We have tried filling in their holes with dirt and rocks, and the only result is that they dig their tunnels again. The most effective tactic is to fill the tunnel with an old pair of blue jeans, pushing it down as far as it will go with a long hoe handle, and filling dirt into the hole on top of the blue jeans. Groundhogs cannot dig out the blue jeans, and die inside their tunnels.

Rabbits can girdle very young trees, but they girdle them in the winter above the snow line rather than below. We have successfully used plastic tree guards around the trunks of small trees to solve the problem. Voles can also girdle trees, but from below rather than above. Tree guards seem to deter these threats as well.

Otherwise, we don't mind too much seeing rabbits. They are fun to race down the lane while riding in our John Deere Gators. We have many hedgerows around the periphery of our farm and between fields. The cover afforded by these thickets encourages wildlife of all kinds by giving them shelter and food. Multiflora roses form nice thick hedgerows and the rose hips on these plants give birds food in midwinter when they need it.

We like to see foxes, for they are allies. When the foxes eat well, we have fewer problems with rabbits and vermin. We had a fox family living in the back fields where we saw them often. One year we had four young kits that would play like puppies at the bottom of the peach orchard. Sometimes we see foxes eating dropped peaches, which they seem to like. Once we saw a fox chase a cat (not ours) up a tree.

Birds like our place. They certainly eat well and they build nests in our fruit trees out of grass, goose feathers (when we kept geese), and twigs. We leave windows open in the Bernie Barn for swallows to fly in and out, and they come back every year to nest among the rafters. Hummingbirds visit all the time. We even had a family of wild geese in residence while their youngsters were small.

Some of the most attractive birds on and around our farm have disappeared. One of these is the quail.

Quails are small, round black and white birds only a few inches long. They lived and bred in grassy fields next to woods or hedgerows. Although they fly, they much preferred to run. It was not uncommon to see a quail running in front of the tractor as we rode down the lane. Instead of running to one side or the other, letting the tractor go by, and peacefully resuming its place on the lane, quails continued to run ahead of the tractor at a pace just fast enough to avoid being run over. If the tractor was going a mite too fast for the quail to run at a comfortable speed, it would fly a short distance until it could again run in front of the tractor. Again, the quail did not fly to one side or the other, but, instead, flew straight ahead. When the lane turned, so did the quail. Only when there was no alternative would the quail leave the path. Quails were amusing to watch, and we miss seeing them.

The other bird that we used to see and hear was the pheasant. Pheasants are also birds of grassy fields that are hunted by many predators. They are not often seen, but the crow of a cock pheasant in the early morning or in the evening carries a long distance and divulges his presence.

There is room for all of these creatures as long as everything is in balance. The ecology of our farm seems to work. Fortunately, we have not had coyotes, wolves, or large cats to menace the sheep or cows. Life would have been much more complicated if we had to deal with these animals. As it is, there are loose dogs that every few years kill some of our sheep. That's discouraging. When sheep were killed, which have been with us a few years, and whose mothers and fathers were known to us for several previous generations, it is like losing old friends. We have much sympathy for those farmers who must constantly contend with predators of sheep.

ART IS PINNED BY A BRANCH

Growth of some apple trees is limited by the rootstock that the variety of interest is grafted on. We don't have any of the most severely limited sized apple trees. That means that our apple trees tend to grow toward the sky, if not checked by annual pruning. Even so, it is difficult to keep their heights to a manageable level. Over the years, it has been easy for the trees to grow ever higher, even without us intending to let that happen. So, there comes a time when the tops of the trees must be cut out to make the tree tops more accessible and let light filter into the interior of the tree for the sake of fruit development. Art had this in mind as he pruned the apple trees in our front orchard one year.

When cutting out the tops of trees, several things must be considered. First, the new heights of the trees must be consistent. This is easily accomplished if the pruner measures the tree heights against the height of the ladder being used for pruning. If the tree is too tall, then pruning of the upper branches can be an overhead job. This makes pruning difficult for cutting off larger sized branches. Second, the branches at the tops of the trees are usually the largest branches on the tree. Cutting out the top of a tree involves removing part of the trunk and some of these upper branches. Because they are not only large in diameter, but also spread over wide areas, these upper branches do not easily fall off the tree. When cut off, they often need coaxing by pulling or pushing to disentangle them from the lower branches on the tree. Art was used to doing this when he lowered the height of a tree.

Art had cut off a particularly large part of the trunk and upper branch of one particular tree, but the branch was stuck in the tree, and no amount of pushing would make it fall to the ground. The only way to remove it would be to tug on it as he stood on the ground. The ground under part of the front apple orchard is sloped, and Art had to stand on the lower side of the tree on sloped ground.

It took a lot of pulling to free that branch and trunk part. Art pulled easily and it did not move. He pulled harder, and it still did not move. So, he gave it his all, and tugged with all his might. The branch came loose with a lurch.

But Art was standing at a Newtonian gravitational disadvantage, with the ground falling away from behind him. When the branch suddenly gave way, he was not able to maintain his balance. The branch came down and Art came down with it, but Art was on the underside of the branch. It was heavy, and knocked him to the ground, falling on top of him. He was pinned. He felt a pain on his upper left side as he hit the ground, most likely a cracked rib. But he had suffered from cracked ribs before, and knew that they healed without much care. Maybe he would have a little trouble falling asleep on his favorite side at night, but there was no other cause for worry. So, he didn't worry.

But, he had to remove himself from that large mass of belligerent apple cellulose, and that was not to be too easy. Art was prone on the ground, with head lower than his feet. He was able to use his arms to raise his upper body and wriggle out from under that weighty opponent. If there had been a referee present, that branch would have been declared the victor by a pin. Art was down for more than a count of three.

SWEETAIRE FARM OLYMPICS

In the SweetAire Farm Olympics this week, Cathy won a gold medal in the blueberry picking event (based on performance with style points). Art got a bronze medal in apple picking (penalized for lack of enthusiasm after the fifth bushel picked) and a gold in strawberry weeding (with an amazing 9.8 out of a possible 10 points). Neither of us qualified for the looking lively in the evening event.

PEPPI'S MEATS

When we moved to Maryland from upstate New York in 1969, Harford County was entirely different from what it is now. The whole county was very rural at that time; farm and forested land were everywhere. There were no major highways like the new Rte. 24, and the U.S. 1 Bel Air bypass did not exist at that time. What is now Md Rte 924 (formerly Rte 24) now follows the same winding path from Edgewood and through Bel Air on Main Street. U.S. 1 used to go straight through Bel Air, as well.

Bel Air was a small, compact hub in the county. There were no malls and shopping centers; cows grazed where a shopping center is now located southwest of the town center, and an old race track was still in evidence where the Harford Mall is now. Many buildings which now house lawyers', dentists', and other professional offices were at that time all private residences. The town was as sleepy as the rest of the county.

Main Street in Bel Air had a courthouse, a hardware store, a major department store, a men's clothing store, a pharmacy, an appliance store, a paint store, post office, print shop, and a movie theater among a selection of various places to spend one's money. The Red Fox restaurant on Main Street was held in high regard by local residents. Walking on the sidewalks of Main Street, and peering in the store display windows, was a pleasurable excursion. A little further on, a Southern States Cooperative and, across the street, the Mill, sold goods and supplies for the nearby agricultural community. A little ways south of town, Preston's stationary store was also known well locally. Bel Air had just about all that county residents needed.

One place that was recommended to us when we first arrived was Peppi's meat store. Peppi's was located off the beaten track, on Thomas Street, across from what is now the parking lot of the Mary Risteau Building. Peppi's building is still there, but housing a much different business.

When one walked into Peppi's at that time, the wooden floor creaked with every step taken. It smelled good inside. There was a long glass case with different meats on display, including various sausages and luncheon meats in bulk loaves. If a customer wanted a pound or two of baloney, the butcher behind the counter would take the meat from the case, put it in the slicing machine, and slice off as much as was requested. While he was doing that, little children were usually offered a slice to eat right there. We liked Peppi's because they were so friendly and good to their customers.

Years later, when Art and Bernie spent chilly fall Saturday mornings selling fruits at the Farmers' Market, Bernie would disappear for a few minutes and return from Peppi's with two containers of homemade cream of crab soup, that, when sprinkled with a little Old Bay seasoning, tasted wonderful in midmorning. There was no reward for standing out in the cold that was any better than that soup. The memory of that wonderful soup is testament to the legacy of Peppi's Meat Store.

The talk was that Health Department requirements became too involved and expensive for the aging owners to deal with. Perhaps there was another reason for the store to close. Whatever the reason, Peppi's is missed by those of us who knew how good life could be when they were still there.

SWEETAIRE FARM DURING THE NOVEL CONRONA VIRUS PANDEMIC

SweetAire Farm in the spring of 2020 during the time of a Corona Virus pandemic was not very much different from SweetAire Farm during any other year. The rest of the state was subject to social isolation, school closures, mandatory mask wear, and working from home, when possible. The only one of these pertinent to SweetAire Farm was the last.

There were still many things to be done, and they were all located one place or another on our farm. We would normally be spending a good deal of time at home trying to do what needed to be done, and would be busy enough to not notice what was going on in the rest of the world. The rest of the world started where the end of our driveway joined the road, and we would not normally be going past that junction except once or twice a week. What was on our side of that intersection was of most interest to us and our daily activities.

What was different that year, however, was the feeling of being trapped on our farm. We could still get Cabin Fever, but our cabin was 49 acres large. As it turned out, it is not the size of the cabin, but the thought of having to stay there. We were certainly very busy with our work, but the sense of confinement remained with us when we stopped to take a breath. We could only be thankful that our "cabin" was large enough to keep us productively occupied during that crisis.

VAN NO GO

It was a little past 6 o'clock one Saturday evening in late November 2020, and Cathy and Art were at the kitchen table, quietly finishing their supper and trying to fill in a difficult NY Times crossword puzzle. They often tackled crosswords and other puzzles found in the daily newspaper as activities to do together. Art heard what he thought was a vehicle door slam outside the house, so he went to investigate. It had already turned pitch dark outside, so he had to turn on some lights in the back room and on the porch to see what had made the noise. It was the Amazon Prime delivery van that had brought a very small package and left it on the porch. The van was in the process of turning around at the end of our driveway, but instead of turning on the blacktop area, it had been driven further into the wet grass and soft ground. While Art watched from the porch, the driver kept trying to drive the van forward, without success. He would then back up a little more and try again. His wheels kept spinning. The ground slopes down in that spot, and as he backed further down the hill, the ground became softer. Soon he reached the edge of our flower bed. If he had gone any further, the back wheels of the van would have been mired up to the axels. Art, who was on the porch all this time, was trying to shout to him to stop trying and just going further backward at each attempt. But the driver had his windows shut and the only sound he probably heard was the sound of his spinning rear wheels. Art was frantically trying to put his shoes on fast enough to get over to the van to give directions. By the time Art arrived next to the van, it was stuck at the edge of the flower bed.

What could be done? The driver was lucky in one respect. He was stuck on a farm, and farms have tractors. Art told him to wait while he started one of his tractors and brought it down the hill from the machinery shed. What else could the driver do but wait there? So, Art went to the house to get his flashlight – he needed it in the pitch dark – and trudged up the hill to get a tractor. The tractor he chose was his largest and the one most likely to be able to pull the van out of its predicament. It was lucky that Art had last started that tractor a month before. He didn't use that tractor often, so when he had tried to start it back then, it had required a jump start. Fortunately, the battery was charged enough this time to start the tractor easily. With tractor started, Art headed over to where he kept his chains and selected one to use. He drove down the hill, and over to where the van was immobilized. Art connected one end of the chain to the tractor drawbar while the van driver tried to find a suitable spot to connect the other end of the chain to the van. That took a while, because the driver had no experience with chains, and didn't know that a chain is supposed to be looped over something and the hook on the end of the chain is supposed to connect over a link in the chain rather than to be hooked to a small hole somewhere. But, after a while, he found a spot under the van in which to insert the end of the chain hook.

It didn't take long from then for the tractor to pull the van out of the soft area and onto the blacktop driveway. It took a little longer and some blows with a hammer to extract the chain hook from under the van where the driver had inserted it. Soon, though, with the driver in the van and with Art out of his way with the tractor, the van drove off, probably to his next delivery. Art heard a relieved "thank you" over the noise of the tractor engine as the van went by. Art drove the tractor back to the machinery shed and parked it out front, not wanting to tempt fate by trying to back it into the shed in the darkness. But, remember, if an Amazon Prime van delivers a package to you in the next few days, it may not have been able to happen if we had not heard that vehicle door slam in the first place.

FARM PAY

A man owned a small farm in the country. Rumors that he was not paying minimum wage to his help had reached state offices, and they sent an agent to interview him. "I need a list of your employees and how much you pay them," demanded the agent. "Well, there's my hired hand, who's been with me for three years. I pay him $600 a week plus room and board. Then there's the half-wit that works about 18 hours a day. I pay him $10 a week and buy him chewing tobacco," replied the farmer. "That's the guy I want to talk to, the half-wit," said the indignant agent. The farmer replied, "Well, that would be me."

OUR OLD KITCHEN TABLE

There is comfort in familiar things, and that includes furniture. There may be some people who would suggest that we replace our old kitchen table, and, if truth be told, we have contemplated doing such a thing a time or two. But, it never happened. Although it is not a piece of fine furniture, our table continues to serve its purpose well.

Our kitchen table is the center piece of most of our inside-the-house activities. We eat all of our meals at the table: breakfast, lunch, and dinner. We drink cups of tea at the table. When we sometimes snack, it happens there at the table. When we entertain guests in our house, we all sit around the table. Lively conversations occur there. Laughter and good times happen there. We have decided business deals there. We have made important decisions while sitting at our kitchen table. We have listened to music while sitting around the table. We read newspapers, catalogs, books, and our daily mail at the table. We have studied and learned at the table. We have spent many good hours around this table. Although our living room has comfortable chairs, sofa, and love seat, we don't use it for life as we do our kitchen table. It is the center-piece of our whole house.

One thing our kitchen table is not is fashionable. It shows signs of wear from years of use. But it was good use, not abuse. Our kitchen table has a metal frame and a wood composition top with a fake wood grain laminated hard surface. The tabletop surface is a little dull with a few nicks from years of work and play that happened there.. Around the metal edges of the table, the black paint has worn off in spots, exposing silvery metal underneath.

The size of our kitchen table is about five feet by two and a half feet, so it is not large by any means, but it fits very well into one side of our kitchen. It can be shortened by removing a leaf in the center, and we used to move the leaf in and out depending on what activities were going to happen at that time, but the leaf has been installed as a nearly permanent fixture for probably thirty or more years now.

Cathy bought this table from a second-hand furniture store in Edgewood when we had just moved out of Army housing after Art returned from Vietnam. We were on a limited budget, and this table served the purpose at the time. With the table came four kitchen chairs, which have long since been ruined and have been replaced with newer ones. The table moved with us when we moved from Edgewood to our present house in Darlington. It has remained in our kitchen ever since.

When we first bought the table, we had two little girls who needed someplace to eat their meals, cut out paper dolls, glue pieces of craft paper together, affix stickers to kids' books, and a place to eat oatmeal cookies or chocolate chip cookies or to celebrate birthdays. When they baked goodies to submit to the county 4-H fair, the cakes and other goods rested on the table until they cooled enough to package up. The table was useful just being there.

We eventually raised four children around our old kitchen table. We ate, sang, played games, talked and just relaxed around our table. The kids did their homework on the table. Art and Cathy wrote letters on the table. Sometimes the only flat surface free of clutter is located on the table, and that makes it prime territory for any of these activities. Sometimes there is clutter even there, but it can be shoved out of the way for a game of checkers or connect four or monopoly or cards.

Our old kitchen table has been the surface for many a card game. We don't need much room for dealing out the cards, and the table works fine for this purpose. Art likes to win his games, but he never blames the table the few times when he doesn't.

There were many luscious Thanksgiving and Christmas meals eaten at the table, and we celebrated many birthdays while sitting around it.

Holidays usually meant that guests would come over to join us and eat, drink cups of tea, talk, and play games. Who cares what the table looks like if we are all enjoying each other's company.

The table has lately accumulated some things that need to be kept handy, such as bills to be paid, a jar of pens to play Sudoku games and crossword puzzles, cups for tea, and a few medicines that are supposed to be taken every day. When Cathy collects the daily mail from our postal mailbox, the pieces of mail end up on our table until they can be sorted into pieces to keep and those to be recycled. Cathy pays our bills at the table, and Art sometimes replaces the chain on his chain saw there, with a layer of newspapers on the table for protection, of course.

Our old kitchen table will probably be with us until the end. It continues to serve its purpose well. It is the site of many happy memories for the whole family. It endures.

FATHER'S DAY: A LETTER TO EVERYONE CLOSE

Dear Friends and Family,

A female friend of mine the other day asked me what I wanted for Father's Day. I hesitated to answer. I thought a few moments and really didn't know how to respond. Finally, I said, "I don't know, nothing really."

So, I thought about it, and when my thoughts had congealed, I thought I'd presume to speak for other fathers as well as for myself.

What fathers want most is that their children do well. They want to know that what they did for their children was, for the most part, good enough so that their children could grow to be successful, happy, and responsible adults. They want to know that the safe environment that they helped to provide allowed their children to explore and mature. They want to know that their adult children are capable of doing the same for their own children. They want respect for that.

There really shouldn't even be a Father's Day, because fathers don't deal with days at a time; they deal with lifetimes. Their timelines stretch from way back when to the far foreseeable future. A day is nothing; a lifetime is everything.

Don't try to make fathers rest on Father's Day. We are used to doing something all the time. We don't want to stop just because someone decided, against our own inclination, to name a generic day for us. Let us be busy. We are happiest that way.

But don't remind us of all the things that have to be done. We already know that list, and even some that aren't on it yet. Let us be free to do something we really enjoy today. The others we'll get to tomorrow or the day after.

So, don't treat us too much differently today than yesterday. We are still the same guys that we were then and will be tomorrow. We don't want a lot of extra attention; we don't want to be kings, just us for another day. Anything else is embarrassing.

So, what do fathers really want for Father's Day? Not a lot, and yet everything that matters. It would be nice to have just a short little report from our kids saying that everything with them is OK.

BERRY PICKER'S LAMENT

The heat is getting to me,
My ambition – it's been shot
But here I'm picking berries,
The sun is just too hot.

In the blazing sunshine,
Comfy, it is not
But I must pick to earn my keep
In the sunshine, I'm so hot.

We'll bring them to the market.
They'll expect to see a lot,
But I can't pick much faster,
In the sunshine, more than hot.

When I die, I hope it's heaven,
And not the other spot,
For I can tell, I know darn well,
The sunshine 'twould be too hot.

OUR TRUCK

Our truck is a 1993 black Dodge Ram pickup truck with a wooden rack on the back and a ram's head hood ornament on the front. The body is in relatively good shape for its age, and the drive train is in good working order. Because of the lack of body rust and the showy hood ornament, our truck has been the envy of Dodge Ram affectionados whenever they catch sight of it; Dodge has not had a hood ornament like this on their Ram trucks for years.

Our truck was bought used from a dealer in 2003 with 120,508 miles on it. It replaced our first pickup truck, a Ford F100 bought new in 1972 and suffering from rusted body mounts that caused it to shimmy and shake whenever it hit a bump in the road. There were rough places along the route to the Farmers' Market where Art knew from experience that he had to slow way down in order to maintain control of the truck. Long after it was time to retire that truck, he went to find a replacement.

The Ram truck had just been traded in to the dealer by its previous owner, and Art was looking for a reasonably good truck as a replacement. He has only bought two new vehicles in his lifetime (one was his Ford pickup), and considers used vehicles a better investment than new ones. So, when he looked at this truck, and expressed interest, the salesperson asked him to make a bid on it. How much could a 10-year-old truck with more than 120,000 miles on it be worth? Prices to purchase used pickup trucks at that time were very low, and Art made, as it turns out, a very generous offer. He was not sorry for the extra-large offer; it was still within his budget, he knew that he usually used his vehicles amortized over an extended lifetime, and he had some needs that required some modifications on the truck as it stood in the dealer's lot. The salesperson quickly accepted his offer, so there was no going back on it at that point.

At that time, we not only used the truck for taking produce to the Farmers' Market, but we also used it to transport cattle and sheep. So, Art asked the dealer to install extra-strong rear springs and good tires to be able to carry the weight of two cows, totaling approximately 2500 pounds. These modifications took several days for the dealer to accomplish, but Art was happy with the results. Our cattle could be loaded on the back of the truck without the truck bogging down or sagging under the load.

We had a wooden rack with oak boards on the back of our previous truck, and, with very little modification, the pieces were installed on our "new" truck. That is the same rack that we use today. It may look a little out-of-place to see a truck with a cattle rack at the Farmers' Market, but there has been no compelling reason to replace it with something else.

When we first brought our "new" truck to the market, in 2003, we were kidded by some of the other vendors. "Oh", they said, "it looks like someone came into some money." That's what they usually say when someone upgrades their old stuff with something better, whether new or not.

Our truck has very limited use these days; it, of course, makes weekly trips to the market, and it is sometimes used in the fall to pick up leaves contributed by our friends and customers. But, it hardly ever goes anywhere else. It has a sheltered bay to itself in our machinery shed when it is not out on the road. And, so, we expect that our truck will give us faithful service a long time yet to come.

SUNRISE

Sunshine is welcomed and valued differently at various times of the year. Sunshine in the deep winter is valued for its mood-boosting brightness, but is usually there because of high pressure and cold air. Midwinter sunshine is best enjoyed from inside the house looking out. Sunshine in the midsummer can be brutally hot; and a few clouds during the summer's day are welcomed. Too many clouds, especially on oppressively dark, cloudy days, can be depressing, and, after a string of these cloudy days, sunshine is again warmly welcomed, no matter how hot, at least for an hour or two. Sunshine in the early autumn can trigger Seasonal Affective Disorder (SAD), causing anxiety and a feeling of unease. But there is nothing more celebratory than sunshine in the early spring, set in a deep blue clear sky, and with a mild temperature. This sunshine lifts the spirits and underscores the wonder of nature and the splendor of life. It is this sunshine that inspires poets, musicians, and creative artists of all kinds.

Sunshine heats our planet and energizes photochemical reactions in our plants and in our skins. In our plants, sunshine supplies the energy for photosynthesis of carbohydrates from water and carbon dioxide, which, in turn, allows growth and reproduction. People harvest these as fruits, vegetables, grains, structural materials, and fuels. On our farm, we benefit with luscious fruits. Warm, sunny days make more available sugars; fruits, especially berries, are sweeter after a string of sunny days.

In our skins the photochemical reaction forms vitamin D3, which benefits immune health and muscle function. Working outside in the sunshine not only profits the psyche, but also enhances physical health. Too much sunshine can harm the skin, but humans were meant to be exposed to at least moderate levels of this natural elixir.

We love to see sunshine early in the morning. Banishing the darkness of the night, sunshine at the start of a new day offers a promise of new energies and opportunities. It comes at a time of a new beginning; it comes at a time to erase the shortcomings and failures of yesterday; it comes at a time to make new plans and to face the day with an optimistic outlook. To see the earliest rays of sunshine can uplift the spirit like none other.

Our large kitchen window faces east, so we can see as the sun comes over the hill and sprays its light inside the room. Until the sun rises so high that its rays can no longer shine directly through the window into our kitchen, it brightens the room like the most dazzling spotlight.

As the seasons progress, sunup appears to move across the sky. This movement is enough to be noticeable over several months. As the days advance, the first rays of the sun appear as a spotlight on different locations in our kitchen. In late December and early January, sunlight first appears on our microwave oven, directly across the room from the window. A little later in the year, the early sunshine migrates counterclockwise around the room to shine on our refrigerator, and then on the entrance to our living room. As the months advance, the first light shines on the kitchen wall where are hung the plaques for Apple of Our Eye awards at the Darlington Apple Festival: from 2001 for Art and 2004 for Cathy. By late April and early May, the movement of the location of the first rays has accelerated, and moved further to hit the pantry door, almost halfway around the kitchen. Within a mere couple of days, it hits the curtain on the side of the window where it enters. Soon, the first sunshine will be nearly orthogonal to the direction of the window, and won't be able to cast its strong rays into the kitchen at all. It stays there for several weeks, until the bright morning spotlight begins to recede in the autumn back toward the microwave oven. We watch at our breakfast table for the first light of the morning sun, and, in this way, the seasons on our farm are made graphically clear year after year.

THE VULTURES WILL GET YOU

Years ago, we developed a family saying, "Ya gotta keep movin', or the vultures will getcha." We came up with this saying for good reason when we had sheep on our farm.

The Conowingo Dam and Susquehanna River are located just over a hill from our farm in Darlington. Vultures congregate at the Dam for extended periods several times during the year. They must stay there to feast on dead fish and animals in and around the dam and around the lake behind it.

Some of these vultures found it relatively easy to fly to our farm and search for meals of dead animals. They were attracted by our sheep, and would perch high on the peaks of our barn roofs, just sit there, looking ominous, and observe our sheep to detect any that did not move while they were on watch. They also roosted high in some of the tall trees surrounding our place. There might be more than half a dozen at a time of those morbidly large black birds peering over us, and it caused us to have an eerie feeling to see them there.

Sheep lie down and chew their cuds at certain parts of the day. They don't move a lot during these times. A flick of an ear or turning of a head might be all the movement that they make. In response to hot summer heat, sheep can become torpid and often lie for hours at a time without moving even a little. Sometimes, they do not even respond to flies crawling over their ears and head. It's especially at those times that the vultures' hopes of a fresh meal were highest, and they watched for hours to detect animals that did not move a muscle.

Every once in a while, an animal would die on our land. Sheep that died were not very common, but we have had one or two over the many years that we raised them. We also had deer die, sometimes after being struck by a vehicle. There were other animals that died, as well. When that happened, the vultures would circle overhead of the still body and land, tentatively at first, and then in a group. They would clean the carcass of all traces of flesh, and then we would later find only scattered bones. It was during those times that we came to appreciate the role that vultures play in the ecological cycle of life. Otherwise, vultures were nothing more than creepy.

One time, as Art was mowing grass in the field between our raised beds, he ran over a piece of welded fence wire that had inadvertently fallen off his Gator on one of his trips. The mower blade picked up the wire and the wire wrapped around the mower blade in a tangled mess.

He turned off the mower blade rotation, and drove the mower back to the barn extension where he usually kept the mower and parked it on the grass just outside. There was a long, hard job ahead of him to extract the wire from the blade so that the mower would be able to function again.

There was nothing else that could be done than to lift the mower as high as he was able, lie next to the mower, and, using intensely raw effort and a set of wire cutters, remove the wire as best as he could. He was not able to raise the mower deck very high, nor did he want to, because an accidental jarring while pulling on the wire might cause the mower to fall on him as he worked underneath. It took a lot of struggling to remove the wire; it was strong wire and it was wrapped tightly around the blade and spindle to which the blade was attached.

It also took a long time. It was possible to cut some of the wire off, but most had to be unwrapped in the opposite direction from which it had been wound. It took him at least 45 minutes to extract the entire piece of wire.

All the while, he had been lying next to the mower, unmoving except for his arm and hand working intensely underneath the mower deck. At one point, well into the time that he was working under there, he took his attention off of the task at hand and happened to look up at the sky above. There were vultures circling around above him. Uh-oh! He had better move his body a little every now and again or else he might have unwanted visitors dropping in.

Ya gotta keep movin', or the vultures will getcha.

COVID FOR CHRISTMAS

It was the week of Christmas in 2023 when Art and Cathy both tested positive for COVID. Neither of us had a severe case, and we were not too uncomfortable. But we spent the holiday isolated and away from family and friends. Both recovered their health soon after.

'Twas the week after Christmas,
And Art and his spouse,
Made it through Christmas,
Confined to their house.

Contagious with COVID,
They sat there alone,
Contact with family
Was only by phone.

We stared at each other,
With little to say,
The time seemed forever,
That very long day.

We weren't that sick,
We felt pretty good,
So we were happy,
Eating good food.

Thanks be to FEDEX,
And Amazon, too.
We still got some presents,
No more than just two.

In the eve, there was football,
The Ravens were on,
Fell asleep before halftime,
The long day was gone.

Now that it's over,
It wasn't so bad,
We still had each other,
And, for that, we are glad.

NEW BEGINNINGS

There is a rhythm to farm life. Actually, there are many rhythms, and each has a new beginning at the start. Before the anticipated event, there is a slight sense of apprehension or nervousness. What if we didn't do something we should have done? Or seen? Or prepared? Or what if something changed, and things go wrong? New beginnings are exciting and relieving at the same time. The sense of apprehension disappears, to be replaced by a sense of peaceful accomplishment and wondrous connection with all of nature and powers much larger than ourselves. New beginnings are the most thrilling and inspiring episodes on a farm. New beginnings sustain a farmer through all the long and hard work necessary to operate the farm.

The most obvious of farm rhythms is the one that begins the growing season each spring. The annual growing season is probably the most important cycle for most farms. Pastures begin to grow, hayfields awaken from their dormancy, fruit trees sprout leaves and new blossoms, and seeds are planted in the ground for annual field crops. Even livestock animals conform to the seasonal cycle. If left to themselves, calving and lambing would occur in the springtime when food again becomes abundant. In the springtime, animals, no longer limited by scarce and dormant forages, flourish and grow. Wildlife populations, too, grow as wild animals produce new offspring. Springtime is an exciting time of the year, a new beginning when all the shortcomings of the previous season are forgotten and dreams of perfection abound.

With less attention perhaps, is the diurnal, or daily, cycle that guides the workday for the farmer, and for the eating, sleeping, and other activities of farm animals. Plants, also, respond to daily cues. They produce carbohydrates in the sunlight during the daytime hours and consolidate their biochemical gains at night. Daily cycles dictate a lot of what happens on a farm. Each new day is a new beginning, with the promise anew of the gift of time, time to make progress and to accomplish the many things that must be done soon, if not immediately. The new day is the best time to be aware of the many blessings that a farm brings to the farmer; it is much easier to remember these at the beginning rather than at the end of the day, when fatigued from the work and challenges of the day.

Each time a seed is put into the ground, or a plant is planted, a new cycle begins. The seed or plant first develops roots so that it can obtain water and nutrients from the soil to support growth and reproduction. Next, the plant expands its physical size, making use of the carbohydrates formed in its leaves through a number of biochemical cycles. Planting a seed or a small plant engenders a sense of optimistic expectations in the person doing the planting. Soon after new seeds are planted, they are watched with anticipation to see if or when they sprout. When they first show their little heads above the soil, they bring a sense relief from the waiting, and then of joy and excitement. Nature's miracle has happened once more!

Each time an animal is bred, a cycle of growth and birth begins there, too. The births of new youngsters promise increase, of numbers, or of income, or of companions. When we kept sheep at one time, lambs born in the winter took much of our attention. They were a lot of trouble, but the sight of cute new little life was exciting nevertheless. When we had cows, new calves were fun to see, as they stood on their wobbly legs and suckled for the very first time. The miracle of new life is awe-inspiring. Again, there is hope that all of these will grow fast and strong, and that all will turn out successful. Before each birth, there is a sense of anticipation coupled with a little bit of apprehension. Something could go wrong, something we may not be prepared to handle, but, once that cute little lamb or gangly calf begins drinking from its mother, then all the nervousness is forgotten, to be replaced in our heads with a sense of relief and faith in the larger scheme of things.

There is an intrinsic continuity on a farm. In the grand plan of the universe, what is here today was usually here in some form yesterday, and the same will probably be here tomorrow. Plants, animals, and the farmer him- or her-self change very little from day-to-day. And the farm itself, the land, the climate, and the environment, were here eons before, and may remain so for farther than the mind can imagine. But, the new beginnings that punctuate this overall existence add all the motivation necessary to tackle the tasks necessary to keep this continuity going. New beginnings contribute necessary interest and excitement to a lifestyle that could otherwise be devastatingly tedious and taxing.

GREETINGS FROM SWEETAIRE FARM

Art and Bernie Mullin stand in front of our truck at the Bel Air Farmers' Market in December. Bernie started helping at the market in 1991, and continued until 2017, when he moved from the area. They sold kiwis that day.

Cathy and Art now shovel snow from the driveway when needed. Art prefers this to using his tractor and plow. A Nor'easter storm on 5-6 February 2010 brought 20-35 inches of snow, known in Maryland as Snowmageddon, to the area. It took several days to clear snow from the entire driveway.

Grandson Gregory Pierson in 2018 on his new zero-turn lawn mower that he used to mow the lawn, apple orchards, and pastures. He spent hours mowing everything he could, and made our farm so neat that it looked like an estate.

Lambs, tuckered out from running around the pasture with each other, paused for a little rest and relaxation in 2012 next to the Bernie Barn. Sheep, as social animals, usually stay with each other throughout the day and night. If they cannot see each other, they usually call to others so they know where they all are.

Cathy took daughter Jodi and grandson Clay for a ride in her new (to her) John Deere Gator. Cathy loves that Gator, and uses it all the time in all seasons for transportation out to the blueberry patch for picking, for carrying prunings from the apple orchard, and as a platform for packaging our berries in the summer. Cathy and her Gator are nearly inseparable.

Our cows and sheep loved apple prunings, and treated them like salad in the midwinter. We would load the apple branches on the trailer behind our Allis Chalmers "C" tractor and bring them to the pastures where the animals were located. The animals frequently couldn't wait until the branches were unloaded before they started to nibble on the ends. This made it sometimes difficult to unload the branches and move the tractor and trailer out of the way. The animals ate the branches at every opportunity they had.

Uh-oh! One of our Chinese Chestnut trees blew down during the 2003 storm, and knocked over the bee hives. Art had to cut the fallen branches back and restore the hives. He wouldn't do that without the protection of his full bee-suit and veil regalia. Even then, it was tricky. The bees were not happy at all.

Granddaughter Emma loved to climb the gate to the summer pasture for the sheep and watch to see what they were doing. The sheep loved to see Emma, because they hoped that she might have some food for them. It all worked out that way. Emma was at least somewhat disappointed when we sold all of our sheep. She keeps coming to visit us once a year from the San Francisco area, but has to find other things to do when she is here.

This is a picture taken at our site at the Darlington Apple Festival in 2008. Bernie Mullin watches as son Paul works to get our apple display ready for the anticipated large crowd of about 65,000 people who will come soon. Art started the Apple Festival in 1986, and was Chairman of the organizing committee for the first eight years.

We had solar panels installed on our house roof in 2014. They are supposed to supply most of our electrical needs through the year. Whenever the sun shines, we often generate more electrical power than we use, sending the extra onto the power grid. The panels also shade our roof and seem to keep it cooler inside the house in the summertime. Because we have no air conditioning in the house, every bit of cooling help is appreciated.

Cathy bottle-feeds a young orphan lamb in 2017. She has the patience to deal with young lambs needing assistance.

Our sheep relaxed and chewed their cuds together several times a day in the pasture. Sheep are social animals and like to stay together. In the background is the machinery shed that took several years for Art to build completely

GREETINGS FROM SWEETAIRE FARM

Each fall after the Darlington Apple Festival, we brought a hand-operated apple cider press to the Bel Air Farmers' Market for customers to make their own fresh, organic apple cider. Most customers loved to process the apples themselves and they really liked the taste of the juice. Here, customer Mark helps his daughter Roxie press the apples. Cathy assists while Art watches.

This is our house in the summertime after the porch and deck were added in 2003. We have rocking chairs on the porch that we sit in to relax after a work day on the farm. We had wanted a porch like this for many years before we could afford to have one built.

Cathy prunes apple trees in the back apple orchard all winter, from late October until April. There are about 250 trees in the orchard to prune. In the background is her John Deere Gator that she uses for many purposes.

This photo was taken at the 2019 Darlington Apple Festival in front of our wagon full of apples. Pictured are (from the left) friend and helper Steve O'Brien, friend and Harford County Executive Barry Glassman, Art, and the very popular Maryland Governor Larry Hogan. It was a beautiful sunny and warm day for the festival.

EPILOGUE

With under 2% of the U.S. population contributing to production agriculture, most of the people in our country do not have the privilege of living and working on a farm. Farm life is a privilege to be sure. Yes, there is hard physical work involved, and, it seems like there is always more to be done, but there are plenty of compensations for the efforts that are required. For one thing, there is the freedom to choose what the farm is to be about, and the opportunity to do all one can to make it happen that way; for another, there is the satisfaction of seeing one's efforts rewarded by results that are clearly due to one's own hard work; for a third, there is the wholesome environment for raising children and their learning a sense of responsibility and the value of hard work; and, for the most part, there is fresh air and sunshine to buoy one's spirits.

Maybe these are some of the reasons that this collection of stories has been put together. We have sent out a weekly email message to customers, family, and friends since 2009, and a lot of the stories in this book appeared first in some form in those messages. Our weekly emails are popular with the people who receive them. We have been told that some recipients send copies to friends and family all over the world. And, when for some reason a recipient is dropped from our email list, they tell us how much they miss the emails, and they try to find ways to reinstate their email addresses on our recipient list. Many among our friends who receive these messages have urged us to compile this book, and we are more than glad be able to do so.

Perhaps these messages give people who do not have the privilege of living on a farm a vicarious experience of farm and rural life. Perhaps, also, the stories that are included in this book give the impression of a simpler and more rewarding way of life different from the complexities of the modern lives of most people these days. We may have given the wrong impression that farm life is simpler than urban life, but farm life is in many ways different, more interesting, and more rewarding.

Each and every farmer has stories to tell to his or her children and grandchildren. We do not presume that our stories are typical for many farmers. We had lives different from many who practice full-time farming; we had opportunities and constraints that are not typical for most farmers; in other words, we had our own lives and experiences to tell about. Yet, there are underlying elements of our stories that can be appreciated by other farmers with their own precious memories.

Now that we no longer have children at home or livestock animals in our pastures, our lives are a lot more quiet. We are now remembering many more stories than generating new ones. So, there will probably not be many additions to this compilation. We could wish, anyway, because it is somehow nice to live a quieter, more peaceful and predictable life.

And so, we hope that you have enjoyed reading these vignettes that came from our lives. We also hope that, in reading these stories, that you develop an appreciation for those who supply the food for your table and products for the betterment of your lives. Farmers are good people who take these responsibilities seriously. We all must do our parts, as we see them, to make our lives, and the lives of others, better for all of us who live on this Earth.

Our stories will go on; as long as we live, we will have some new ones to tell. And so will you. We hope that your stories will be remembered with pride, happiness, fondness, and affection. In the meantime,

Stay well,
And, do good.